in the
MEANTIME...

finding yourself

and the love

you want

IYANLA VANZANT

A FIRESIDE BOOK
PUBLISHED BY SIMON & SCHUSTER

FIRESIDE
Rockefeller Center
1230 Avenue of the Americas
New York, NY 10020

First Fireside Edition 1999

FIRESIDE and colophon are registered trademarks
of Simon & Schuster Inc.

Designed by Bonni Leon-Berman

Manufactured in the United States of America

20

The Library of Congress has cataloged the Simon & Schuster edition as follows:
Vanzant, Iyanla.
In the meantime—: finding yourself and the love you want / Iyanla Vanzant.
p. cm.
1. Love—Religious aspects.   2. Man-woman relationships—Religious aspects.
3. Intimacy (Psychology)—Religious aspects.   4. Marriage—Religious aspects.   I. Title.
BL626.4.V36   1998
158.2—dc21   97-40971   CIP
ISBN 0-684-84136-3
ISBN 0-684-84806-6 (Pbk)

ACKNOWLEDGMENTS

o god! how great thou art! You have brought me from a mighty, mighty long way. For this I am so grateful! I am also grateful for the visible and *invisible* angels You sent to guide, protect, encourage, and support me. With sincere gratitude, I would like to acknowledge my visible angels:

My children by birth, DAMON, GEMMIA, NISA;

Their children, ASOLE', OLUWALOMOJU, ADESOLA, NIAMOJA ADILAH AFI;

My children by acquisition, J. ALEXANDER MORGAN, MAIA, LUMUMBA, ATIBA, COUJOE, KOBIE, GAMBA, and NWANDU BANDELE;

My godfather, AWO OSUNKUNLE ERINDELE;

My elders, who put up with me for more than thirty years, OMI RELEKUN, OSUN TOLEWA, BABATUNDE, CHIEF and BARBARA BEY, STEPHANIE WEAVER, and OSEYE MCHOWI;

My life coach, DR. DAVID PHILLIPS;

His wife, MRS. PEGGY PHILLIPS;

My rebirthing coaches, KEN KIZER, RENE KIZER, and DUJUNA WUTON;

My prayer partners, DR. BARBARA LEWIS KING and REVEREND LINDA BEATTY-STEPHENS;

My dear friends who have provided me with excellent relationship models, JOIA JEFFERSON and RASHID NURI, STAN and TULANI KINARD, FREDDIE and MARGE BATTLE, REVEREND COCHISE and VIVIANNA BROWN, NATU and FATIMAH ALI, SUSAN and KEPHRA BURNS, STANLEY and CHEMIN BERNARD, RALPH and JEANNE BLUM;

My agent extraordinaire, DENISE STINSON;

My editor from heaven, DAWN MARIE DANIELS (you really earned your halo on this one!);

My fellow writers and teachers, NEALE DONALD WALSCH, PAUL FERRINI, JOHN RANDOLPH PRICE, EVA BELL WERBER, Foundation for Inner Peace, MARIANNE WILLIAMSON, WAYNE DYER, TOM JOHNSON; ALEXIS DAVIS of Ketcum Public Relations, MICHELLE BUCKLEY and KIMBERLY GRAHAM of Mahogany Cards, Hallmark, Inc., and VALENCIA SCOTT of 7-Up for providing me with up-to-date relationship information.

The invisible angels I would like to acknowledge are ESU, who brings the blessings; OBATALA, who tells me what to do with them; SANGO, who makes sure I do what I am told; YEMOJA and OSUN, who have taught me to maximize all blessings; OYA, who helps me to transform nonblessings into blessings; and the Master JOEL GOLDSMITH, whose work is a blessing in my life.

And I would humbly like to acknowledge my Self for being willing to move through the fear, denial, confusion, and anger required to figure out why I had to write this book.

this book is dedicated in love
and with love to

DR. BETTY SHABAZZ,

who taught the world how to live in

the meantime and do something

very valuable with it;

COLEEN GOLDBERG,

who prayed for me without ceasing and

spent the last days of

her life traveling to my wedding;

REVEREND FERNETTE NICHOLS,

who brought forth the sermon that

gave birth to this book;

and to my husband,

IFAYEMI ADEYEMI BANDELE,

who helped me realize that

the meantime does pay off!

CONTENTS

Introduction
13

THE JOURNEY BEGINS

There will come a time in your life when all you can do is love. You will have done all you can do, tried all you can try, hurt all you can hurt, given up so many times that love will be the only way in or out. That day will surely come. Just as sure as you are reading this page. In the meantime, here are a few things you can do to get ready for the most joyous day of your life: the day you experience true love.

Chapter 1
LOVE'S GOT EVERYTHING TO DO
WITH THE MEANTIME
23

Chapter 2
KNOW WHERE YOU LIVE
51

CONTENTS

THE BASEMENT
Chapter 3
SPRING CLEANING
81

THE FIRST FLOOR
Chapter 4
DOING THE LAUNDRY
109

Chapter 5
CLEANING OUT THE REFRIGERATOR
131

THE SECOND FLOOR
Chapter 6
LET'S DO A LITTLE DUSTING
157

Chapter 7
GET THE RING OUT OF YOUR TUB
186

Chapter 8
TAKE OUT THE TRASH
215

BETWEEN THE SECOND AND THIRD FLOORS
Chapter 9
CLEANING OFF THE DRESSER
237

CONTENTS

Chapter 10
CLEANING OUT THE CLOSET
254

THE THIRD FLOOR

Chapter 11
PULL UP THE SHADES
AND LET SOME SUN IN
281

Chapter 12
REARRANGE THE FURNITURE
301

THE ATTIC

Chapter 13
PUT YOUR FEET UP AND RELAX!
319

INTRODUCTION

what do you do in the meantime? Somewhere in the back of your mind you know the day will eventually come when the relationship you are in will become all that you want. Or all that you want in a relationship will one day show up. The question remains, however, what do you do in the meantime? There's a funny thing about love. It will find you in the most unusual circumstances, at the most unlikely times. Love will come upon you, throw its arms around you, and transform your entire existence. Unfortunately, most of us won't recognize the experience or understand the impact when it's happening. It's like being in therapy. You keep talking, searching, questioning what's going on with you and in you while being totally ignorant of the fact that you are being blessed. Perhaps it's because love rarely shows up in the places that we expect it to or looks the way we expect it to look.

He was my love counselor. Tall, slim, very quiet, almost shy. I was short, stout, and quite, shall I say, boisterous. I was forever doing, saying, or experiencing things that attracted attention to me—usually negative attention. He was seventeen. I was thirteen. He was a group leader at summer camp, and I was a summer worker who had not gotten paid. An administrative foul-up deleted my name from the payroll roster. He was assigned the task of making sure I got paid.

It seemed that no one knew what was going on, except him. As far as I was concerned, he knew everything. He walked me through a process that took two weeks to unravel. As we went from office to office, supervisor to supervisor, he was patient, always amenable. I was angry with a lot to say. He was comforting, and did I really need comforting! My love counselor constantly reassured me that it would all work out just fine. I believed him because it gave me the opportunity to be in his presence. That belief and his persistence finally paid off. I was issued three Summer Youth Corps paychecks for forty-five dollars each. It was a thrilling moment for me. It was an accomplishment for him. He was just doing his job. I was just being in love. He had twenty-five other youth workers to think about. I could think about nothing else but him. Now that I had my paychecks, I realized there was one small problem I would now need to resolve. This young man, with whom I was madly in love, was dating one of my best friends. It was the beginning of my *meantime*.

I spent thirty years of my life being in love with this man. I call him a counselor because he helped me search, question, and heal myself. He taught me many lessons about life and love. When we met, other people had me convinced that what I felt was not love. They said it was infatuation. Because they were older and, I thought, wiser than me, I believed them. I thought it best to ignore what I felt. I moved through that phase of my life believing that I knew nothing about love—after all, I was just a child. I concluded that we would never, could never be together. He was too old for me. I moved on with my life feeling hurt and being angry about what I had been told and what I believed I had lost. In the end, I concluded that I was not *good enough* to be loved by him or anyone. In this moving, believing, conclusion-drawing process, I also made some decisions.

I decided I would never be hurt by love again. Although I wasn't quite sure what it was about love that had hurt me, I knew I never wanted to experience it the way I had when I was thirteen years old. I also decided that no man would do to me what my father had done to my mother. What he had done was none of my business, but I made it my business by watching, judging, and trying to figure out what no one seemed able to come right out and tell me. Who knows the truth about love, loving, or relationships? Was I really wrong about what I felt, what I saw, what I believed, and what I concluded from the relationship models I had seen? Good questions! But, in the *meantime,* I had to figure out the answers.

At age sixteen, I really thought I had found love. Instead, I got pregnant and was left alone to raise a child. At nineteen, I just *knew* I had found love, so I married it. Wrong again! At twenty-one, love called me up on the telephone, took me out on three dates, and moved in. That was when my *meantime* got real ugly. In the process, I got very, very clear. I became clear that all the things I thought about love had nothing to do with it. I realized that I couldn't recognize love because I had never actually seen it. Oh, I had a picture in my mind of what it should look like, but that picture had been cracked a long time ago. I also discovered that love is more than just a good feeling. It is more than just being needed or having your needs met. In a thirty-year meantime experience I came to realize that love is an inner, personal experience of total well-being that did not match any picture I had ever seen.

When I was with him, my love counselor, I felt like I could fly, and it didn't even matter if the people on the ground could see my panties while I was flying! The mistake was believing that he made me fly. After many crash landings, I realized that flying was something I did for myself, within myself, when I was able to relax. That's right, relax! Relax all the fears, hurts, angry decisions, judgments, and conclusions. Relax the demands, expectations, and fantasies. Love, I discovered, is being still enough to feel all that is going on inside you and then learning how to acknowledge and accept what you feel.

In the presence of my love counselor, I was okay. Unfortunately, I thought *he* made me okay. In the meantime, I spent fifteen years trying to find someone who could do the same thing he had done—make me and life okay. Once I realized that I was just fine just the way I was, things got a lot better. The meantime got a lot easier. It was then that he walked right back into my life.

The age gap between us had miraculously closed, and we thought we were ready for love—and each other. We thought that because we needed and wanted each other everything would be just fine. That's what we thought! In reality, we were still too confused, too needy, and too afraid that we weren't good enough for each other. All of our "too's" were topped off with a lot of other baggage we were both carrying—childhood baggage, image baggage, you name it, we had it. We spent five years together acting out our stuff—anger, guilt, shame, love fears, and love fantasies. Eventually the stuff fell in on our heads. We were in the *meantime* together!

That's what usually happens in the meantime. Things fall in on you and they fall apart! In the meantime, you will have an experience, or a series of experiences—earth-shattering, heartbreaking experiences that are designed to eliminate your false needs. It is a process divinely designed to help you clear out your stuff. Clearing out stuff is hard work. It is like spring cleaning where you have to pull everything out, sort through the mess, throw stuff away, and get the entire house in shape. In the meantime, cleaning, clearing, and elimination can look like dishonesty, infidelity, betrayal, and abandonment. It's not! It is all the stuff that you hold on to that keeps you from a true and honest experience of love.

When we finally separated, I was wounded. I was afraid. I had spent most of my life silently praying that this man would love me. When he finally said he did, it didn't look anything like the way I expected. The meantime is like that: You get what you want only to discover that it is not what you thought it would be! Now you're stuck—or at least you think you're stuck! I was not only stuck, I was disappointed about my failed love affair, and it was my fault! I spent the next ten years trying to figure out what I had done wrong. Why couldn't he love me? What was wrong with me? If you are anything like me, these are just a few of the questions you will ask yourself in the *meantime.*

As time goes on, you will come up with answers. Believing each answer is the right answer, you will incorporate certain new behaviors and beliefs into your life. As each one proves to be a little off the mark, you will find new beliefs, parameters, and conditions to place on loving and being loved. It's called *meantime hysteria!* The truth is that you are probably angry! The truth is that you are probably afraid! The truth is that until you learn to face the truth, you are never going to find the love you so desperately want. The truth is that love is buried in your soul, and no relationship with anyone can unearth it or activate it in your life. This is the very truth that it took me ten years to discover.

I have had what I once thought were disastrously dysfunctional relationships during my many meantime experiences. What I now realize is that each experience taught me a little more about myself. You see, there are stages and levels of the meantime. You learn a little and use it, but there is always more for you to learn. You figure out one thing and put it into practice, but after a while, you will notice that what you are practicing no longer works. That's the beauty of the meantime. It does not allow you to stagnate. It forces you to grow, and grow some more. In order to grow, however, you must work. It is the work we are called to do on ourselves in order to experience love that makes the meantime so challenging.

Nowhere do we learn more about ourselves and life than in relationships. Let me speak for myself—I don't! I learned to be very grateful for my teachers/lovers/partners and the lessons they taught about fear, anger, and need that were often camouflaged as love. Once I learned my lessons and applied them, my life took off in an entirely different direction. I no longer needed to do things to prove myself worthy of being loved. I was no longer afraid to ask for what I wanted for fear that I wouldn't get it. I was no longer angry when things didn't go my way.

Most important, I was no longer angry about what I could not and did not have in a relationship. In the meantime, I learned how to mind my own business. The business of loving myself and being excited about me. I learned how to fly on my own.

Relationships are not contained. What you are going through in the name of love, for the sake of love, will show up in every other area of your life. You cannot tune out the channels of your brain or heart as if they were channels on a television where the program on channel two has nothing to do with channel ten. The various channels of our lives are intertwined and interdependent. Let me speak for myself—mine are! The same confusion I had about loving myself and loving my *him* showed up in my career. It affected the relationships with my children. It affected all of my relationships with men. In much the same manner I had him and lost him, I had jobs and lost them. In much the same way that our time together was disappointing, unsatisfactory, my career was disappointing. I spent forty-seven thousand dollars to go to law school, only to discover that I hated practicing law.

The interference from my relationship channel was creating static on every other channel of my life. Even from a distance, my love counselor was teaching me lessons about myself, and I had to figure out how to apply those lessons to my entire life.

I had to work very hard to become aware of myself and to accept myself for all and everything that I am. I must admit to you that it was not easy work! It was painful and very frightening. Reflection, evaluation, and unlearning require a willingness to do the grunge work. I had to sift through and discard many of my beliefs and ideas about myself and love. In other words, I had to change the picture. It was like cleaning house, trying to identify things that were dusty or broken, throwing out things I didn't need anymore. What the heck is this?!!! I had placed so many conditions on loving and being loved. It was like going through the dresser drawers and closets of my mind. I had to throw away those things which had sentimental value but were no longer practical. I had to admit some things simply did not fit, and would never fit again. Like the laundry, I had let the old hurts and fears pile up, and the pile was overwhelming. Slowly, methodically, I had to cleanse my heart to prepare myself for true love. In the meantime, I had to plow through the mess— the huge mess.

I had to start in the basement of my house where all my things from childhood were stored. This meant I had to polish up my self-image, which had been buried under a lot of stuff my parents gave me. Once I caught a glimpse of my real *Self,* I moved up to the first floor, opened the curtains, and let the light of truth expose my fears and fantasies for just what they were—distortions and shadows of the past. When I saw the truth, I had to take responsibility for letting the house get so messy, and I had to own up to the fact that I was the only one who could clean up the mess. The time had come for me to roll up my sleeves and do some real grunge work. Believe me, it took a lot of courage to go up to the second floor, where I had neatly tucked away the vision of how I wanted things to look. With a little faith and a lot of trust, I was finally ready to get rid of the old, faded drapes, rugs, and furniture, acknowledging all the costly mistakes I'd made. Looking around, I felt like I had wasted so much time and energy, but I knew the truth. The truth is, we all do the best we can do until we are stronger, wiser, willing, and ready to do better. Boy, was I ready!

I let myself be creative, using new styles and colors, weaving a new pattern of living that lifted me right out of the old familiar stuff up to the third floor. It was a place of breathtaking color and light. It was a place I had hardly visited before; guess I was too scared, too confused, or a little bit of both. Finally, my vision had been restored, the hard work was paying off, and I knew I was exactly where I was meant to be, at peace. I was so proud of myself, I invited some friends over to share with them what I had learned and where I would be living from now on. Some of them didn't like my new house. It was too different, all the stuff was gone! I was too different, standing on truth, living without fear! They wanted to leave. That was just fine with me! I cleaned up the little messes they'd made, believing with all my heart that if I kept the house clean, those who came in love would stay. In fact, I made the attic of my house a sanctuary for love. I choose everything I did and said with the greatest care. When I finally finished smoothing the bed and plumping the pillows, I turned around and my love was there. A little older, a lot wiser, my love counselor and I were ready to settle in together.

I just kept praying that it wouldn't rain. It didn't rain, but it was as cold as it could possibly be. I didn't feel the cold. I was warmed from the inside out on that beautiful May day, the day my love counselor and I were married. The people who told me it would never work were there. Those who had prayed with me for it to work were there. Some were there because they just couldn't believe it! Others were there because they knew it was right. In the meantime, I was warm and glowing, the way brides usually are. It has taken thirty years and three marriages, collectively, but we are both wiser, stronger, clearer.

More precisely, we are in love with ourselves and with each other. We knew it was right now. We knew that the picture was clear and that the meantime had been an absolutely necessary part of our relationship. Now we can spend the rest of our lives together, trying to remember what we forgot in the first place. That is what the meantime is designed to do: help you realize what you know and don't know about love.

In this book we are going to clean your house, the place you keep all the *stuff* you believe about love. We are going to disinfect your mind and sanitize your heart in order to prepare you to have what you say you want. We will examine love and what it looks like when it is active in your life. What it feels like when you discover it. How it transforms our humanness into divinity and how it catapults you into rewarding and fulfilling experiences in every area of your life. We will examine love gone wrong, love gone astray, love in disguise, and all the things that are cleverly disguised as love. My hope is that we will do this from a functional and practical perspective, taking into consideration those situations and people that have had the greatest impact on the development of our beliefs about love. Most important, we will examine and explore the things we sometimes do to find love, keep love, and experience love. We place our search for love in the frame of reference we're calling *the meantime.*

Chapter 1
LOVE'S GOT EVERYTHING TO DO WITH THE MEANTIME

she was not looking for him. He was not looking for her. As a matter of fact, they were both somewhat *attached* to other people. Yet, the minute they saw each other, their body parts began to twitch, and their eyes began to sparkle. The *meantime* was brewing. They worked their way across the room, neither aware that the other was doing the same thing. He spoke first. No, *she* did. She asked him a silly question to which he and his twitching body parts were more than willing to respond. He ducked his *attachment.* She ducked hers. They needed some time to talk. They did, and they laughed, something neither of them seemed to do very often with their *attachments.* They exchanged telephone numbers to their places of employment. Although they both knew, they both acted like they didn't. Reluctantly, they both rejoined their *attachments,* and together they entered a simmering pot of *meantime* stew.

When you are not happy where you are and you are not quite sure if you want to leave or how to leave, you are in the *meantime.* It's a state of limbo. You are hanging on, ready to let go, afraid to fall, not wanting to hurt yourself, afraid you will hurt someone else. In the meantime, you pray the other person will let go first so that you will not feel guilty.

The other person keeps dropping hints, letting you know that it's time to go. You deny it! Why? You don't know why, but I can tell you that the meantime is fraught with *don't knows* and *can't do's. Don't know why I can't go. Don't know why I should stay. Don't know where I'm going. Don't know how I am going to get there, wherever there is.* Ambivalence, confusion, reluctance, and paralysis are all characteristics of the meantime. If you knew the answers to these questions you would be just fine. In the meantime, you are many things, fine is probably not one of them!

Life would be so much easier if, when we hit a snag in a relationship, any relationship, we would stop, address it, and move ahead smoothly. The truth is, in most cases, we could do just that. The reality is, we don't do it! We keep moving. We allow little insults to become raging angers, little arguments to become festering feuds, little pains to become deep wounds, and we keep moving. In many cases, we keep hurting. When the relationship at issue is an intimate, loving one, the attempt to move forward without addressing the pain only complicates matters, further poisoning the relationship.

How can I stay and not get hurt? How can I go without hurting? You cannot answer these questions if you are in pain. What you can do is make the effort to discover the truth about love, because it is the only thing that can help you move through the experience. In the meantime, if we can remain loving of ourselves and toward other people by staying in conscious and honest communication, a disruption, snag, or delay in a relationship becomes a healing process. When we cannot, we engage in *meantime behavior*—hurting, fighting, not telling the truth, and moving forward in confusion. Confusion begets confusion.

Back to our meantime lovers. Two weeks later, she called him at work. He had already called her twice, but hung up when her voice mail answered. In the *meantime,* they each tried to convince themselves that they should not call each other again, but they desperately needed to see each other. He invited her out for a drink. She set the date, time, and place. He showed up with a rose, a single pink rose. The minute she saw it and him, the twitching body parts began to thump. Her attachment became a blur, and she didn't know what to do. He did. He said all the right things, in just the right tone of voice, at the right moment, which created a corresponding thumping in his corresponding body parts. She told him about her attachment. He told her about his. Well, not exactly. Although there was *someone,* his someone knew what the deal was. That's when she realized she was headed for trouble. Quickly, she made her excuses and took her thumping body parts home. In the meantime, he had two more drinks and tried to figure out what he was going to do and how he was going to do it.

LET'S TALK ABOUT LOVE IN THE MEANTIME

Life is all about love. Love is the only true meaning of life. Being alive means that we are occupants in love's house and are accountable to love's rules. Neither life nor love requires us to give up our dignity, self-worth, career objectives, favorite television program, or our good common sense. For some reason, we don't always understand this. We believe in the necessity of giving up one thing in order to get something else. We especially believe this about love. We do not understand that the highest expression of love is the experience and realization of more—more of who you are, what you do, what you believe, and what you have. Love has the ability to bring all of you together under one roof, at one time, as one experience. Love is the experience of oneness, a union of the mind and heart. Unfortunately, we believe we can establish this union with others only if we give up something. We attempt to create this union with others before first creating it within ourselves. This is absolutely impossible. You cannot *get* love from the outside until you *are* love on the inside. In the meantime, we do many things in the name of love, for the sake of love.

We live in the *meantime* while we are learning about love. We flounder around, involving ourselves in strange alliances, making up rules as we go along, in the name of what *we* think love is, or should be. We watch and listen to others, believing they know all there is to know about love and relationships. The truth is that they, like the rest of us, are learning by trial and error. At best, we pick and choose who to love and how we will love them. At worst, we discover that it is virtually impossible to do enough fast enough, for enough people, in enough situations to receive from them the love, admiration, or acceptance we seem to need. In the meantime, while we are learning the truth about love, we can make a pretty big mess of most things. Nowhere do we make a *bigger mess* than in our so-called loving relationships.

They were at it again! He and she both knew that they needed to make a swift but loving departure from the relationships they were in. Neither of them had the courage, strength, or presence of mind to do so. He didn't leave because his attachment had been so good to him. In the three-plus years they had been together, they had really been through a lot—a lot of hysteria about whether or not they should stay together! In the end, they stayed together because they had nowhere else to go. She stayed with her attachment to avoid facing the fear of spending time alone. She had been there and done that so many times before. It was not a very pleasant possibility to look forward to, and she surely did not want to subject herself to it voluntarily. In the meantime, she kept hoping against hope that somehow, some way, her attachment would miraculously disappear or become the love man of her dreams, meaning that she would live happily ever after. That's how she convinced herself, time and time again, to stay. In the meantime, she kept looking elsewhere for something else, although she was not quite sure what it was she was looking for.

Love is the only thing we need. Love is our peace. Love is our joy, health, and wealth. Love is our identity. We go into a relationship looking for love, not realizing that we must bring love with us. We must bring a strong sense of self and purpose into a relationship. We must bring a sense of value, of who we are. We must bring an excitement about ourselves, our lives, and the vision we have for these two essential elements. We must bring a respect for wealth and abundance. Having achieved it to some satisfactory degree on our own, we must move into relationships willing to *share what we have,* rather than being afraid of someone taking it. Joyful sharing and excitement. Value, purpose, and vision. That's what love is about. When we bring these things to the relationship, love becomes a great multiplier and enhances the experience of life. When we do not have these things in place, the search to find love sets up the experiences we need to discover what is true about love and what is not. The discovery process is called the *meantime*.

We enter relationships looking for love, expecting someone to love us or accept us lovingly. This makes perfectly good sense if you consider that we are each born to express and receive love. In some unfortunate situations, we can want love or acceptance so badly that we will do almost anything to get it. We break love's rules. We disregard love's house. We forget to set love boundaries. We allow people to step in, be in, move in, live in our lives in ways that have nothing to do with love. Even when we have boundaries or standards clearly defining what we will do, how we will do it in the name of love, and what we expect in return, there never seems to be enough love to fill the void we have all, at one time or another, felt in our hearts. When we believe we do not have enough love in our lives, we enter the *meantime*. What we fail to understand is that we are the love we seek. Until, however, we can recognize ourselves as love and live in harmony with our true identity, the void grows deeper, wider, and more painful.

They just didn't get it! He called several times during the next several weeks. At first, she refused to return his calls. She was struggling to shake and break her attachment. He had already shaken his, although he had forgotten to tell her that she had been shook! *"Surely she knows!"* he thought. *"She has to know!"* In the meantime, people often forget to say what they mean or mean what they say because they assume you already know. He did not assume that he would pass her on the street, but he did. The moment they saw each other, the thumping started—his mind, her heart, and their body parts. They spoke. Actually, she spoke first. He responded by talking to her about the calls. Feeling guilty, as we often do in the meantime, she agreed to call him later. She did, and they agreed to meet.

When you're in the meantime you want an escape route! You want something to do other than all that meantime stuff. They wanted to do something about their thumping body parts. They wanted to be attached to one another. They thought it was love. It had to be love! Why else would it keep showing up, thumping and giving them the perfect excuse to break all other *attachments*. The meantime is not about breaking up attachments. It is about creating attachments honestly and lovingly. However, in the meantime, the thumping body parts are completely unaware of this little tidbit of information. He made the offer. She accepted. On opposite sides of town, both of their other attachments were fed up with excuses and ready to do another kind of thumping of body parts!

IN THE MEANTIME,
KEEP YOUR NEEDS TO YOURSELF!

People cannot fulfill your needs. They may want to, they may try to. They may convince you that they can, but they cannot. What people can do for one another is make the need seem less urgent. We distract one another so that we forget, temporarily, what we need. We help one another replace a pressing need with something else. In the meantime, the need does not disappear. It dissipates. In a nutshell, people need love. God is love.

What we need is God, but that's too esoteric for most of us to handle. It's also pretty frightening!

To say we need God conjures up some pretty frightening images for most of us, the most frightening of all being those things we believe we will have to give up to get to God. Instead, we say we need the love of another person because this is the kind of love most of us believe we can handle—to some degree or another. We also think we need a house, a car, a few kids, and a job so that we can feed the kids. Of course, these things are important, even essential to our well-being, but what we really need to live on, and live in, is love. We also think that things and people bring more love into our lives. Do they? On some level they do. What they do in actuality is provide us with the opportunity to share the love we are and the love we have within, which is God's love.

We are not always aware of how our needs lead us into dark corners. Try as we might to be alert, strong, and positive when it comes to love matters, many of us seem to always end up someplace we do not want to be—alone in the meantime, looking for a relationship.

Over the years, I have heard absolute horror stories about the goings-on called love. At times I have been amazed that we could believe that something as divine as love could show up looking so ridiculous. In other situations, I have been appalled at the foul things people do in the name of love. Finally, I had to stop. To smack myself. To realize—there is a pattern here! The players are different. The events are different, but some-where underneath it all there is a sameness. Men and women have a tendency to do the same things when they are trying to get their needs met. I decided to keep a list. I wrote down the thirteen most common things we do in search of love or a relationship in which we want to be loved. Each of these things will inevitably fail to meet our needs. They will take us to a hellish meantime experience:

1. All the signs say this is not the one, but you ignore your internal alarms, and move ahead into a love fantasy.
2. Because you fear being alone, or because you believe you cannot have what you want in a relationship, you accept the first person who comes along, only to be left, beaten, ripped off, or impregnated and then left, beaten, ripped off.
3. You confuse friendship and niceness with romantic love.
4. Because someone is nice to you and you are not used to it, you don't know how to say no to them when you realize they are not who you want.
5. You get caught up in the packaging and promises.
6. You force your desires for a relationship onto another person, or issue an ultimatum. Because the person does not know how to say no, s/he goes along with you . . . for a while.
7. Because the other person expresses an interest in you, you respond without really exploring if this is who or what you want.
8. You allow blind faith, which leads to *blind love,* to take you into a relationship that is unhealthy.
9. You choose to believe that what your partner has done to another person, s/he will not do to you.

10. Sexual compatibility is mistaken for love.
11. You stay in a relationship although you are miserable, trying to work things out even when your partner shows no interest in working through the difficulty.
12. You don't express what you really feel because you believe it will hurt your partner's feelings.
13. You choose to believe your partner's lies even when you know the truth. You act like you do not know what is going on when you do.

LOVE IS NO*THING* THAT GIVES YOU EVERYTHING

What can you do when a relationship is not going the way you would like? When things are not working the way you want them to work? How do you learn to take· what you have and make it work to your advantage? As I ask these questions, I am reminded of a story I heard about a woman named Luanne Bellarts, who was born with cerebral palsy. As a result of this disease, Luanne had full use of one toe, on one foot. Raised by very religious parents, she learned a great deal about truth, trust, patience, faith, and love as it related to her capabilities. I am sure most of us would consider this kind of physical limitation to be an insurmountable or monumental defeat. Luanne, however, learned to type on a computer keyboard using her big toe. She wrote the story of her life, *Bird with a Broken Wing*, in this way. Her book was her testimony to the power of faith, in which she eloquently described how to turn trouble into triumph, tragedy into victory. She wrote about the *meantime*, about learning how to take what you are, what you have, and what you can do, and make it work for you.

Luanne's story is not about relationships per se. It is, however, about principles. Truth, trust, patience, honor, and faith are the cornerstone principles of all life's relationships. They are also all the things we receive in the presence of unconditional love. Having learned so much about family relationships, friendships, and, more important, the *selfship,* Luanne documented how to develop and nurture all relationships with the vigilant employment of loving principles. What she learned while lying flat on her back, sitting in a wheelchair, and being totally dependent on others is exactly what we able-bodied beings stumble over, muddle through, fall into, and fail to recognize about relationships. Although Luanne never experienced an intimate, loving relationship with a man, the way we believe it should be, she did with one toe, on one foot, what we spend most of our lives trying to do. She discovered love. Love for herself. The love for and of others. The love of God. She figured out what love *looks* like and what it should not look like. She understood what love *felt* like and what it felt like when there is an absence of love. She discovered how to find love, nurture it, and make it last in yourself, for yourself, and within your life. At age thirty-six, Luanne died of cancer. In the meantime, during the course of her life, she lived in and for love with a tremendous amount of dignity. Finding love and maintaining our dignity is something we often struggle to do in our relationships. The experience of the struggle is called *the meantime.*

Anything you resist will persist! Of course our meantime lovers got caught! Now they and their attachments were all in the meantime! All the things they had ignored, denied, avoided, and resisted were staring them in the face. It was a classic meantime scenario—getting caught, lying, resisting. He got caught because he lied. He told his attachment he loved her when he wasn't sure. He said he didn't want to leave when he did. He told her he was sure when he wasn't. To cover up his guilt about lying, once he got caught, he told his attachment that she had no right to question him! People who get caught in a meantime lie will usually become belligerent and self-righteous. He reminded his attachment that he was grown, with every right to do what he wanted with whomever he wanted! This is another characteristic of those in the meantime: they act very mean.

She got caught because she was resistant and guilty. She resisted being alone. She resisted telling the truth. She resisted doing anything that would make her feel guilty! Guilt is like a big red neon sign sticking out of the middle of your forehead! You know it's there, but you try to act like it isn't! In the meantime, when you are trying to act innocent, you inevitably say something to prove your guilt. She told her attachment that she had done it because he had done it in the past. It was her stuff that she was trying to put off on him. In the meantime, all the stuff you thought you could get away with and from is looking right at you. The question is, *"What are you gonna do about it?"*

In the meantime, one of the things we do is become bold enough to say and do the things we would never say or do under normal circumstances. It's not that we should not say or do them, we choose not to. When things are at the least tolerable in a relationship, we believe that hiding, avoiding, denying, and resisting are the right things to do. We think we are saving someone we love from pain and suffering. The truth is, we are suffering! We are choking on our words! Suffocating our feelings! Twisting our truth! Banging our heads against a brick wall and picking on ourselves—Why?!!! Why?!! Why can't I get this love stuff right?! Picking on yourself is the height of meantime behavior, and it is the very behavior that will make you say or do something you really don't want to do—just like they did.

Whether you are in the midst of a divorce, separation, break-up, or a heated argument, the most loving thing you can do for yourself is to avoid the temptation to blame the other person for what you are feeling. It's you! It's you! I know that's a bitter pill to swallow! I know because I have swallowed many doses of this myself! Sooner or later, we must all accept the fact that in a relationship, the only person you are dealing with is yourself. Your partner does nothing more than reveal your stuff to you. Your fear! Your anger! Your pattern! Your craziness! As long as you insist on pointing the finger out there, at them, you will continue to miss out on the divine opportunity to clear your stuff. Here is a meantime tip—we love in others what we love in ourselves. We despise in others what we cannot see in our-selves. Often when a relationship goes sour we become blind, immune, or resistant to our stuff by making an admirable at-tempt to dump it on the other person. People will resist having your stuff dumped in their lap because all too often it is also their stuff—the stuff they can't see. They resist by fighting or running away. Now get this! As crazy as it seems, the person who stays to fight with you (this does not mean physical fighting or abuse) is usually the one who really loves you. They love you and are willing to duke it out with you and your stuff in order to facilitate mutual healing.

Unfortunately, when you are fighting in a relationship, if you are not clear about your intent, or if you are resistant to knowing the truth, you will get hurt. On the other hand, if the person you are fighting with throws in the towel and runs away, you will also get hurt. You will remain unhealed. Your stuff will settle down for a while, but it is sure to come up again, in another relationship. In the meantime, while you are resistant, unclear, or in fear, please know that fighting is normal and quite common. Being mean to others is to be expected. Never believe that what you do in a meantime situation is the truth about you. It is not! The truth of the matter is, if you are willing to go through the process of fighting, being mean, getting hurt, and realizing *there's got to be a better way!* you will eventually shift out of your pattern into a state of consciousness where you will be healed.

WHERE AM I?

It is important to state clearly and emphatically that the meantime is not a bad place to be. Nor should you assume that if you are in the meantime, you or anyone else has done anything wrong. The meantime is not a signal that you have messed up again or been messed over again. What the meantime is, and will always be, is a catalyst to a deeper awareness of love for yourself and others. It is a therapeutic review of your beliefs, notions, ideas, and perceptions of what love is all about. When we are alone, without a love attachment, we have a pretty good idea about what we feel and where we are as far as love is concerned. When, however, we are in a relationship, having a meantime experience, the picture is often a lot less focused.

As it relates to relationships, most of us don't know where we are most of the time. That's because our ideas and beliefs keep changing according to our experiences. In response, we keep trying to figure out what to do and how to do it. We keep asking, Why? Why did it go wrong? When? When will I get it right? Who? Who will I end up with? How? How will I know *this one* is *the one?* These are pretty run-of-the-mill meantime inquiries. Regardless of what your relationship looks or feels like, if you are asking these questions, you are having a meantime experience. Sometime, however, we will resist asking ourselves probing questions. It doesn't matter! You can be pretty sure you are in the meantime if:

- You know what is wrong with all your ex-lovers, but you are blind to your own weaknesses.
- You are crying for no apparent reason, and you do not want anyone to know you are crying;
- You have been fired or laid off;
- You are separated or recently divorced;
- You were recently robbed or ripped off, sentenced to prison, or recently released from prison;
- You have had six dates with five different people in the last nine months;
- You haven't had any dates in the last nine months;
- You are married or share toothpaste with another person, and you are still looking for a date;
- You are not married but have been sharing toothpaste and closet space and still aren't sure this is what you want to be doing;

- You are not married, do not share toothpaste, and have given up on dating;
- Your mother keeps asking when are you going to have children;
- Your mother keeps asking when was the last time you saw your children;
- You have forgotten how children come into being.

Although there are hundreds of other scenarios, these are common everyday situations signaling that you are having a meantime experience. It is also a pretty sure bet that if you live in one of these situations, you are experiencing turmoil, inner turmoil, as you try to figure out what to do next.

The internal conflict and turmoil of a meantime experience is a direct result of your failure to do one of the following four things for yourself and in your relationships:

1. You failed to be clear and articulate exactly what you wanted, needed, or expected from yourself and from others;

2. You failed to tell the absolute, unedited, microscopic truth to yourself, to another, about yourself, about another, with regards to what you wanted, needed and expected in any relationship;

3. You failed to ask for what you wanted and accepted what was offered while being fully aware it was not even closely related to what you had in mind;

4. You moved forward in a relationship in a consciousness of fear.

Now you are in the meantime, which is life's opportunity to get clear, get real, and heal yourself in preparation for giving and receiving the one thing we all want—pure, honest, unconditional love.

IT TAKES TIME

There is no prescribed period or length of time you can spend in the meantime. It is not a matter of "If I do this, I'll get out quicker!" Or "If I do it this way, I'll never experience this again!" You are always your own experience. What is happening to you is happening through you. You will stay in the meantime for as long as it takes to get your inner workings in order. You will also be there for as long as it takes, not only for you to get ready, but for someone else to get ready. In other words, you may be ready, but your divine mate may not be ready. You may be healed of your insecurities, but your perfect partner may not be quite healed yet. You may have done all the forgiving you need to do, but the person you are waiting for may not have even begun to do forgiving and releasing work. Consequently, you will be in the meantime until the divine person you are preparing for is also prepared and ready for you. Do not be dismayed! This is a good thing! The meantime is *protective* as well as *preparatory*.

Patience is the healing elixir for the meantime blues. Your challenge, whether you like it or not, is to learn to be patient with yourself while you are developing patience. Don't get mad at yourself for being mad or upset, or for feeling bad. When you are in the meantime, there is a tendency to beat up on yourself for what you should or should not be feeling and doing. In the meantime, feel what you feel and allow it to pass. Don't judge your feelings or yourself for having them. Do not label your feelings good or bad, right or wrong. Drop your hands to your sides and give yourself permission to ride out the emotional tidal waves that are sure to surface every now and then. Once you have had enough of feeling bad, or once you are able to understand the core issue that supports the emotion, it will go away. Each time an emotion surfaces, this is a sure sign that you are working through it in order to release it. If you resist the feeling, it will fight you, grow teeth and claws, which it will then use to fight you—it will be fighting for its life! In the meantime, when old feelings and patterns are fighting you for their lives, the most loving thing you can do is be patient with yourself and with what you are feeling.

Patient preparation for loving and being loved unconditionally does not mean you must sit around waiting and twiddling your thumbs. It means that even while you are in the meantime waiting for the divine experience, you can and will have meantime experiences, meantime relationships that are valuable and meaningful. Never believe that what you do in the meantime, even when it means you have short-lived relationships, is a useless waste of time. Every relationship is the relationship you need at that time. Everything you do in every relationship you have prepares and brings you closer to the grand experience of total, unconditional self-love and love for others. Many meantime experiences and relationships are designed to do just that, to bring you closer, not take you all the way. Your job is to avoid the temptation and the trap of thinking that every relationship has to be the relationship that lasts forever and ever Amen.

Remember that you are always being prepared for something better or protected from something worse. When the divine reason for the meantime union has been fulfilled or when the divine season for the meantime experience comes to an end, you will move on to exactly where you need to be.

THE FRUIT AND THE TREE

There is a very good chance that most of us will go through life having one relationship experience after another—some pleasant, some not—without any real awareness of how we got locked into the pattern of moving and hurting, hurting and hiding. We believe we are responding to what has *just* happened or what was *just* said. We believe that the people we have *just* met have influenced the positive or negative experience we have *just* had.

Few of us understand that who we are and what we feel are what we have been and felt for a very long time. It's our *stuff*. *Stuff* is what the meantime is made of. All the stuff you need to know, need to feel, need to sort out, and heal comes to life in the meantime. This is the stuff that makes us overly aggressive or passively self-destructive in the search for love.

Our passive/aggressive behavior patterns are born when we are born. Largely, they are set by the patterns of our birth. Otherwise known as the *birth pattern*. As we move through life we unconsciously re-create the incidents, energy, and environment that existed before and at the time of our birth. Our responses to our birth patterns are often unconscious, which is the very reason we can't always recognize what we do, why we do it, when we are being passive, or why we are being aggres-

sive. If we took just a little time for self-reflection and examina-
tion, we could easily connect what goes on in our relationships
with the pattern of our birth. While we are unaware, we become fixated on trying to figure out what *just happened* and why
it is affecting us so deeply, and often painfully, in the meantime.

My mother was an alcoholic. Shortly before I was born, my
mother was diagnosed as having breast cancer and leukemia. As
it turns out, when she was not drunk, she was sedated because
cancer threatened to rob her of two things she loved, her breasts
and her life. I am told that my mother was very proud of her
breasts. They were, I am told, large and firm—a real source of
her pride in her appearance. When she was not pregnant, they
accented her narrow waistline, which meant she attracted a
great deal of attention. My mother, I am told, thrived on attention. The fact that my parents were not married to each other
also drew a great deal of attention. My father was married to
another woman who lived two blocks away from the home my
parents occupied with my paternal grandmother. My mother was
his mistress who bore his three children. Needless to say, there
was *a lot going on* in the atmosphere into which I was born!

In the womb, we marinate in the energy that becomes the
foundation of our beginnings, our sense of self. Some people
marinate in care, concern, and loving excitement. I marinated
in an internal and external atmosphere that was laced with fear,
confusion, guilt, dishonesty, and dis-ease. Perhaps that is why I
have been a *Type A* personality for a good part of my life. I must
admit that my earliest relationships were strangely similar to
the kind of dysfunction my parents displayed. My first love was
emotionally unavailable. My first marriage was an experience of
verbal and physical abuse. How can something you love cause

you such pain? How can you give up something you love so dearly? These were probably my mother's questions, and they were among the first questions I asked about love and relationships in a very aggressive manner.

You may not know the exact conditions of your birth, or they may not have been quite as dramatic as mine. The fact remains that you learned and experienced things in the womb, and once you left the womb, you probably continued the pattern of behavior in your own life. I was an adult when I learned that my father was verbally, and sometimes physically, abusive to my mother. He tried to get her to stop drinking. She would not. He tried to get her to take care of herself. She could not. He was aggressive in his *love* for her because all accounts indicate that they fought like cats and dogs! Violence is aggression manifesting itself in a very physical way. If you think about it, birth is violent too. It is an act of aggression that pushes you out of the only place of comfort and security you have physically known. In many relationships we confuse aggression and/or violence with demonstrations of love.

WHO WROTE YOUR BOOK OF LOVE?

When a pregnant alcoholic goes into labor, there's a good chance that her senses are dulled. I believe this was the case with my mother. She was drunk, either on liquor or pills, when the pains began. This, I believe, is why she waited until the last possible moment to let someone know I was on the way. Once she let them know, she had to descend four flights of stairs to get out to the street to hail a taxicab. Although we lived only four short blocks from the hospital, it was too late! She had waited too long! By the time a taxi stopped, her water had broken. They say dry births are very painful and very hard. Mine was a dry birth. I am told that my mother fought to hold on to me, but much to her surprise and the cab driver's dismay, I was born in the taxicab right in front of the hospital! Now that's aggressive.

There was quite a commotion, as there usually is at the beginning of any relationship. There was a big mess in the taxi. My mother was out of it, and I was sort of on my own, on the floor of the taxicab trying to figure out what was going on. I can imagine it was like going home after the first date, wondering if you were going to be invited out again! There were people around, but I suspect that they were frightened. That's it! There is always a little fear in the midst of being loved. I am told that one of the nurses who rescued me from the taxicab looked at me and said, "You just couldn't wait, huh? *Impatience!* Now look at this mess!" *I did it wrong again!* There was also the tiny issue that my father wasn't there to help my inebriated mother have his baby. My mother and I were both ashamed of that. Since then, I have had innumerable experiences of being ashamed of myself.

This was my birth pattern, which probably resulted in my perceptions that:

- I am always the one to be blamed. I wish I had a dollar for every time I have said, *"Oh, I see! So now it's my fault!"* in a relationship.
- I have to do everything for myself, by myself, because there is never a man around when you need one! Did I mention that independence has frequently been an issue in my relationships?

- Loving and being loved is something to be ashamed of.
  More specifically, I am ashamed of myself for what I have
  done in the name of love.

It happens to many of us in one way or another. The most
loving experience of our lives, our birth, can quickly be over-
shadowed by everything else that is going on that has nothing
to do with love. Our birth is one of the most profound demonstrations of God's love for us. It is a time when we are loved
and ask for absolutely nothing in return. While we are being
born, however, there's lots of rushing around, noise, fear, and
excitement. There's also pushing, pulling, and screaming. It's a
very aggressive, often violent atmosphere, couched as a natural
expression of life and love. What happened to most of us who
are old enough to read this book is that some element of our
birth or childhood was traumatic. In my case, the trauma left a
lasting impression on my soul that has worked itself out in my
relationship with myself, my parents, and most profoundly, in
my love relationships.

In the womb, we are shaped and molded by God. We are
nurtured, protected, and loved unconditionally by God. At
birth, it is our turn to demonstrate that the love of God has
paid off. We must breathe. Breath, the gift of life, is given to us
by God with no strings attached. It's God's way of saying, "Here
is My life. Take as much as you want. It is the life I give to you
because I love you." What do we do as God is offering us this
precious gift of love? We cry!

Screaming your little head off in God's face is a very, very
aggressive act. This is how people, not God, expect us to demonstrate that we know we have been, and are being, loved.

Crying is what we do when we do not feel nurtured, protected, and loved by people or in relationships. Crying is also what we do when someone looks into our eyes, the mirror of the soul, and says, "I love you." Somewhere in the process of being born, we came to expect people to do for us what God has already done for us—give us life and love, with no strings attached. Somehow, somewhere, we learned to expect from people what we can actually only get from God. Yes, people are God's representatives, but remember, they were born the same way we were born.

LOVE HAS EVERYTHING TO DO WITH IT!

It's not completely our fault, you know. Most of us can't remember back that far, to our birth. Besides that, since the day we were born, there have been very few experiences in which we have been loved totally and unconditionally without having to give anything in return. This is how God loves us from the time we are born until the time we die. In the meantime, most people who come and go in our lives attach tiny little price tags to their love. Sometime the tags are so small we don't recognize that they are tags with strings attached until it is time to pay. Some of the price tags are attached at birth by people and through the environment into which we are born. They become the prices we demand and the prices we pay in our relationships.

Our parents, doctors, and nurses were worried about us. Why is it that people who really love you worry about you? They wanted us to show signs of life—crying, screaming, and turning red instead of blue. When you cry for someone they really believe you love them! Those present at our birth really wanted us to be okay, but they also didn't believe we knew how to do it on our own. How many times have you stayed in a relationship, telling yourself that if you left the other person wouldn't make it? Or, that you won't make it without them? At birth, those who love you or are aggressively worried about you try to help out—they stick something up your nose! Pry your eyes open! Blow in your face! If you don't respond the *right* way in the prescribed amount of time, they can get so worried that they smack you on the behind. *"Hey! Wait a minute! Love hurts!"* How many times in your life have you stumbled, fallen, or been pushed to the conclusion that love hurts?

The truth is that love is supportive and nurturing, not aggressive or demanding. It is protective, not overwhelming. Love expands, gives, and heals. For most of us, our entrance to life was a fairly standard medical procedure. As a result of that process, we have unconsciously concluded that love is painful, confusing, invasive, aggressive, and sometimes violent. You had no idea that there was a great deal going on that had nothing to do with you or love! At birth, while God was freely giving you the gift of love called life, all the other *stuff* robbed you of the experience of His unconditional love. Very often, our *stuff* robs us of the experience of total self-love and unconditional love in our relationships with others.

A friend of mine, Ken Kizer, who helped me understand the impact of the birth pattern, told me he was a forceps baby. Somebody had to come into the womb and drag him out—by the head! Of course, it was done in concern and with love, but the impact on him, he realizes, was profound. He admits that for most of his life he would go into projects and relationships with great enthusiasm. About 75 percent of the way in, he would get pooped. He would stop. He simply could not find the strength or the presence of mind to finish what he had started. As a result of his birth pattern, he had taken a passive approach to life. Aren't many life experiences and relationships like that for some of us? I'm sure we all know someone who has to be dragged kicking and screaming into a relationship. Once there, just when things seem to be going along just fine, the person will bail out. It is sometimes called *fear of commitment*. It is a demonstration of passive behavior, the result of a birth pattern.

I believe that there is a direct correlation between my birth pattern and the fear that resulted in shame in many of my relationships. My friend Ken admits that he was more likely to be passive. I was usually ready to fight. He would throw his hands up in despair just when things were getting good. I was obsessive about getting what I wanted, exactly the way I wanted it. In life, there are times when you have to be passive and times when you must be aggressive. In relationships, this usually translates into not knowing when or how to let a partner support you or when you are being dysfunctional or co-dependent. In and of themselves, neither passive nor aggressive behaviors are inherently inappropriate. When, however, you are in the meantime learning about self-love and unconditional love of others, the goal is to break your birth pattern. The realization has now set in that what you have been doing in your relationships does not work. You also realize that it is up to you to break the mold and unlearn what you have learned in order to create a new love model based on new information.

In the meantime, you want to become conscious of your

patterns and what triggers them. You want to be in touch with what you are feeling and what you do in response to what you feel. You have come to the meantime to facilitate a shift in your consciousness from the passive/aggressive model to a receptive/active one. You want to become consciously aware of yourself and receptive to new information that will lead you to new behavior. Once you are aware that you can do something else, you must become willing to put this new information into practice in your life. When you are receptive you actively want to know what is going on with you. It may be impossible for you to go back to the beginning to find out what was going on at the time you were born. That doesn't matter. You have all the answers you need. Look at your life. Examine your relationships. Examine your expectations about love. Reflect on the prices you've paid, to whom you have paid them, and what it *really* has cost you. You must also examine how your behaviors and expectations have paid off in terms of what you have allowed yourself to do in order to get what you thought was love.

What you know and believe has unfolded through the patterns in your life. Look not only to your relationships with other people, look at your relationships with yourself. Look at your career. How do you respond to the pressures of life? Of love? How do you demonstrate love? What are your expectations for returns on your love investments? When it is time to nurture, support, and shower yourself with love and attention, what is going on that takes priority over you? *The answer always lives in the same room as the questions.* You are the answer. Your soul is saying, "Learn how to love yourself unconditionally no matter what is going on!" The question for you may well be,

"How the heck am I supposed to do that?!!!!" For some the question is, "How can I learn to activate and demonstrate self-love?" For others it may be, "How did I get off track?" or "How can I get back on track?" In the meantime, while we try desperately to answer these and other questions about love and loving, life goes on, and so do our relationships.

Chapter 2
KNOW WHERE YOU LIVE

francine had aggressively done all the right things in the right way. She obeyed her parents and never missed sending a card on their birthdays. She had always paid attention in Sunday school, and never spent her offering money on candy. She had gotten all A's in grade school, and had been the valedictorian in high school and the class president in college. Now she had a good-paying job that offered lots of growth potential. She drove her own car, belonged to the right organizations, recycled every Wednesday, and volunteered some time at the senior citizens center during the holiday season. She had a checking account, a savings account, and a pension fund, and she went to the gym every other day. Francine was on top of her life, in good physical shape, fairly, no, very attractive, and she was also still single. The one thing she couldn't get right was finding a man, and when she did find one that she liked, she couldn't keep him. This is the most miserable meantime of all! The one you sit in, stew in, find yourself in when you have done all the *right* things and gotten the *wrong* results! It is the result of not knowing exactly where you live in relationship to love or how to move to another neighborhood.

There are hundreds of thousands of meantime scenarios that give depth and meaning to life. The meantime between jobs, the meantime between the argument and the reconciliation, between the separation and the divorce, between the test and the results. Each of these meantime experiences, although fraught with anxiety and stress that make them seem unbearable, are emotionally and spiritually profitable. A honeymoon is a meaningful meantime. Likewise, the period of labor preceding a birth is a meaningful but painful meantime. There are those meantimes which are immediately identifiable as being worthwhile and empowering, and there are those that wreak havoc on the soul. When you are in the meantime, you must not make time an urgent matter. Time is of absolutely no consequence when you are doing healing work directed toward inner growth. We make time an urgent matter by using age or status as a measure of accomplishment. *"I should have done this by now!"* or *"I should know/have this by now!"* Nothing could be further from the truth! In the meantime, the clock stops and you are put on God's divine schedule.

MAMA SAID . . .

Gail knew it the moment she met him. Paul knew too, but as the story goes, they had to act like they didn't know. They had to play the game—get to know each other, see if they liked each other, see what they had in common. They had to "take it slow." Paul's mother said, "Make sure you know what you're doing." Gail's mother warned, "Don't be in such a rush!" Gail's script was written. "What if I'm wrong!" Paul's ego screamed. The bottom line is that they both knew love was in the air, wrapping its arms around them. In the meantime, their minds were filled with cautions and precautions from well-meaning loved ones and the world at large. What they had been told had a far greater impact than what they knew within themselves. They had been told what to do and what not to do. They knew what they felt, but still they danced around the truth as if it was a snake poised and ready to bite them. When you dance around or avoid the truth, you will more likely than not end up in the meantime, trying to figure out what you did or did not do right.

When you know, you know! When it is time, it is time! There will be no doubt, no questions. You will instantly be willing to do what is necessary—to act or acknowledge that you are not willing to act. When entering a relationship, you must be able to distinguish between what you know and what has been written into your script by others. There will also be those occasions when you think you know, when you think it's time, when you think you know what needs to be done, but you are not sure of what it is or how to do it. Each of these scenarios is meantime activity. It is designed to make sure you know where you are, what you want, and what you are willing to do to get what you want with as little drama as possible. Where you are in the meantime, the key is to stay in touch with your heart and mind. Think what you are thinking, and allow yourself to have a complete thought. Do not allow your script, your pattern, fear, or any other toxic emotions to stop a thought or feeling in midstream. Do not convince yourself that you cannot do what you need to do or that doing it will not produce the results you desire. In the meantime, ride it out!

Ride out the thoughts, the feelings, the fear, the anger. You are healing your patterns, my dear! Healing is serious business and serious work. Take your time to feel and think. Be patient, remember? You can afford to be patient if you remember that love and all of its glory are patiently waiting for you to break your pattern and do a new thing.

It had been four years since Pat and Eddie had broken up. They spoke to each other at least once a week, but he was seeing other people. She was trying to do the same, but something was wrong! Something, somewhere was terribly wrong, and Pat wanted to know exactly what it was so she could *fix it*. People were starting to stare at her, she thought, every time she went out alone. She didn't want to be alone, but she hated the dating game. Meet someone, go out a few times, decide you like them, but they don't like you. Start all over again. Meet someone, go out a few times, you like him, he likes you, but nothing happens. You get bored. You move on. You meet another someone, go out once, discover he's married. Here comes another one, almost like the other one. You go out, discover he's an idiot, a jerk, or that he thinks this about you. It can be maddening! In the meantime, you don't know what to think about yourself. Is it your hair? Your breath? The spinach that you didn't know was stuck in your teeth while you were grinning at dinner? It's a mystery to you, but it's a mystery you are determined and *destined* to uncover.

While you are playing the dating game, you will have platonic friends of the complimentary gender—the opposite sex. These are the guys you treat like one of the girls, or the girls you treat like one of the guys. You can go out with these people and have a real good time. You can talk to them about any and everything. Although they are fun to be with, they will not, cannot satisfy the romantic cravings you are sure to have in the meantime. Although they have no problem telling you how beautiful or handsome you are, they have made it very clear that they don't want to buy a house or have children with you. In one smooth move, they can give you a much-needed hug and say, "Pass the popcorn." This is why you feel safe with them. You know you can ask them questions and get honest answers. The one question you ask them over and over again is, "What's wrong with me? Why can't I find or keep a relationship?" These friends love you. I mean really, really love you, so they can tell you the truth: "Don't worry about it. You are not ready yet." Correctamundo! You are in the meantime! You are not ready because you have some healing and cleaning to do!

WOULD YOU LIKE TO KNOW THE WAY HOME?

I once heard a story about a little boy who asked his minister, "If we all come from God and he wants us to find our way back home to him, why doesn't he just keep us there in the first place?" Right out of the mouths of babes! If we come from the love of God, why can't we just stay there? What is the purpose of being born, forgetting where we come from, only to discover it so we can go back? I have asked myself this question at least a million times. The answer, as best as I can make of it, is that the journey through life helps us rediscover and remember what home looks like. Life is home. Home is God's house, the place where God keeps all Godly possessions and creations. At home, we are allowed to explore and examine the architecture of the house from top to bottom, inside and out. The exploration is called living. The purpose of this exploration—and everything in life has a definite purpose—is to learn to stand firm upon life's foundation. The foundation of life at home is to remember and experience pure, unconditional love.

Relationships are the tour guides that move us through various levels and parameters of home. They are like rooms, each one a little different, offering a little more or a little less than we want, or need, to remember. Relationships also give us the opportunity to choose and decide where we would like to sleep and how we want to be treated during the exploratory journey through life. In order for us to help ourselves along the way, we are given a map in a tiny suitcase called a heart. The map contains the floor plan of our true home and is filled with directions that lead to the truth about love. Along with the map, we come prepared with a compass. It is called the mind. The purpose of the mind is to support us in the use of the map. Somehow, along the way through the rooms of the house, we get confused. We allow the compass filled with thoughts, be-liefs, judgments, and, of course, patterned perceptions about the house to take over as the guide. In the meantime, while we are trying to read the compass, we leave the packed suitcase in the corner of some room, while we drag ourselves up and down the steps of the house, trying to figure out the right direction. Using the compass without the map takes us over obscure lumps in the carpet, into frightening cracks in the wall, through rooms that are under renovation, and into dark, lonely closets.

From time to time, we will admit that we are lost. We realize that what we are thinking about and doing is not getting us where we want to be—in the attic. This is when we check to see if the compass is in good working order. Most of us do not stop to think about what we are thinking about until we find ourselves in a deep hole in the floor, or amongst the clutter of some pile of garbage. It's also about this time that we will remember the suitcase, the heart. We remember that it is the heart that we have been ignoring that gave us the first warning. It is the heart that we have been afraid to hear, that has helped us find our way through the twists and turns of the house. Even when we are brave enough to hear and trust the heart, we behave as if its guidance is only a fleeting idea. An idea to which we pay very little attention, because we have been told by those who have taken the journey before us, *"Do not under any circumstances trust your heart!"* In the meantime, while we are trying to make the compass work and give us an accurate directional reading, we continue to explore, search, and rummage through the house, missing the treasure buried within it.

BELOW THE BASELINE

We all start out in the basement of life. This is where we are first programmed and indoctrinated about worldly affairs and love affairs by those who love us. It is here that we develop our self-image. Amid blue lights in the basement is also where we bump into issues of self-value and self-worth. These are the attributes that are essential to our ability to develop and maintain wholesome loving relationships. It is in the basement that we develop issues related to survival, where we learn and act out the passive/aggressive behavior patterns that ultimately determine our approach to life. Whether or not we dance and have a good time or spend the night holding up the wall in the basement becomes a pretty reliable relationship barometer.

What we learn in the basement carries over into every aspect of our lives as adults, and most of it does not a good relationship make! Our task in life is to sift through the programmed clutter, the mental garbage, and emotional junk accumulated in the basement and find our way to the attic, where love reigns supreme.

When you live in the basement, you don't know what's wrong with you. You may know that you are not happy, but you have no clue about what to do to make yourself happy. You also have no idea that in order to be happy, you must tell yourself the truth about who you are, what you want, and how willing you are to do what is necessary to get what you want. In the basement, you must allow yourself the privilege of feeling what you feel and expressing what you feel. Most basement dwellers, and those who visit there frequently, are so programmed about what they *should* want that they don't know what *to* want. When they do know, they are afraid that what they want from life will make somebody mad. Rather than do that, they suffer silently. Silently doubting themselves. Silently denying themselves. Silently doing what they think they should be doing, while they want to be doing something else. Silent suffering is a sure sign of a dysfunctional compass.

The basement of life's house can be a pretty miserable place, and your environment always affects your nature. In the basement, you are more than unhappy. You are miserable. When you are miserable you blame yourself, you blame other people, and you name names! You believe that the world is against you, so you keep saying it—over and over to anyone who will listen. *"No one wants to see me get ahead! No one wants me to have anything! No one wants to see me happy! No one wants to love me!"* Even those who are closest to you are out to get you. You don't know why, so you ask, *"Why me?"* The basement is the storage place for the *Why Me Syndrome.* *"Why does everybody hate me? Why does everybody want to see me down, keep me down, want me to fail? Why is it that life and love are not going the way I want them to go? The way I've worked so hard to get them to go."* Why? Because you have been working with the wrong equipment, for the wrong reason, with the wrong intent—that's why!

The purpose of your tenancy in the basement is to learn to recognize the things about yourself that need to be healed, to understand what role you play in your own misery. While you are in the basement, you have no clue that you need to be healed. It's them, not you! It's the family pattern with which you have been cursed! While you are in the basement you are working through all of the programming, the indoctrination, your mother's stuff, your father's stuff that has, through synthesis, become your stuff. In the basement, you must learn to look at the relationships around you as a reflection of you in order to figure out where you want to be in any relationship. The only way to do this is to become willing. You must be willing to release the things that are not working by opening yourself to hearing the things about yourself that you have heretofore not been open to hearing. Willingness is the spiritual cleanser you will need to make your way out of the basement.

The moment you become willing to see yourself, to recognize what you are doing, you will move upward, swiftly. Willingness is the only way in which you can cleanse your heart and mind from having gone through so much hardship for so many years, in the name of love. Love is not about survival. It is about growth, and if you insist on staying focused on survival, your growth will be stunted by those experiences which seem completely useless. Willingness, on the other hand, is your key to remembering that after all of the bad things, the good things will show up. When they do, the so-called bad years, the difficult experiences, will become memories. Memories of what *not* to do, and what *to do*. Those bad experiences were the only way love could get your attention. They were also the routes you chose, instead of consciously moving through life's house, trying to clear your mind of old patterns. There was so much stuff going on, how were you supposed to know that you were being prepared to love yourself and share your love with another person? In the basement, however, you want truth and clarity real bad! The question is, are you willing to do the work required to get it?

The only thing you actually have to do to get out of the basement is admit you need help and be *willing* to receive it. In other words, shift out of the passive/aggressive pattern into a receptive/active mode. You must be willing to look at your own crud without avoiding it or making excuses about it. You must be willing to stop saying, *"This is how I am! And this is how it's going to be!"* That is *willfulness*, insisting that things are the way you see them. This is not the best way to demonstrate a willingness to see things from another perspective, a higher perspective that will take you up a healing path to the highest experience of love. You must be willing to pick up the broom, the mop, and the dustcloth and get to work cleaning yourself up and out. Cleaning out the old thoughts and behavior patterns so that you can get an accurate reading of your heart with your emotional compass. The good news is that in the basement, you will not actually do the work. The only requirement is for you to be willing to do it. Once you become willing, you shift. You will find yourself on the first floor of love's house, which is where the cleaning actually begins.

FIRST FLOOR! GOING UP!

The first floor of life's house is where we live when we know we need to heal, but we don't know exactly what it is that we're healing. What I mean to say is, we don't know what's wrong. During this phase of the journey through life, we are at least willing to admit that we have thus far been involved in miserably dysfunctional relationships, but we are no longer blaming other people—what they did, what they didn't do, how good and innocent we are, how low down and rotten they are. It is here that the realization has finally set in; the finger you are using to point at them must be used to probe within. This can be a very frightening place to live! It is on the first floor that you must admit to yourself, "I know I have played a role in my own unhappiness, but I don't know what the role is or why I have chosen to play it." This is a good sign! As a tenant in life's house, you finally understand, whether you are aware of it or not, that love is listening to your every word. In the most sacred part of your being, you want love to know that you are very serious about healing yourself and your beliefs about love.

It is the asking of the probing questions that opens the floodgates of healing in your soul. When you ask, it means you are open to receive the answers. You are also willing to know the truth. On the first floor, the spiritual cleaning product you must employ is truth. Truth helps you to see beyond the veil, beyond the distortions. Truth is like an antibacterial disinfectant that will keep the germs of fear, fantasy, and unconscious choice from spreading any further in your life. In order to disinfect yourself using truth, you must learn to listen to your body. You must recognize when you are feeling uncomfortable, unhappy, dissatisfied about what you are doing to get or keep love. This is a good sign! As the feelings intensify, you will continue expressing your bodily and emotional discomfort in the form of questions. Questions will facilitate reflection upon your past actions and experiences.

It is here on the first floor of love that we find the wisdom of experience to be our greatest teacher. Reflecting on your past choices is the key to understanding the inappropriateness of your approach, as well as the fallacies and fantasies that have been holding you down. You will ask, *"Okay, what am I thinking? What am I feeling?"* You will get an answer because you have become willing to know. More than that, you are now willing to accept responsibility for what you know. Responsibility is the detergent you must use to discover what you do, when you do it, how you do it, and why you do it. The answers will reveal to you exactly how you ended up in the meantime loveless and/or confused!

On the first floor, you are engaged in an information-gathering process, and you must take total responsibility for gathering the information that you need. With this information you can begin cleaning the germs and fungus of programming, negative self-talk, misery, and unhappiness. You will recognize yourself in what is going on around you. You will realize that *you* have attracted the emotionally unavailable person, the abusive person, the unsupportive person. You will recognize that *you* seem most interested in the very person who is not the least bit interested in you. You will understand all the things *you* have done to try to make an unworkable situation workable. You will eventually become aware that your experiences are the result of what you have been thinking, saying, and doing. As this clutter is cleared, you become better equipped and willing to acknowledge, *"Hey! This is me! This relationship is me! This unhappiness is me! This is my stuff! It's here in my face, and I have to start cleaning it up!"* Learning to accept responsibility for cleaning up your first-floor mess is exactly why you must spend some time in the *meantime*.

Before you can leave the first floor, you must know what works and what does not work. You must understand that shutting down when you have a disagreement doesn't work to make things better. You need to realize that hiding, running away, or avoiding difficulties in a relationship does not get you what you want. You will have the revelation of, "This is what I'm doing to create friction and stagnation in my life and relationships." This revelation is your *Ah Ha experience*. Ahhh Haa! This is what I do when I am afraid. Ahhh Haaa! This is what I do to avoid telling the truth. You will see all of this as the result and reflection of your experiences and patterns. Unfortunately, once you see it, you won't have a clue about what to do about it! It doesn't matter, that was not your assigned task on this floor. The first floor is where you live in order to discover what's wrong. The second floor is where you learn what to do about it. Once you have all the information you need, pack. There is a place opening for you on higher ground.

AIN'T NO MOUNTAIN HIGH ENOUGH!

On the second floor of life's house, you know you need to be healed. As a result of reflecting on your experiences without blame or feeling victimized, you have a new level of insight about yourself. The challenge of living here is that you know you must do something, but you don't know what to do. You realize if you do not know what to do, you could fall back through the floorboards into the dank basement. It's not such a long fall, but you want to avoid it at all costs. It is here that you will start reading books on love, life, and anything remotely relevant to the two. You will begin to attend workshops in an effort to improve yourself. You may be running around like a chicken without a head trying to figure out the right way, path, and method to your healing. Your healing has become an urgent matter. You want to do it, but you also *must* do it. You will feel anxious, perhaps desperate. You start to turn everything, every little experience, into a big thing. You watch yourself under a microscope, afraid that if you blink your eye for one second you are going to fall miserably, hopelessly in love and get messed over again. Not knowing what to do to get or keep a love relationship makes us all a bit crazy!

The second floor of life's house is the most important level of all, for it is here that a deeper level of learning begins. The first, last, and only lesson you must master at this level is, *There is absolutely nothing wrong with me!* Or anyone else! You now understand that every experience, every relationship, every heartbreaking or dishonorable event in your past was a necessary element of your growth. You will discover that God has always and will always love you, no matter what you have done or what you may do. How do you know this? You will know because you realize that only God and the love of God could have picked you up out of the basement. You couldn't have done it on your own, because you did not know what to do!

Now that you've got that, get this: Your progression has been phenomenal! In the basement you didn't know what was wrong. On the first floor, you learned what it was. Here on the second floor you will learn that there has been absolutely nothing wrong with what you have been thinking, believing, saying, or doing, other than the fact that it did not get you what you want. In essence this means that *you know what not to do.* While you thought you were at a complete loss, the fact is that *knowing what not* means *knowing what to.* It's called *change your mind.* If what you are doing does not get you what you want, change your mind! You must change the floor tiles, draperies, wallpaper, room arrangement, the entire decor of your mind. You will do that by surrendering everything you once thought was true —true about you, and true about love. You will now know that it is not true, so rather than try to fix it, you are willing to give it up! That is what surrender means. Not doing a single thing, not making a single decision, not engaging in a single activity based on what you once believed. Surrender is an abrasive cleanser, and it is the spiritual cleanser for the work you must do on this floor. A word of caution: Surrender works best when it is used in combination with forgiveness.

Be willing to hear the unpleasant. Be willing to face the uncomfortable. Surrender the belief that you cannot deal with confrontation, rejection, or abandonment by forgiving yourself for ever believing such things. You are more than equipped to handle any situation when you stand in a consciousness of surrender and forgiveness. You know why? Because you no longer have a need to be right. Your only goal will be to live, love, and be happy. Your broken pieces will be healed by love. Your mangled mind will be repaired by love. Your house will be cleaned by love. You now know that hiding, avoiding, judging, shutting down, and living in fear does not make you happy. In response to wanting love, you will choose not to do these things anymore.

On the second floor, you are really shifting from the passive/aggressive model to a receptive/active approach. This is a floor of major transition. Transition is the result of surrender and forgiveness. As you give up one thing, it must be replaced with something else. In order to replace what you release, you must be receptive. That is why you are reading so much. It is also why you will invest so much in workshops. You will gather new information to replace the old programming. You will search for new approaches to old situations. Having cleared a great deal of mental clutter, you can now hear yourself think, and you are willing to hear other people. You will be willing to express yourself without fear of judgment and allow others to express themselves without shouldering the responsibility for what they do or feel. My, my, how you have grown! It's the beauty of surrender. It is the blessing of forgiveness. With these two cleaning tools under your belt, you will begin your ascension to the third floor.

THE POSSIBLE DREAM

You are now well on your way to discovering the truth about yourself and love. At this point you will know what's wrong and what to do about it. That in and of itself is difficult, but there's another catch. On your climb between the second and third floors, each time you apply what you know, another situation will arise to test if you trust what you know. The basement is willingness. The first floor is truth and responsibility. The second floor is surrender and forgiveness. In order to make it to the third floor, you will need trust and patience. Patience will be required in order to know what, when, where, and how much of what you have learned needs to be applied in every experience of your life. Trusting yourself to *know that you know* is a very necessary step toward developing patience and self-love. You must give yourself time to grow and nurture yourself while you are growing through life and love experiences. What makes the experience of the climb from the second to the third floor even more challenging is the fact that each step between the second and third floors is covered with your stuff! Childhood stuff! Fear stuff! Ego stuff! In order to complete your journey without becoming beat down and worn out, you must learn how to walk through your stuff, embrace it, accept it, and love it. This, my dear, is no easy task!

For some there may be two or three steps between the second and third floors. For others there may be two hundred or three thousand. The steps will be the number of new, similar, or repeat experiences required to help you get it. You must get that loving yourself is all that really matters. When you love you, you can love everybody and anybody else. This does not mean that people will not make you mad. Instead, you must learn how not to get mad or how to love people even when you are mad. On this leg of the journey, you will not always feel up to making the climb. You will want to whine, pout, and have things your way. It's just a temporary mood swing. Know that it will pass. There will be times when you feel totally ill-equipped. Know that you can do it! You will review the steps you have taken and celebrate how far you have come. It may not be easy, but you've got this book and loads of experience you can share with someone who is down in the basement. Sharing what you've learned and helping others is a good source of renewal.

One day, when you are not even expecting it, you will see the light! You will hear the words, feel the feeling, experience the splendor of living on the third floor of life's house. You will be in love with yourself and with life. You made it! Even though you will not be fully healed, you know what to do, how to do it, and why it is necessary to keep love at the center of every-thing. You will begin to teach other people what you have learned by sharing your own very personal stories without fear of what they will think about you. You will talk about your experiences in and out of love without pain or anger. You will know in the deepest part of your soul that while you were learning, remembering, and re-creating your ideas about love, love was standing by your side, listening and watching. When you get this, when you really understand that love has always been and will always be the only thing you need, you will be completely at home on the third floor. The work is not over, but you are now able to do a lot more a lot faster.

THERE'S NO NEED TO BE AFRAID OF HEIGHTS!

The third floor is where you will live when you still have healing work to do but there is no urgency or anxiety attached to it. This is a state of consciousness in which you know *what* needs to be done and are now mastering *how* to do it, all of the time, in every single situation. You live on the third floor when all things and every thing makes absolute sense. And when they do not, you don't worry about it. At this level of your development you will be willing to surrender, you become open to forgiveness, and you trust yourself. You have enough love in your heart to be an active participant in any further healing that needs to be done for yourself or anyone else. You come here, to the third floor, to perfect how and why you do what you do.

By the time you reach the third floor you have learned the importance of telling the absolute truth all of the time. You can relate every experience back to your true thoughts and honest feelings. You will recognize that your poor choices, faulty decisions, and bad judgments were made in fear or impatience rather than in pursuit of love and truth. The good news is that you rarely do this anymore because prayer, meditation, and reflection are a staple diet for you. On the third floor, you develop the courage to accept total responsibility for every aspect of your life, without the need to beat up on yourself for what you think or feel. When you are not feeling bruised and battered by life, you can look at yourself in the mirror every morning and be pleased with who you see. This is what is called —easy living! What may not be so easy are the adjustments that will have to be made. You see, on the third floor is when *shift* really starts to happen, when you are doing what you have learned, the people around you will have to adjust. You have learned what to do and you are doing it in a different way. People are not going to be happy about this! They liked the old you, the predictable you, the hysterical you. Now you are trying to be different, and people won't like it!

On the third floor, everything you know will take on a different meaning. Surrender, for example, will now mean that you are willing to surrender every relationship you have. That's right! Every relationship that is based on the old you must shift, change, or be released. These are the relationships that tempt you to engage in basement or first-floor behavior. These are the conditional second-floor relationships born in the chaos of your stuff. By the time you reach the third floor, you are consciously aware that as you shift out of your old patterns, some people and things are going to fall away. The things that once made you happy can no longer make you happy. The attitudes and behavior that once occupied your life, making it a dramatic production, will no longer be worth your time and energy. This will probably be the hardest stuff you will ever do, because it is here that the old you is going to challenge the new you. It's called internal conflict. Don't let this worry you! You will know exactly what to do. If you don't, rest assured that is why you are here, on the third floor of life's house, to practice and master how to do it.

As you casually move around in your new dwelling space, you will realize that because you have new information you now have the perfect opportunity to do things in a new way. This is miraculous! You will know that your role in life is to serve and support people while honoring yourself. These are the only spiritual cleansers you will need from this point on— acceptance, service, support, and honor. You will also know that as long as you use these four cleansers as the basis of your decisions and actions in your relationships, everything you do will turn out just fine—eventually. When it doesn't look the way you thought it would look, you now know better than to worry about it.

How did this happen? How did you get so wise? Somewhere, on the steps between the second and third floors, as you diligently work to clear away your stuff, you will come upon a startling realization. You will realize that you are not alone, have never been alone, and will never be alone. In response, you will no longer feel isolated. Your mind and heart will be united through the power of unconditional love, which means you can be perfectly content being with yourself. You will love yourself just that much. This is really, really good for you! From this point on, all you have to do is remember that everyone in your life is a reflection of you and a reflection of God. This will make it very easy for you to determine how to treat people and how to expect them to treat you. When unconditional love is your reality, you will treat all people the way you would want to be treated, the way you would treat God. And you know what? They will treat you the same way.

Many people become permanent residents of the third floor. This is perfectly acceptable. You can live in this place and state of consciousness for many years and be totally satisfied. You can live here following the death of your life partner or after the termination of a long-term relationship. You can live here whether you are straight or gay, black or white, male or female. The third floor is like a retirement community—you come here to rest, rejuvenate, reflect, and deepen your awareness of life. You will find things you love to keep you busy, and you just don't worry about life anymore. Instead you live it. You will work on the house, in love. You will work in the house, with love. You will have wonderful neighbors, good friends, and your life will be a pleasant dream. You will realize that there is a floor above you, and you also realize the only thing you need to do to get up onto that floor is make a slight shift. That floor is the attic.

CAN YOU SET THE TABLE?

Before we explore the attic, here's a simple "Know Where You Live" test. After reading the following scenario, select the letter response that best describes your natural response to the situation. Unless you are quite sure that you live in the basement, please make a concerted effort to tell the truth.

Rose and John met in their freshman year in college. They started out as study buddies. Their relationship grew and blossomed as they endeavored to study each other's body. They were both quite mature, very dedicated students, looking forward to bright and successful futures—he as a mechanical engineer, she as a communications specialist. By the time they were seniors, they were more than buddies, less than fiancés. They had more than a casual loveship, but not the level of commitment needed to become engaged. They were at the "in between" time of their relationship. It was serious, but not that serious. They had plans, individually and together, but they just weren't ready to act on those plans yet. They had been monogamous, not by agreement, but by choice. Things just sort of worked out that way, and they were both pretty pleased.

During the first half of their senior year, John told Rose that a junior student had caught his eye. In many ways, she reminded him of Rose. He went on to say that he was interested in exploring the possibility of a relationship with her. He told Rose that he wanted to be honest with her, he respected her just that much. If you were Rose, being the level-headed young woman that you are, considering the length and depth of your relationship with John, you would answer in which of the following ways?

A. I want you to be sure about our relationship. Because we've been together for four years, I think you should explore possibilities with other people. If, however, you decide to have sex with her, please use protection.

B. If that's what you want to do, do it. I trust you to do the right thing. I don't feel threatened in any way. (She says this to John but she doesn't really mean it!)

C. Are you some kind of nut! What the heck are you talking about? You can't do that! You think I'm just going to sit here picking my nose while you run around with some chicky from LA? I hate you! I hate you! I thought you loved me! How could you even think such a thing?

D. You remain silent. Leave the dormitory. Walk down the road to the railroad tracks, where you lie face up on the tracks and drink scotch straight out of the bottle!

If you answered A, you are exhibiting third-floor behavior. You know how to do what you need to do, which in this case is surrender and trust. You realize that love is not possessive. You know that you cannot lose what is meant for you and that if something is going to happen, it is going to happen. You appreciate John's honesty and feel confident that your friendship will remain intact, while your *loveship* could very well be altered. You send him off with your blessings, knowing he will keep you informed of the progress of the relationship. When he leaves to go on his first date, you pray for peace of mind and then continue studying for your exam.

If you answered B, you are exhibiting second-floor behavior. You know what to do, but not how to do it. Your stuff is in the way! You are saying one thing when you really mean another. You are not expressing your truth, because you do not trust John to honor and respect your feelings. If you told him how you really felt he might get mad at you. As soon as he leaves, you start crying and call your girlfriend to tell her what happened. She tells you what you should do, how you should do it, and why you should do it. You listen. You cry. You do nothing else.

If you answered C, you are exhibiting first-floor behavior. You don't know what to do or how to do it. You feel betrayed, disrespected, and you are definitely in fear. You really want to hit John, but he's much bigger than you. Instead, you throw him out, scream at him while he's leaving, and call home to momma. She tells you don't worry about it, he'll be back. You know your mother never lies, but you don't believe her this time. She tells you to come home this weekend to have a good home-cooked meal. You hang up, go to bed, and cry yourself to sleep.

If your response is D, you are definitely exhibiting the drama of basement behavior. In this case your brain is flatlined, which means you don't know what the problem is, but you are sure there is one. *"Why me? What did I do? Why does this kind of stuff always happen to me? What's wrong with me?"* You have no faith in John, no confidence in yourself. Lying on the railroad track, threatening to kill yourself is how you plan to pay John back for what he has done. Of course, you are not really sure what he has done. The liquor, you hope, will make you drunk enough so that you will not feel the pain when the train runs over your body. Of course, there hasn't been a train down these rusty old tracks in forty years, but who knows that?

THE QUALITY OF YOUR MIND!

Love has prepared a wonderful suite for you in the attic of its house. It is called the *Love Is Sweet* suite. Thoughts about living in the attic may conjure up images of a dark, dank, dismal, uninhabitable place. In life's house, however, the attic is the haven of unconditional love. It is a beautiful and expansive place, with a great view of life's grandest images. It is a quiet, serene place that fosters a perpetual expression of love. The journey up to the attic facilitates a shift in perception. It is this shift that helps us to establish relationships based on the unconditional love of self. It is also this perceptual shift that enables you to demonstrate not only that you know what love is, but that you are able to act in love all of the time. The *Love Is Sweet* suite is located at the tippy top of life's house, which is why we probably liken finding true love to a "mountaintop" experience.

At this level of living, love is all there is. There is nothing else. Your job is to put love into action in every single aspect of your life. You will shower yourself with love. You will allow others to shower you with it. In the attic, you may recognize that there are still some loose ends hanging around in your consciousness, but you can leave them hanging. You will know that love will handle them in the appropriate way, at the appropriate time. If while you are in the attic you fail for any reason to demonstrate love, the response will be so quick and disruptive, the pain so excruciating, you will be forced to resume a posture of love. At this level of living love is your peace. Love is your strength. Love is your abundance. Love is your health. Love is all there is for you. You will absolutely shower everything and everyone with love. This is where you will live when you surrender your total being to love.

There is only one way to shift your consciousness from painful conditional attachments to peaceful unconditional love. You must create new love expectations based on honor, respect, and support. Honor what *you* feel by believing you can have what you want. Respect where *you* are in your life, understanding that when you are ready to move forward you will. Support yourself by refusing to accept less than you want. This is your foundation—what you do and how you treat yourself. In order to establish this new foundation in your consciousness, you must create new responses to life's challenges that are based in love. Your level of self-awareness and commitment to love will be matched by those you attract. When it is not, you have a choice to make, and you have no fear of making it in a way that is honorable to you.

Living in the attic does not mean that you will never again be tempted by the basement, first-floor, or second-floor experiences. What it does mean is that you will recognize the experience for what it is and make the shift. It means that as you shift, you will facilitate healing and growth for someone else. That is the beauty and ultimate purpose of living in the attic—you will now become a teacher. You will be a role model. You will teach others the full and true meaning of love by being a living example of love. This is where Jesus lived. This is where Buddha lived. They taught love by living love. This is where Mother Teresa lived. They each gave of themselves selflessly in the name of love, for the sake of love. The attic is where we are all born to live. It is where we will live when we stay in love no matter what else is going on.

It's time to pick up our mops, brooms, and dustcloths and do some spring cleaning!

THE BASEMENT

it's that wonderful time of the year again when every-thing outside starts to perk up and look beautiful. It's also the time that we begin to notice that all of the things inside look dank, dark, and dusty. It's just plain old dirty! We scramble to clean up our messes, and while we hate to admit it, that's what our relationships often look like—a mess!

When we look outside it seems as if everything is perfect for everybody else. Then we look at what we have . . . there's dirt and clutter everywhere! We have accumulated so much stuff over the years, it has been impossible to keep up with it or know what to do about it. Our house, our relationship house, needs cleaning. It's that springtime cleaning! Time to pick up, sweep out, get rid of the old, useless, worn-out stuff that we have been hanging on to.

Chapter 3
SPRING CLEANING

it had been fourteen years. Fourteen long, passive years. They weren't all bad. As a matter of fact, they hadn't been bad at all, just long. It was three days before the fifteenth year when he realized he just couldn't do it anymore. Jack could not stay with her or listen to her constant complaining and badgering one more year. He had to go and he knew it. Now he would let her know it too. Helen would think he was kidding, again. She would accuse him of having another woman, again. She would scream, cry, and swear at him again. The same way she had done in years three, seven, and twelve when he had made similar announcements. He loved her, but there was something that just didn't click between them anymore. Perhaps it wasn't her at all. Could be, he thought, that it really was him. Maybe he was stupid, weak, or as she put it, *dismally dysfunctional.* He would take the weight, the blame, and be the bad guy, but he knew he could not, would not, stay another long year. He knew he *loved* her, but he wasn't in love with her, and he had to go.

He would keep *loving* her as he was walking out of the door because his meantime had been too long.

It's time! You've been putting it off long enough. Things are piling up, and you can't find what you are looking for. With regard to relationships, this means you cannot figure out what went on, what's going on, or what to do about any of it. There's a foul odor, the origins of which you do not know. You have become aware that there are little holes in the walls of your life. Termites, perhaps? Something eating away at the very core of the structure, your structure, which is your life and affairs. As you scan the space your life occupies, things look pretty dusty. Your mind is cluttered, congested, and you need some breathing space. You have come to the realization that you must, *you simply must,* clean out the corners of your mind, dust under the bedrock of your heart, rearrange your beliefs, ideas, and perceptions, which, like dresser drawers, contain all the goodies you have accumulated. It's time to air out every room so that you can take a deep breath and not choke. It's spring cleaning time.

Why couldn't Jack get himself together? God knows she had tried in every way she knew to help him. She told him what to do and how to do it. She had told him at least a hundred times or more how they could move ahead faster and have more joy and excitement in their lives. Did he listen to her? No! He made excuse after excuse—he couldn't leave the city, change his job, buy a new house, make more love. She was sick of it! She was sick of him! But she loved him. There was something about him that she loved. Perhaps it was her. Perhaps, she thought, he had been right all along. Maybe she was selfish, or as he had said, *incredibly insatiable.* She had tried her best to change, but it didn't work. She liked to travel. He liked to read. She liked money and nice things. He liked secure investments. She liked sex. He liked television. This was a mess! A real mess! She would have to clean it up before their fifteenth anniversary party.

IT'S A DIRTY JOB, BUT YOU'VE GOT TO DO IT!

A total housecleaning is a pretty tall order, but it is something we all have to do. As we are all aware, the longer you avoid doing it, the more pressing the need becomes. We are talking here about getting rid of the dust bunnies in the crevices of your brain. These are the old hurts and pains you have accumulated. We are referring to the removal of the mold and fungus that has become lodged in your heart. This refers to the people with whom you are *still* angry after all these years. Let us not forget the need to throw out the old, those things you did in all of your yesterdays, and those with whom you did it. Yes, we are referring to those things you are still beating yourself up about, and allowing others to beat you up about. The purpose of this cleaning is to learn to appreciate what you have and to make space for something new.

What was he thinking when he married her? Thinking is the operative word here! Jack admitted that he hadn't been doing much of that at all around the time he met Helen. He was lonely back then. He felt like a failure at that time. He felt like his life was going nowhere really fast, and then Helen came along. She gave him hope. Helen saw something in Jack that he did not see in himself. She motivated him. She inspired him. When she was younger, she could really light his fire! Now she got on his nerves. Now she picked on him. Now she said to him all the negative things that he always believed about himself. She was just like his mother: a go-getter, a social butterfly, a royal pain in the butt! He was just like his father: a company man, content with a beer and a good television program, a penny-pincher who was concerned about the future. His parents stayed together for the children's sake. Jack and Helen, thank God, did not have any children. The one they tried to have was stillborn. Helen was never willing to try again.

We don't like to do it—cleaning, that is. We particularly don't want to do it when it's nice outside, when things seem to be going along pretty smoothly. Who wants to be bothered with sweeping, dusting, mopping, and moving furniture when they could be reading a good book or sipping iced tea at the country club? Perhaps that's why we put it off for so long. We know it needs to be done, but we just can't seem to get motivated to do it. That's what happens in our relationships. We know there are things that need to be said, need to be done or undone, but we just can't seem to get motivated. Like cleaning the house, cleaning a relationship can be overwhelming, like there's too much to do and too little time to do it. For some reason, when the house or the relationship gets really bad, we believe we are simply not equipped to do what needs to be done. We want help. Somebody has got to help us do the work. That help usually comes in the form of a problem. Problems provide great motivation for cleaning up relationships, love issues, and the house.

Helen's plan had backfired big-time. She really thought that if she got involved with another man, the man she really wanted would come and get her. That is the only reason she started dating Jack. She thought she could make Jamie mad enough, jealous enough to come back. She was wrong! In the process things got out of hand. People started telling her what a nice guy Jack was and how happy they were for her. How could she disappoint the people! That's what her mother had told her, never disappoint people. Before she knew what was happening, Momma had planned the wedding. She couldn't back out. She could have, but she didn't have the courage to do it. Besides, over time, she had grown to like Jack, even love him a little bit, notwithstanding the fact that he was not who or what she wanted to marry. But she did. She married Jack, and now she was trying to figure out why.

YOU CAN'T PLAY IN A DIRTY BASEMENT

When you don't do what makes you happy, you eventually become angry and resentful. Many basement dwellers are this way. They take a passive approach to their happiness and then blame other people for their misery. What they are actually doing is making excuses for themselves. Basement dwellers have lots of excuses to explain why they are the way they are and why they cannot do what they want to do. They are victims— victims of life and, of course, victims of love. They can never seem to find anyone to love them the way they want to be loved. They are always being cheated on, treated badly, used up, and dumped. They can't for the life of them figure out the reason. Why? Because basement dwellers have done it to them- selves. They have abandoned their heart's desires to do what they think is the right thing to do. Jack and Helen were both basement dwellers. Neither was doing what he or she wanted to be doing, and neither was telling the truth about it.

They were three years into acting like things were just fine when the disaster happened. Helen discovered that she was pregnant. It was also around this same time that she heard through the grapevine that Jamie was about to marry one of her high-school friends. At first she was hopping mad. *"How could he?!!!"* Then she remembered that it was she who got married first. *"How could I have been so stupid?!!!"* Now she was beating up on herself, feeling sorry for herself. The anger and self-flagellation grew into a catatonic state of depression that almost killed her and did, she believed, kill the baby she was carrying.

In some ways, building a relationship is like preparing a meal. You must have the right ingredients in the right combination to ensure a successful outcome. As a precautionary measure, while you are cooking, you must taste the dish to make sure everything is going okay. If, at any point, the dish does not taste right, you may have to add a little something. This addition, however, does not ensure that the dish will turn out right. There are times when adding too much or too little can ruin the entire effort. There are also times when you add the wrong thing. In an attempt to rectify this error, you add something else. Your good sense tells you to throw the dish out and start all over again, but you don't want to waste what you have. This is what you tell yourself to hide the fear that you may not succeed in making the dish correctly. Overcompensating or undercompensating for what you did or did not do at the beginning sometimes works when you are cooking. It rarely works in relationships.

The proper ingredients must be present at the start of a relationship. Along the way, tasting or assessing helps to keep you on track. If, however, the right ingredients were not included at the beginning, adding more stuff can make matters worse. If you want to know the end, look at the beginning! It rarely works to add a baby to a bad marriage. It hardly ever works to move a failing relationship to another neighborhood. Making more money does not make irreconcilable differences reconcilable. Buying a new house with a big mortgage does little to improve communication. When these problems are at the root, the core of the relationships, adding something to them is like putting a Band-Aid on cancer. In these instances, adding something may make it appear to be better. In the long run, however, a Band-Aid cannot heal cancer! Cover-ups do not address the core issues in a bad relationship. The only way to heal a sour relationship is to admit that there is something very essential missing. Once you make the admission, you must be willing to do the work to find out what that essential ingredient is. You must retrace your steps, remembering what you did or did not do. Once you discover what's missing, it could very well mean that you will have to scrap the entire thing and start all over again.

When the baby died, Jack was beside himself with grief. He had put so much hope in this child. He had hoped the baby would make their relationship better, give them something in common, something in which they could share an interest. How could their baby die just like that? Jack wanted to know why. He demanded to know why! Helen knew why. She did not want to have Jack's child. She wanted to have Jamie's children. She was convinced that his marriage had killed off that possibility, and she was sure it had killed the child in her womb. Jack and Helen had to hang on to each other just to make it through the day. It was then that they confused need with love. Exchanging needs in the absence of a commitment to build an honest relationship, they became even more confused. So confused, in fact, that they thought they could make the marriage work. In an attempt to do so, Jack became totally passive: *"Just let her do what she wants to do, and don't make trouble!"* Helen became impossibly aggressive: *"I'm going to do what I want to do, and he better not say a word to me!"* Jack took up residence on the couch, feeling sorry for himself and asking, "Why me?" Helen became preoccupied with doing whatever was necessary to survive—survive the guilt, the shame, the fear that Jack would find out what she had done. They both realized that the marriage was a mistake. He thought it was her mistake—she should not have married him. She thought it was his mistake—he should not have married her. Those who live in the basement really don't know what's going on. They were both mistaken.

IN THE MEANTIME, HEAL YOURSELF!

The presence of love is a healing power. The effects of this healing are what we are all born to discover and experience in every aspect of our lives. It is sometimes difficult to realize this because, in the meantime, we are not getting the love we want, in the way we want it. The meantime is often a time of vagueness. You are experiencing a vague anxiety that you cannot quite pinpoint. It's in your head. No, your chest. No, in your heart. You may look okay on the outside, but on the inside there is something else going on.

Sometimes that something else is sadness. It's like you are walking a tightrope, about to fall. You are trying to hold on, to stay grounded, but slowly, bit by bit, you realize that you or your relationship is falling apart. You are sad about it, but there doesn't seem to be anything you can do about it. In the meantime, you must remember that just when things look like they are falling apart, they are actually falling into place—the divine place they should be for everyone involved. When you are in the meantime, you are in a time of healing preparation. You are being prepared for the grandest experience of your life— unconditional love. In the meantime, you must be willing to endure the process of feeling vague confusion and helplessness. Remember, however, that the meantime is not a permanent condition. It is a healing process.

There is always a process involved in any healing endeavor. The first step in the process is to be willing to pray and ask questions. We must stop trying to figure out what is going on! Sooner or later you should realize that if you knew what you were doing to make yourself miserable or crazy, you would not be doing it. Stop! Pray! Ask! In order to do this, you must be willing to stop moving, talking, thinking, and thumping. It would take about thirty seconds, but thirty seconds can be a long time when you are in fear, when you are hurt, or when you are confused. The good news is that prayer helps to alleviate confusion. Once your mind is clear, it is imperative that you ask yourself three probing questions:

1. What am I feeling?
2. What is it that I want?
3. What am I feeling about what I want?

Once the questions are asked, the healing begins, and the answers will pour forth. *The answers are always within reach of the questions.* You, however, must be open, receptive, and willing to receive answers.

What you are feeling is always at the core of your experience. Feelings and emotions are the energy that motivates us to act and speak. Feelings are often the answers behind the questions we have in our relationships. When you get in touch with your feelings, you have a major clue to why you are doing or have done certain things. Feelings are the seeds. Experiences are the fruit. By the time the seeds bear fruit, we are usually in the middle of a mess. We react to the mess by getting busy, trying to clean it up when what we should be doing is digging up the seeds—exploring our feelings. In a relationship, it is imperative that you stay in touch with what you are feeling in order to determine what is motivating your behavior.

What you feel usually determines what you want. More important, what you feel about what you want always determines what you do. If you feel that you can't have what you want, you may be acting out toward others in anger or resentment. If you have judged what you want as wrong or believe that you are wrong for wanting it, you may be acting out fear —the fear of being found out. In any relationship, what you want and what you feel or believe about what you want will determine the quality of your interactions. At a very personal and intimate level, these feelings and beliefs help you determine your boundaries, the ways in which you will allow yourself to be treated and how you treat others. When a relationship goes sour or falls apart, you must examine yourself by asking questions. This is not an attempt at self-analysis. It is, however, the only way to ensure that you do not lose you in the process of becoming or staying united with someone else.

What you do in response to what you feel is called meantime behavior. This is the behavior that gets you into trouble in your relationships. This is the passive behavior that makes you feel bad, weak, dumb, or stupid, and the aggressive behavior that makes you angry with others, and makes you feel guilty or ashamed of yourself. It is the experiences you have in response to such behavior that lead you to believe that love hurts. Love does not hurt! It heals! What hurts is what you do or fail to do in the name of love. These actions, or nonactions, are the origins of the passive/aggressive behavior patterns that drive you nuts! And you know what? This behavior has absolutely nothing to do with love. It is, on the other hand, the very essence of the fears and fantasies that take us all into the heart of the meantime experience.

STOP PICKING ON YOURSELF!

The healing process that leads you to the ultimate experience of self-love and unconditional love works whether or not you are involved in an intimate relationship. You can always stop what you are doing and check in on yourself. This would help you to determine if you are moving through an experience toward healing or responding to the motivational influence of a toxic emotion. You need to know why you are doing what you are doing so that you can begin to clean house. This personal, internal, emotional housecleaning involves the removal of some junk, clutter, and trash in your mental and emotional closets. *"I can't live without you, baby!"* is junk! *"Something must be wrong with me!"* is absolute trash. *"Something must be wrong with you!"* is the outgrowth of clutter in the mind. Ninety-nine percent of what you see around you has its origins in your mind!

We want to feel good about ourselves, and we think we need someone else to help us do it. We rush into relationships hoping it will happen. Love, however, has another agenda. Love wants us to heal! Love is determined that we will heal. It urges us to clean, sweep, and put out the garbage of past pains, shames, and confusion. The relationship experiences we have are a part of love's healing and cleaning process. Like mirrors, relationships are designed by life to reflect your stuff and help you claim it. Of course, we are not aware of this, so in the meantime, while love is trying to heal us, we are trying to hide under the rug.

Hiding what you feel and think and trying to hide what you do in relationships is the epitome of meantime basement experience. Hiding is among the many games and gimmicks we have devised and employ in our search for love. Hiding motivates us to do things that are not in our own best interest. Sometimes the hiding and avoiding games work. They enable us to *think* we feel better. They allow us to *believe* things are going the way we want. We feel good temporarily, but it rarely lasts long. Sooner or later we will become either passively defective, unable to express what we feel, or aggressively angry, reacting to an experience in an inappropriate way.

We get angry when relationships do not work out the way

we planned, but we are not always sure of what to do about it. Love, the healer, is forever saying through our experiences, *"Stop! Ask! Tell yourself the truth!"* Do we listen? Of course not! We make excuses. We keep hiding. We refuse to check in, to identify or discover the truth about what we feel and what we are doing in response. The next thing you know, the rug is ripped away! The heart is bleeding and love, or what we thought was love, has blown up in our face—again. In the meantime, we want to be brave, but we're hurt. We want to move on, but we're angry. Somewhere in the back of your mind there is an annoying voice. It is the voice of love, whispering, *"Get a mop and broom so we can clean up this mess. Let's begin by telling ourselves and everyone involved here the truth."* Healing begins with truth.

THE GREAT DOWN UNDER

Everyone will find out what love *is not* on their way to finding out what love *is*. Little feelings often tell big stories. Love is not about ignoring your feelings. Love is not trying to control what someone is doing. Love is not remaining silent in fear. Our parents demonstrated their love for us by providing for our basic needs while we were growing and learning to stand on our own. That is the deal parents make with life when they agree to bring new life forward. Life does not expect us to transfer the needs-provision performance into the love-relationship equation. True love can exist only between equals. This equality is not specifically limited to income or education. It includes a commonality in what people expect of themselves and want for themselves in and out of the relationship. It is for this reason, among many others, that it is important that we are willing to tell the truth about what we want. Telling someone what they want to hear in order to get what you want is a big no-no.

Our souls call forth those experiences and people who will foster the growth or restructuring of our soul's identity. That identity is the pure essence of love. Love is a choice. We either choose to live as a reflection of the love that we are or we choose not to. The people in our relationships come to show us what we need to do to choose love. The experiences of our relationships unfold as the means by which we can learn how to choose self-love first. Right in the middle of it all there is God's voice in your soul, gently reminding you that *"you are made in my image and likeness, now act like it! Clean up your act!"* Our lives are God's love ministry, and it is our duty to live our lives in a way that will save our souls through love. You must first be willing to be saved. You must also be willing to be loved.

WHAT'S IN THAT BOX UNDER THERE?

In the basement of life's house we come face to face with our survival issues: how to survive, what is necessary to survive, what others will demand from us, and what we must give them in order to survive. Survival issues are usually rooted in experiences related to physical well-being and expressions of love. As children, the first things we become consciously aware of are our physical bodies and the bodies of those around us. We learn this by how we are handled; what, when, and if we are fed; and by what we see, hear, and feel. Early on we learn how to navigate our body around other bodies in order to be

safe. Singularly and collectively, these navigational issues related
to our physical survival and satisfaction show up in our relationships. They are the issues from which we develop the gauges on
our mental compass. The basement, or the early experience of
life, also teaches to what degree we must rely on or give up
parts of our mental and physical welfare in order to get love.

By age five, we have a well-developed sense of the mind-
body-survival connection. You know the sounds and movements that will result in your being popped on the fanny or
banished to the corner. You have probably learned about sharing. That it means you must give away what you have in order
to make someone else happy. If you love people you want them
to be happy, which means you must learn how to give away
your *stuff*. You tell yourself that you're happy they're happy.
While you are learning about sharing, you are also learning
about what's yours and what's not, and what could possibly
happen to you if you confuse the two. It adds up to more
information about how you could get hurt.

Now you are seven or eight and you've learned that your
little body, which was once cute enough to be exposed to anyone, anywhere, is now somehow offensive. As a child, it is quite
understandable that you would translate this into *"Something's
wrong with me!"* You must keep it covered and never, never
make reference to it in public. This is how we all learn to hide
ourselves. You may not be quite sure what "public" is, but you
know it lives on the other side of the bathroom door where
there are strangers. Strangers look like the other folks who love
you, but strangers can hurt you. They will hurt you either
because you are cute or for no good reason at all. In order to
survive being hurt by a stranger or even by some of the plain

old folks you know, you learn what to say, how to say it, and when to say it, because the last time you got those things confused, you experienced either wrath, rage, or pain. In many ways, your life has become a very large playpen in which you have learned a great deal about your ability to survive with as little pain as possible. Through our childhood experiences, we learn that love can be a win/lose situation in which you stand a good chance of doing most of the losing and much of the hurting. In order to avoid the pain, we get very clear about what we must do in order to survive.

In relationships, basement dwellers are obsessed with issues related to survival. They hang on to people in order to survive. They also hang on to relationships, no matter how unpleasant or dysfunctional they may be, in order to survive. A battered spouse lives in the basement. Someone in a codependent relationship with an alcoholic or a drug-addicted partner is a basement dweller. Infidelity is a basement technique. You sleep around to ensure that the feelings for your partner survive. As you experience a basement meantime, you blame all of your outlandish beliefs and behaviors on the need to survive.

When you hear someone or yourself say, *"I have no choice! I have to do what I have to do!"* know that you are in the company of someone who is having a meantime experience in the basement of life's house. Also realize that this person has no idea about the nature or cause of the real issues with which they are being confronted. Where there is no choice, there is no love. When you are preoccupied with life and death issues, it is very difficult to make a conscious choice grounded in love. Survival choices are reactions rather than creations. Survival motives are born out of desperation rather than desire. Survival instincts are the exaggerated and aggressive energy of the birth pattern. When you believe your survival is at stake, you do not care what you do or how you do it. You scream your little head off, flinging your arms around, because you must survive.

We cannot have an honest, honorable, or loving relationship with ourselves or anyone else until we clear our survival issues. As long as we believe that another person has or can withhold some element of life essential to our survival, we will not tell the truth or cannot express our emotions; our self-value, worth, and esteem are diminished; and we deny the natural, normal reflexes and instincts of the mind and body. When you believe that you must give up pieces of yourself in order to avoid being hurt or to survive, you are having a meantime experience in the basement of life's house. Living here makes you a victim. Children must often feel like victims of "big people." In the basement you feel sorry for yourself, or you pout and stomp your feet. You want to get it together, but you believe that the circumstances of your life are beyond your control. Somebody else is in charge.

When you live in the basement you whine and complain about how bad it is. You focus on all the "bad things" that could happen if you try to change your station in life. As far as relationships go, you have given up or convinced yourself that *a piece* of a relationship is better than no relationship. You must take what you can get. One day, you will figure out that what you have been thinking is *out of order,* or perhaps you have not been thinking at all. You have been reacting, hiding, trying to survive. Slowly you will come to the realization that there is a better way to live. You want to change your living conditions. The key is to realize that survival is no longer an issue for you. You have survived. You are now willing to grow. To flourish.

WHEN VISION IS OBSCURED, DEEP CLEANING IS REQUIRED!

A basement meantime is more than just an experience of uneasy feelings. It is an experience of bringing feelings to the surface with as much pain and drama as you can stand. After all, survival can be painful and dramatic. A basement dweller may attempt to eat or drink away the misery. It rarely works! When there is something *wrong* inside you, it comes to the surface. When it does, people notice it. They may mention it to you, but when you live in the basement, you cannot stand criticism. You think people are just picking on you. You are confused, and your life tends to be a little chaotic. You are angry, and you always seem to have experiences that make you even more angry. In the basement, you have not been paying attention to what is coming up in you or going on around you. As a result, people are staring at you because they know that something is very wrong. They know, you do not.

If you find yourself in the basement or in a basement type of relationship where you believe you are a victim, where you feel that your survival is at risk, where you are focusing on every unpleasant thing that has happened in your life—STOP! There is a problem about which you may be completely unaware that is coming to the surface. A part of the problem could be your own fears and beliefs. Another contributing factor could be that your childhood programming is surfacing. It could very well be that you are repeating what you heard or doing what you saw being done when you were a child. When this is the case, you must take a moment to examine what you are feeling and thinking. This helps to make you aware of the pattern. Once you recognize the pattern, what you usually do under this or similar circumstances, you can choose a new course of action. The old ways cannot survive your choice of a new way. It will, however, take repeated and consistent practice before the new way can be incorporated into your consciousness. Practice makes perfect!

Love is the experience of joy, peace, fulfillment, purposefulness, harmony, abundance, and service. These are often the very things we try to find in a relationship. They are usually the very things we consider impossible to find in our relationship with ourselves. Few of us are taught that the very things we seek are within. We must de-program ourselves from the old love recipes that we have been given. *Do this for love. Do that to get love. Be this to keep love.* Love is not at all what we do. It is the experience of being who we are. Love relationships are the way we seek to experience more of ourselves, the truth of ourselves. We must pour new ideas, new concepts, and more truth about our identity into our relationships. In the meantime, while we are de-programming, relationships can be trying. It can be very challenging to realize where you are and where you want to be, and all of the work you must do in order to get there.

What you believe about yourself is reflected in the people with whom you choose to align yourself. Each choice provides you with the opportunity to act in accordance with the highest essence of your being, the soul. Our relationships, and the people in those relationships, are the tools that God uses to give us a *soul lift*. God, the creator of your life, wants you to elevate the way you view yourself and treat yourself, and ultimately the way you treat others and allow them to treat you. God's desire is for us to raise our love consciousness and love vibration to match the energy that has been implanted at the deepest level of our souls. Relationships are the most readily available means to bring us in touch with or take us out of touch with our own definition of love. Whether the relationship is with your parents, family members, professional or social acquaintances, your children, or strangers, it can shape, mold, and restructure what you do and how you do it in the name of love.

God is love! But how many of us really know what that means? How many of us have a distorted perception of God or an even worse concept of love? Many of us do, which is probably why our relationships look so strange. Relationships always reflect what we saw, heard, and learned at home. In other words, whatever loving and being loved looked like at your house, whatever you were taught was required to get or maintain love, will be the primary ingredients in your love recipe. There are also those of us for whom God was nowhere in the picture. As a result, we are working in the dark about love, God, ourselves, and the truth about all of these things. At some point, we will all discover the truth. In order to do so, we will have to bring God back into focus. When we do, our relationships will be transformed into deprogramming mechanisms, helping us remember, learn, and practice the truth about God, ourselves, and love. The key to getting the work done with as little pain as possible is willingness.

WILLINGNESS IS A GREAT BASEMENT CLEANER!

Once you become aware that there are cracks in your foundation, and that they have led to the hazardous nature of your actions, you must become willing to clean up your act. You have survived your basement meantime experiences and relationships, and although you may still not have a firm grasp on the nature of your problem, you realize you are faced with an excellent opportunity. This opportunity has been reserved as a blessing for human beings. You can change your mind—about you, about life, and about love. Willingness is the key to taking advantage of the opportunity to clean yourself out of the basement. Because you are willing, you now understand that your meantime basement experiences were preparatory devices. They were the devices used by life to prepare you to do the serious work that lies ahead of you. You are about to undertake an exciting journey—the journey through love's house.

I am sure you already know that this will be a working journey. What you may not know is that it offers many great rewards. In order to take full advantage of everything that is about to be offered to you, you must be sanitized. Willingness is like an antibacterial disinfectant that will clean away the fungus and cobwebs that have accumulated as a result of your past experiences and relationships. If you have spent lots of time in the basement, you may find that you have layers of anger. Willingness is an excellent cleaner, and it can be used to eliminate anger. Once you become willing to grow, you will discover that you are not at all angry with someone for doing something to you. You are actually angry with yourself! You are angry because you now understand how you helped to create your own experiences. You also recognize that the purpose of those experiences was to teach you the truth about yourself, and to remind you of the truth about God, the love that lies dormant in the essence of your soul.

Willingness is also an excellent vision cleanser. It gives you the ability to see yourself in other people. When you enter a relationship, you are going to meet yourself in the actions, behaviors, and beliefs of those involved in the relationship with you. In some way, those people are going to do and say to you the very things you have been doing and saying to yourself. You will come face to face with all the things about you that you know, and a few of which you are completely unaware. You are going to meet your good side, your bad side, and the side for which you probably have no name. Because willingness works like an antibacterial agent, it will remove the germs of guilt, shame, anger, fear, and resentment, which could deny you the opportunity to get really clear. Once you are clear, you will be able to see exactly who you think you are by looking at what you expect and tolerate from other people.

If used liberally, willingness will remove the scuff marks from the walls of your heart. If, on the other hand, you display any signs of resistance, you may find your toilet clogged! If at any time on your journey you find yourself stuck or clogged up, you may want to sit down, take a deep breath, and remind yourself, *"This is not a true reflection of me! I am going to make another choice! I am going to change my mind!"* This would be an admirable display of willingness. You may, however, at times discover that there are some stuck-on stains or ground-in dirt in the crevices that require heavy-duty cleaning. When this is the case, cry! While you are crying, forgive yourself for believing that you ever did anything wrong. Remind yourself that everything you have done was in response to what you needed to unlearn. Once you have finished crying, forgiving, and remembering, run, do not walk, to the nearest mirror, look yourself squarely in the eyes and say, *"I love you very much!"*

WHAT YOU GIVE, YOU GET!

That's how Jack began the conversation, by telling Helen how much he loved her. Then he told her that he was leaving. Before she could open her mouth, he went on to say that he was grateful for the time they had spent together, but that he thought it best, for both of them, if they separated. Acting as if he didn't hear her laughing or see her shaking her head, he confessed. That's right! He confessed that their marriage was his attempt to feel better about himself. It seemed like a blessing at the time, but now, all these years later, he realized how unfair it had been to both of them. She was standing up now, so he sat down and continued.

It was the baby's death. After the baby had died, he couldn't find the strength or courage to leave. He kept hoping against hope that she would change her mind and have another child. Did she remember that they had talked about having children? She was sitting down again, so he stood up. Perhaps children would have given them something in common, something to do besides pick on each other. Why didn't she want to have children with him? Was he really that bad? Is that why she always acted so indifferently toward him, even when they were making love? It always seemed that her mind was somewhere else. Off in space, or with somebody else, anybody other than him.

She was crying, so he sat down right next to her, put his arms around her, and he cried too. What happened to his friend? He remembered what good friends they once had been. He could point out all the things that she had done and not done over the last fourteen years to destroy their friendship, but none of it mattered now. He knew she was unhappy, and so was he. He was unhappy with himself and his life. He needed some time to think, to regroup, to detox from the television. He was willing to give her anything she wanted. He wasn't angry, he was miserable! He was miserable deep down in his soul and needed to do something about it. He did not think he could do that in the marriage. He did not want to do it in the marriage. He wanted to leave. He needed to leave. He was sorry he had not left before. If he had, perhaps it would not be so painful now. Could she please let him go without a fuss? Even if she made a fuss, he was leaving. What did she want? What could he do?

What is in your soul will set up the circumstances and experiences of your life. Those experiences will either heal you or cripple you in your soul. When love and willingness are added to the life equation, you will, despite all of your bad choices and poor decisions, be healed. For the first time in their fourteen years together, Helen told Jack exactly why she married him. When she heard herself say that she was trying to make her childhood sweetheart jealous, she was dumbfounded. When you are willing to be healed, you will find yourself saying and doing things you would not, under normal circumstances of fear, say and do. Helen went on to admit that she did not want his children because she had lived with the hope that Jamie would someday come back for her.

She also confessed that marrying for such a reason was a horrible thing to do, and she would be eternally sorry. She had spent their entire marriage in anger and pain. Helen realized that she had never gotten over the fact that Jamie had rejected her. She also realized that she never gave Jack a chance. For that too, she was sorry. She did not want Jack to go, but she did not want him to stay. She was afraid. She was confused. She, too, needed some time, to think, to regroup, to figure out what to do with the rest of her life. The only thing she wanted from him was for him to go quietly and not tell her mother. In the meantime, he could stay until he found a place to live. Jack stayed in the house with Helen for about two years. He left about the same time that Jamie divorced his wife.

THE FIRST FLOOR

what is that smell?!!! It's horrible! Has it dawned on you that the only time you smell it is when you open the refrigerator? Something is rotten in Kenmore, honey!!! The problem is, you don't have a clue what it could be. Could be that green stuff in the bowl or the brown stuff in the foil. Perhaps it's that fuzzy pink stuff that was once red and is now fermenting on the side of the vegetable crisper. Don't you just hate it—cleaning out the fridge. It is a nasty and time-consuming chore. You've been putting it off for days, no, weeks, and so has everybody else. Why are you always the one who gets stuck doing the dirty work? Now you have to do it, because everybody knows you've got a problem. Each time you open that door, everybody, including company, knows that there is something very nasty and foul growing in your midst. Well, you can't put if off any longer. It's too embarrassing. Thank goodness the same is not true about the laundry! At least you can hide that. . . .

But why? Why do we let it pile up? Whether it's the laundry or an issue in a relationship, it would be so much easier if we would deal with a little at a time. We promise ourselves, every time we stand before the mammoth pile, or have a heated argument, that we'll do it that way. Liar! Liar! Pants on fire! Your dirty pants are on fire—all twelve bags of them! Even those you tried to hide in the bottom of the closet are on fire! Don't you know by now that the longer you put something off, the worse it gets! Eventually the foul smell will seep into everything, or the bag will burst, spilling all of your soiled undies into the middle of the floor, or pent up anger will lead to an argument. Whether it's the fridge, the laundry, or the little issues turning into fuzz on your relationships, *take care of it! Now!* Before you get embarrassed! Or hurt!

Chapter 4
DOING THE LAUNDRY

lynn and steve had been married forever—nineteen years. They had two wonderful children, a boy of fifteen and a girl of thirteen. Steve was the only man Lynn had known, if you know what I mean—he was her first lover. Now he was her husband and, she thought, her best friend. They had a pretty decent marriage. Lynn was a very, very intelligent woman. Brilliant, as a matter of fact. Steve was a blue-collar worker who wore a tie. A high-school graduate. Not a lumberyard worker, but an office worker for a government agency, one level above the basement. Lynn worked full-time and went to school at night. Things were a little tight financially, but they weren't really struggling, if you know what I mean.

Around the middle of year nineteen of the marriage, Steve started acting like a certified idiot. A certified idiot believes he has a license to *act a fool*. He was not coming home during the week! It's one thing to stay out on the weekend, but only a fool stays out on a week night. He never had any money. How many times can your pocket be picked in one month, even in LA!

Lynn couldn't figure out what the heck was going on. After a little *wifely interrogation,* she discovered that her best friend, her husband, had a problem with cocaine. He was spending all his money on it and hanging out in the places in which it was sold. Shortly after this startling revelation, Steve messed up so badly at work that he got fired. It was actually because of the drug situation—it was discovered that he had drugs on government property.

Life can be hard, but God is always good! Because Steve had been on the job for so many years, they didn't exactly fire him. They *invited* him to resign, with no marks on his record. Lynn asked very few questions, and Steve offered no explanations. After a little *wifely insistence,* Steve entered a drug treatment program, and Lynn lived through that with him. Nine months after the fifteen-month treatment program, Steve still hadn't found a job. Lynn was doing everything in her power to hold the marriage and the household together. Now they were struggling! Friends were lending them money because Lynn was the kind of person you wanted to do everything in your power to support. Steve, on the other hand, was not coming home at night.

YOU MUST KNOW THE RULES
IF YOU WANT TO PLAY THE GAME!

You are the love you seek. You are the companionship you desire. You are your own completion, your own wholeness. You are your best friend, your confidant. "You are," as poetess Audre Lourde wrote, "the one that you are looking for." You are the only one who can do what you are looking for someone else to do. When you go out into the world, looking for love or work or melons, realize that you are bringing your goods to the table —your soul, your mind, and your body. If you do not feel good about who you are and what you have, how can you expect your goods to be matched pound for pound, stitch for stitch? If you are on the *love block* without knowing the truth about you, you, my dear, are in a lot of trouble! Pack up your goods and go home! If you don't, what you are likely to find out there in the world is going to knock you for a loop.

When you know a thing, you do it, you live it. When you *know of* a thing, you try to figure it out. Most of us are trying to figure out what to do to make our relationships better, to make them work, because we have skipped over *loving me* into *love you.* Self-love means taking the time to smile at, listen to, and tenderly embrace yourself. Without time spent this way, the thing we search and hope for in relationships will continue to elude us. That experience—the total acceptance, honest acknowledgment, trusting support, and honoring of self is all the experience we need to make any relationship a good one. When we have this kind of self-love, we are more than willing to do the work, the sometimes nasty work, required to establish, build, and maintain a relationship. Without it, we are bound to get lost in a pile of mess.

If you were looking for a new home, you would spend time identifying the specifics—the size of the kitchen, the number of bedrooms and bathrooms—and the specifics would be identified before you went into the marketplace. The same is true of the search for love. You must know what to look for before you start to look. Some of us rush into the market, squeezing plums and buns, accepting what feels good, looks good, or smells good, without really understanding *what is good*. What's good for you matches your specifics. What's good for you expands the greatest experience of yourself. What's good for you lifts your awareness to a higher recognition of your *all-rightness* in life. What's good for you will ultimately prove to be good for those you have invited into your life.

After several weeks of Steve's idiotic behavior, Lynn decided it was time for a little *wifely investigation*. One night she followed Steve and found their car parked on Beacon Street, a street full of apartment buildings. A few nights later, Lynn elicited the help of a friend who had a car. Just as she suspected, they found the car parked in front of a Beacon Street building at 2:00 A.M. Every other night for the next two weeks, Lynn and her friend would go car shopping on Beacon Street. Each night the car was parked in front of a different building, which made it a bit difficult to determine exactly where Steve was going—but he was going *straight to hell!* if Lynn ever got her hands on him. Since they had never seen him going into or coming out of any one of the buildings they had no idea to whose or what apartment Steve was visiting. Lynn told her friend that *wifely patience* is rarely outdone.

In the meantime, Lynn never said a word to Steve—she didn't confront him or ask any questions. Lynn was trying to maintain her dignity, which was being dragged up and down Beacon Street. While she was holding on to the best of her ability, Lynn's driver friend kept reminding her, *"He snorted up his paychecks for the last two years."* And, she continued, *"He's not working."* Besides that, she pointed out, "You're feeding him, and *while he's eating your food,* he has nothing better to do than to get another woman!" She wasn't finished yet. "Get a grip, girl! If this is love, hate me, please!" As she always did, Lynn listened intently before she gave her pat answer, "No divorce! It's a sin! My children love their father, and I won't do that to my children. He's my husband, and we can work this out." In the meantime, Lynn kept praying. At one point, she even considered going to a psychic reader to get some insight on the right address.

Eventually, with the help of the friend, of course, Lynn went to Beacon Street at eight o'clock in the morning—she had figured out the pattern. He would leave home just before 5:00 P.M., before Lynn came home from work. He would stay out all night and be home by the time Lynn called the house at 9:00 A.M. from her desk at work. That meant he must be leaving his Beacon Street hideaway at around 8:30 in the morning. It was the friend's idea that they hide in the bushes—literally—and wait for him. The suspense! The drama! The cute little doggie they almost scared to death when he began to relieve himself on Lynn's leg! It was almost worth the day's pay it cost them both to pull it off. Bingo! At 8:20, Steve came out of the second building on the right side of the street, got into his family car, and drove off. Now they knew the building—all they needed was an apartment number.

HAVE YOUR EYES CHECKED REGULARLY

What are you looking at? What are you looking for? What are you looking with? These three questions are essential to discovering true love. If you are nearsighted or farsighted, or if you suffer from blurred vision, you run the risk of missing love when it shows up. If you don't know what to look for or where to look, how will you recognize what you want when it shows up? If you have an old picture that is cracked, faded, and rolled at the corners, you may miss certain small details essential to the whole picture. It is for this reason you must constantly check your vision, version, and projection of love.

If you cannot detect what is hurting you, it may be that you have been trying to squeeze yourself into a situation in which you did not belong, a situation that you have outgrown. If you cannot see the source of your confusion, it could be that you are looking *at* the wrong thing, looking *for* the wrong thing, or looking *with* the wrong intention in mind. Love never looks vengeful or violent. It never looks to strike out or knock down. Love is an expansive energy that leads to sharing, giving, building, and healing. Love energizes and encourages you to do more, commit more loving acts, to be more, behave in a more loving way, and to give more and more love to more people.

Loving and being loved is a big responsibility. This means that you must look at yourself, as well as those you love, with an expansive view, knowing that nothing stays the same. Things will expand sometimes beyond our vision or reach. Loving and being loved also means that you must always look for the good. The good qualities, the good potential, the good that has been done with you and for you. It means you must look with merciful and forgiving eyes, trusting and truthful eyes, gentle and kind eyes, that always see beyond the behavior to the core, the essence, the soul. You may not always want to do this. There will be times when you do not know how to do it. The key is to always affirm that love is your guiding force. In this way, no matter what you do or how you do it, love will be present.

Once you have accepted this degree of responsibility for

yourself by forgiving yourself for what you have created, it will be easy to love those who played a role in your creation. With that done, you can move to the next step, receiving unconditional love from others. For many, it is much easier to give than receive. To receive means recognizing that everything that comes to you is a reflection of what you deserve. Water rises to its own level, and so does love. People will give you things, opportunities, resources, their time and energy in response to the amount of love you have for yourself, and the amount of love you give others. This can make receiving very challenging because you must believe that you deserve what you get.

It is very difficult to receive when you are suspicious about the motives of others. It is for this reason you must learn to trust—trust yourself and trust other people. Trust is the main ingredient of unconditional love. If you do not trust, you will be suspicious. You may suspect that you are indebted to people. Once you believe you are indebted to someone, it will be hard, if not impossible, to be honest with them. It's hard to tell the truth to someone you are afraid of or dependent on. It may be difficult, if not impossible, to express what you feel, believing as you do that you owe them something for the love they have showered on you. If, and only if, you remember once again that you are loved will these thoughts dissipate. You will remember that you deserve love in any form it comes in.

In this state of mind, you can accept what is offered to you with an open heart and no feeling of obligation. If someone tries to make you feel obligated you can remind them and yourself that *God uses people!* God uses people to let you know where you are in love's house. It is not wise to deny God the privilege of showing you how much you are loved! If you find it difficult to receive, it could be that you have missed a few steps. Don't worry, you will be provided with an opportunity to retrace your steps and clear up the stuff you have missed.

Armed with this new little tidbit of information, Lynn kept praying. She also went to a psychic reader after her friend jumped ship. The friend had had enough of the secret spy games. It was wreaking havoc on her own relationship. The psychic didn't tell Lynn anything that she did not already know, and she did not give her the apartment number. It didn't matter, because the friend came back. This was a *real friend* who thought Lynn was about to fall over the edge. Besides that, *real* friends don't desert their friends. Without any advance warning, the friend called one Friday night to say she was on her way to pick Lynn up. They were going to church. It was an old Baptist church in a storefront on a corner. The sermon was about not letting lost people get you lost. It was a bull's-eye hit with regard to what Lynn was going through. After the sermon, the friend took Lynn by the hand right up to the front of the church where all the church matrons were congregating. Approaching the biggest, most serious, and most powerful-looking matron in the group, the friend blurted out, "My friend needs you to pray for her! Please!"

Instantly the seriousness was transformed to loving concern. The matron never responded, never asked questions. She took one look at Lynn, summoned the other matrons with a wave of the hand, and they went to work. The matrons surrounded Lynn and began to pray—actually they were moaning or singing or doing something neither Lynn nor the friend had ever heard before. By the time they were done, Lynn was on her knees, crying in the middle of the circle. The friend was plastered to the wall—doing the same thing—crying. It was quite an experience, Lynn told her friend later on. She also promised that the car shopping was over.

HAVE COURAGE UNDER FIRE!

It would seem that with all you have been through, lived through, and grown through, the job would be easier. This is not the case in love's house. The truth of the matter is, few make it all the way to the top, because the work gets progressively more difficult. Those who are very good students, the best students, always get the hardest tests. You see, love is nothing to play around with. Thus far this is what many of us have been doing. We have been playing with love and at being lovable. There comes a time, however, when you have to put your money where your mouth is! You say you want to enjoy the benefits of total self-acceptance. You believe you want the blessing of a loving, committed relationship. You think you can live and exemplify the true meaning of unconditional love. Well, prove it!

In order to get to the second floor in love's house, you must be willing to give total unconditional love to everyone, under all circumstances. That means being willing to be totally responsible for what you do and how you do it. Total, absolute, and complete responsibility for the expression of love, under all circumstances, is the only spiritual cleanser that can get this job done.

When you are willing to take responsibility, you can look at your life and learn to listen to your experiences! Your experiences will provide you with a workable formula that is applicable to any and every situation in which you need more information about yourself. When you invite experience to be your teacher, you are able to sit and reflect on all you have learned, as well as what you have missed. This sitting is sometimes called meditation. The reflection is called willingness to grow. Used in combination, these two spiritual cleansing products, meditation and reflection, produce responsibility. When you are ready to take total responsibility for bringing love into your life or back into your relationship, your work on the first floor is just about complete.

Several days later, Lynn was going through some mail and old papers on the dresser when she discovered an envelope with the Beacon Street, name, address, and apartment number. It had probably been in the junk on the dresser all along! The telephone hadn't hit the cradle before the friend was blowing the horn. She had come to accompany Lynn on what promised to be their last Beacon Street shopping trip. Lynn just wasn't herself. She was mysteriously quiet, almost serene. Her eyes were fixed, and she never said a single word. Before the car was shifted into park, Lynn was headed toward the building. *"Where the heck are you going???"* Her glazed eyes had the friend very concerned. *"What are you gonna do? What are you gonna say to him?"* Lynn never looked back. Never said a word.

It was as if she had radar. She zeroed in on the appropriate bell and pushed it—several times. The friend kept asking the same dumb questions. Lynn kept ringing the bell. "Who is it?" *"Oh my God!!! It's Steve! He answered the doorbell! What a flaming idiot!"* thought the friend. "It's Lynn," she replied, as calm as if she were going door to door selling Mary Kay. To the total astonishment of her friend, the door buzzed, and Lynn went into the building. Of course, the friend's mouth had fallen to the floor by now! It was as if she were cemented to the very place she was standing. Lynn was out of sight—in the frickin' apartment! It was a first-floor apartment, not more than ten yards from the front door.

Forty-five seconds later—I swear, forty-five seconds!—Lynn reappeared, with Steve walking right beside her. He had a white shirt slung across his left shoulder. (Isn't it amazing the details that catch your eye even when you're in shock!) He followed Lynn right out of the building. On their way out, Lynn reached over and grabbed the friend, who was still standing right where Lynn had left her and whose mouth was still hanging open. For the first time throughout the entire ordeal of the day, Lynn spoke to her friend. "I'm going home to take care of some laundry!"

HOW DO YOU MEND A BROKEN HEART? MIND? SPIRIT?

Truth is love's mother, and we all know it is not wise to lie to anyone's mother. Somehow, some way, Mother always finds out that you are lying. When she does, there is hell to pay! One of life's most difficult challenges is being able to look at yourself honestly, acknowledging and accepting what you see. What makes the task all the more difficult is the belief that what we see translates into *"What's wrong with me?"* There is nothing wrong with you! The truth is that there are some aspects of you and some areas of your life that require attention. Some need a little work. Others may even need intensive care. This is nothing to be ashamed of or guilty about, because the same is true for all of us. The truth is that until we are able to accept and acknowledge our own truth, without shame or blame, we will be on Mother's bad side. It is, therefore, absolutely essential to our survival and evolution that we take a look at ourselves, what we do and why we do it on a daily basis. Until we are able and willing to do this, the true and fullest meaning of love will continue to escape our grasp.

If you are experiencing confusion, it could be that you need a shot of truth. Failure to tell, resistance to hearing, and inability to recognize the truth will cause great mental and emotional confusion. All too often, in love relationships we withhold the truth in fear of causing hurt to others or revealing too much of ourselves. In some cases we believe in the *wrongness* of our truth. *It's wrong to feel this way. It is wrong to say this or that.* No truth is wrong. If it is true for you, if it is an accurate reflection of what you feel, it is not wrong. It may be that your truth, based on your experience, is a little out of focus. It may require some tuning up, but that still does not make it wrong. The truth always is what it is. Love, truth's first-born, allows us to acknowledge, accept, and express our truth without fear. It also enables us to hear another's truth without being devastated.

Your truth will not always be easy to express, but this year's feet may not fit in last year's shoes. The truth is we will not always like the truth we hear from others, but we must be willing to hear it. Speaking and hearing the truth is another form of acknowledgment. If we want to discover the true meaning of love, we must be willing to hear, acknowledge, and accept another's truth. When we cannot, love is absent, and we are operating in fear. It is at that instant, the instant we shift into fear, that we must pray for healing.

Dear God:

Guide my words that I may speak the truth from a conscious-ness of love. Open my mind and fill it with love. Open my mouth and fill it with love. Let the words I am about to speak be heard with ears that are filled with love. Keep me in a constant and conscious state of love so that I might speak my heart in a loving and healing way. I know that the words I speak are from my experience. I pray for the ability to speak them with love and to be endowed with love by speaking them. Thank you, God! For I know that you have heard this prayer.

Or,

Dear God:

Open my ears that I may hear what is being said in a con-sciousness of love. Fill my mind with love. Fill my heart with love. Allow love to encircle me that I may hear clearly and lovingly. I honor the words that I am hearing with a consciousness of love so that this can be a healing and loving experience. I know that the words being spoken are the truth of the experience of another. I pray for the ability to hear them with love and to be filled with the courage of divine wisdom. Thank you, God! For I know that you have heard this prayer.

A daily dose of truth serum enables us to speak the truth and hear the truth without fear. It means we are willing to acknowledge and express our emotional experiences and to allow others to do the same. In speaking the truth of your experience to another, it will serve you well to realize that how they *choose* to respond is not your responsibility. The choice to respond with love or in fear is just that, a choice. In hearing the truth of another's experience realize that you cannot take it personally. When we listen with an open mind and a loving heart, the truth will open the door for healing, not hurting. It is only from a truth-filled state of conscious, the willingness to speak the truth and know the truth, that we can build a firm, lasting, and truly loving relationship with ourselves and others. Anything less than this is not love. It is fear.

It was three days of hell, silent hell, before she had the courage to ask him—How long? When? Why? Who? Everything Lynn finally asked him, he answered. He answered it all! —with eyeball to eyeball contact and honesty! Steve took full responsibility for his actions, although he started out by saying that Lynn didn't care—she was too busy to care. When your partner commits infidelity you may feel betrayed, hurt, and taken for granted, and your self-esteem may sink straight through the floorboards to the basement. Notwithstanding this and more, you must never allow yourself to be blamed for the inappropriate actions of another. Lynn had not said anything because she did not want to accuse without proof. After all, she was a criminal law student. Actually, she did not want to run the risk of his lying. She would have lost all respect for him had he actually opened his mouth to lie, and she knew that it would be very hard to love a liar. She was, however, willing to assume her share of the responsibility for the difficulties in the marriage. When you take responsibility for what you've done, or what you haven't done, when you take responsibility for what you want, without judging it right or wrong, when you are willing to tell the absolute truth, you will know whether to stay or not.

LIFT THE THOUGHTS ABOUT YOU!

When I lived on the first floor of love's house, I was still preoccupied with physical love and satisfaction. Not for survival reasons, but because I still didn't know any better. I kept asking myself why I wasn't pretty, why I wasn't desirable, and why I couldn't find someone to love me. I wanted someone to treat me special and make me feel special. In the absence of a meaningful love relationship, I went through my days feeling incomplete and worthless. Of course I never said one word. I couldn't say a word, I was trying too hard to convince myself that I was okay and lovable. There was one small problem, however: I didn't believe it! I thought I was in some way damaged. I won't *blame* my childhood, although I will say it made a healthy contribution to my conclusion. I had never seen real affection displayed between my caregivers, and I had rarely been shown real loving affection by them. Once again, I was on my own to figure things out. I must admit that I didn't do such a good job of it.

Did I mention that I was chubby? When I lived in the basement, I tried to eat myself out of misery and unhappiness. I was willing to stop eating, but I hadn't actually done it yet. Eating was my excuse. It was the excuse I gave myself for the reason people did not love me. I couldn't figure out any other reason, so I decided to create one on my own. I decided that if I were fat, people would have a reason to treat me bad. I told myself that fat people didn't deserve to be loved. Mind you, I didn't say any of this out loud, I just figured it out in my own mind and unconsciously acted on it. The mind really is a terrible thing to waste! Being fat didn't help matters, but it did provide me with a feasible explanation. However, even with this explanation, I kept asking myself questions. I kept asking God questions. I did not think I was getting any answers, but I have since learned that within the question *is* the answer.

Eleven years later, Lynn and Steve are still together. It took them almost that long to sort through their laundry. In the end, their meantime paid off. They both learned a great deal, and they were both willing to do the work it took to clean and heal their relationship. Lynn had avoided the problems for a long time and finally had to admit that she had been in denial. She could not admit to herself that she was just not everything that her husband needed or wanted. Rather than face that, she opted for a state of vagueness. It wasn't intentional. Her husband, her best friend, was in trouble—not just drug trouble, but moral, emotional, and spiritual trouble—and she didn't know what to do. She had taken his load on her back and carried it to the best of her ability. They had never really addressed the drug problem, and Lynn still doesn't know why he did what he did. Steve has refused to share any details. Reflecting back on the experience, Lynn admits, she just didn't know what to do.

She had seen it happen before—her mother and her father's drinking problem. Her sister and her brother-in-law's violent temper. Her brother's wife and his children born outside their marriage. Lynn had watched these women move through their difficulties in pain, with tears, only to lose their marriages and large pieces of their minds. Lynn was determined not to go that route. She would juggle whatever she needed to juggle in order to save herself and her family.

What Lynn came to understand was that they never had addressed their responsibilities or roles in the marriage. As a matter of fact, they had never really discussed anything. They loved each other, they enjoyed each other's company, and everything else would work out in its own course. It was only when a problem came up that they would come together to talk about an issue. On the good days, however, neither of them took responsibility for working on the marriage. Steve took no responsibility for working on himself, and Lynn didn't assume the responsibility for raising certain issues with him. When the affair happened they had to sort through their laundry—the hard feelings, the disappointments, the feelings of failure and inadequacy on both their parts.

Lynn really had to work hard to forgive Steve. More important, she had to forgive herself for being lazy, for not taking responsibility for her own happiness, and for not putting her foot down with Steve. Perhaps if she had done that early on, things would not have gotten so out of hand. That is something she would never know, like one of those socks that disappears in the dryer. Steve and Lynn's story demonstrates that there are times, those very special *meantimes*, where if you are willing to do the work, the hard nasty work, you can save the relationship. It really took a lot of willingness, particularly for Steve. He had to be willing to face the truth and tell the truth, regardless of the outcome. Lynn really was his best friend, too. They used their spiritual cleanser called *responsibility* and applied it to all the stains, dirt, and hurt that had accumulated in their marriage. In that way, they were able to use the truth to clean and heal the relationship.

What made it work was that at the core of it all, they really loved each other—not in need or fantasy, and not in fear. They just simply loved each other. As you can see, love did not keep them from acting crazy, but it was definitely the unconditional love at the core of their relationship that gave the spiritual cleanser a boost. Lynn says that sorting through nineteen years of mess was just like sifting through laundry, separating the whites from the colors—this is yours, that's mine, what's this doing in here? But they were both immediately willing to do the work that needed to be done. Unfortunately, the same is not true for JoAnn and Paul.

A PART OF THE PROBLEM!

JoAnn and Paul had been married only three years, but it was an intense three years. They were in grad school together. They both worked full-time jobs. They had a lovely little apartment, two cute little cars, and one big problem. JoAnn couldn't shake her ex-boyfriend. Every time Paul turned around, JoAnn was talking to him on the telephone, helping him with some project or another, taking his mother to this place or that place, and disappearing with him for hours on end. Paul tried his best to understand that they were just friends and that they had been friends for more than fifteen years. However, no man in his right mind can be okay with his wife hanging out so frequently with the man she used to sleep with. Well, maybe a man in his right mind could. Paul could not.

"*He's my friend, Paul!*" JoAnn would say each and every time Paul went off about him. "I married you! I am in love with you! I love him, too, but he is my friend. You are my husband!" Paul would calm down, temporarily, until the next time he called. Then the argument would escalate, and JoAnn would be reduced to tears. "You are not my jailer! You are my husband, and you cannot tell me who I can have as a friend." Paul insisted that he could, and would. It was then that he forbade, that's right, forbade his wife to see the guy ever again—forever and ever, amen! You see, we are getting off to a real bad start. Whenever there is a problem in a relationship, ultimatums don't help.

In a relationship, what your mate does to annoy, upset, or make you angry is like having the headlights of a Mack truck shining in your face—it's glaring! What this person is doing to you always seems much more shocking than anything you would even consider doing to them. You may not consider it, but because the lights are in your face, you do it. You do your number on them to such a degree that you may be completely unaware of it. This is a major stumbling block in our relationships—not being aware, not wanting to hear, not realizing what we do to our partners in response to what we think they have done to us. We usually criticize people for the things we do and the things we do not like about ourselves. We are so busy looking out, looking at them, that we cannot see what we do and are therefore not willing to take responsibility for it.

This was the case with Paul. In the three years he had been married to JoAnn he had slept with two other women. One was an old college friend, the other his ex-girlfriend. Of course, he never bothered to tell JoAnn this, but he was so afraid that she would do what he had done, he pushed her right into doing it —wait, that comes later. JoAnn felt she had a responsibility to her marriage, but she also had a responsibility to herself. She and this man had a lifetime relationship. They were a mutual support system. Yes, they had been lovers at one time. Now, by mutual consent, they were friends. He was very close to her family, as he was to his. He knew everything about JoAnn, including the fact that Paul was quite disturbed about their friendship. He advised JoAnn to listen to her husband, honor his request, and send him a Christmas card if she remembered.

GIVE UP THE FIGHT!

Perhaps it really does have something to do with the way we are born. It could be, it just could be that because of all the pushing, pulling, and being slapped around in the birth process, we think that we have to fight. It's particularly interesting that we think we have to *fight to get* love and *fight to keep* love. Fighting is painful! Loving is not, or at least it shouldn't be. Love is gentle, kind, sensitive, and supportive. It is the conditions that we place on loving and being loved that make it a rough, tough, shoot 'em show. It's what we do, not what love is, that makes us believe that love is painful. The corresponding belief is that *the more I love, the more painful it will be.* In order to avoid the pain, we believe we must fight to keep from getting hurt in love. It makes absolutely no sense! If you add to the equation something or someone who is threatening to take love away, then what you have is an all-out war! Unconsciously we regress into a state of combat, doing what we think will be required to ensure that love or life survives.

We must give up the fight in relationships if we want to be healed on our journey through love's house. Some of us are so accustomed to *fighting* to get what we want, *fighting* to get what we need, *fighting* to get ahead, and *fighting* to stay on top that we are like soldiers on the battlefield, looking for the enemy under every rock. The fight is often woven into our words, the way we say them, as well as the energy behind them. At times we expect a fight when we ask for what we need or want. When we don't get the fight, we'll pick one. We will find something to say and say it in such a way that a fight is the only natural outcome. When the person we are trying to fight with won't fight back, we become enraged—we go looking for someone to fight with. When we find it, we don't want to assume the responsibility for starting it.

The same way we fight with one another, we fight with ourselves. I admit, I have been guilty of having a raging battle going on in my own head! I would fight with myself for what I did or didn't do! If I lost, I would fight with myself about the way I did it! When that got tired, I would fight with myself about whether I should do it over, or ever do it again. The sad part is, I never won! How can you beat yourself? I would usually leave the fight mortally wounded, until I could find something else to fight with me about. In the same way I would fight in my mind, I would fight my feelings. There are certain things I simply would not allow myself to feel. I would fight to hold it back. I would struggle to keep it from coming up and spilling across my lips. I would fight rather than feel, because I knew I could survive getting beat up. I did not know if I would survive going to the depths of my emotions. That, I am told, could blow your mind.

What stopped me from fighting, mentally and physically, was a statement made to me by my dear friend, colleague, and teacher Ken Kizer. He said, *"God will agree to help you fight or struggle if you ask Him to.*" Each time we act on an impulse other than love, we are asking God to help us fight. We will fight our guilt, our shame, our fear, and our dishonesty. We fight to keep from being found out, from being called out, and to keep from being wrong. When we, like Paul, do something of which we are not proud, we must take responsibility, like Steve, and tell the truth. Truth is like an invisible warrior. It will save you from the battlefield.

Paul did not tell the truth. JoAnn was not prepared to fight. Instead she lied. She continued meeting her friend. She stayed very angry at Paul. And since he never stopped insinuating that he knew she was still seeing her friend, JoAnn eventually did the very thing Paul accused her of doing all along. She slept with him. I am in no way saying that he forced her to do it. Nor am I saying that what she did was a reflection of her highest identity. I am simply saying that in the end JoAnn fought back. Two days before they graduated, JoAnn told Paul what she had done. Suffice it to say, Paul was not a happy soldier! Although JoAnn begged for his forgiveness, Paul left—without ever saying a word about his little indiscretions. When I last heard from them, they were fighting in divorce court. It seems that Paul wants all the furniture he bought for their cute little apartment.

Chapter 5
CLEANING OUT THE REFRIGERATOR

bruce and david were lovers. They were lovers of wine, running, art, and each other. Bruce thought that theirs was a match made in heaven. They had, however, one small, tiny, almost insignificant problem—David was not openly gay, and Bruce was. Scratch that! David was still in the closet, living as a bisexual, and living with his *very* heterosexual girlfriend of four years. Bruce knew that this one little obstacle put their relationship in jeopardy, so he tried in every way he knew to convince David of the necessity of admitting to himself and the world that he was gay. Bruce went on an all-out campaign to address this one tiny flaw in the man he loved. Each time he did, David's response would be the same: "I'm going to tell my family and leave Diana soon."

Words can ease your mind for a little while, but when there is a crisis the mind needs action. You have to do something to back the words—particularly if you have been hearing the same words for two years. This lack of action was creating quite an undercurrent in an otherwise wonderful romance. It became a major issue the day they saw David's sister in the department store, and he acted as if he didn't know Bruce. When Bruce asked David if he was going to introduce him, David shot him a glance that would crack stone, and said, "Do I know you from somewhere?" The sister was appalled that some "gay" guy was trying to pick her brother up in broad daylight. It was disgusting, she thought, and David agreed with her. He agreed to such a degree that he left Bruce standing at the Dior counter with his mouth hanging open.

A few days later when David had the decency to call, Bruce really let him have it. It was bad enough that David was denying his own sexuality, but how dare he deny Bruce in the process! At his age, which, by the way, was well over thirty, he should have been man enough to stand up for what he believed. Why was he denying himself to protect his family? What was he protecting his family from? Homosexuality was not a disease, it was a lifestyle. It was the way Bruce had chosen (or been born, depending on which way you look at it), and he felt absolutely no shame. It was bad enough that Bruce had acquiesced and let the man he loved live and *sleep* with a woman, but to have his lover of two years deny him publicly was a downright abomination. David kept apologizing and begging for forgiveness, but Bruce was hurt to the bone. "Come out! Come out! If you want us to build a life together, come out! I will not, I refuse to spend my life in denial, and I love you too much to enable you to do it." The conversation erupted into a screaming match when Bruce told David that if he did not come out to his family, he would come out for him!

Well, that got David's full attention! Don't be confused. David really did have feelings for Bruce. He was more comfortable, more at ease when they were together, but he had a responsibility to Diana. Bruce knew the truth. He knew that the big responsibility was to his mother. David was an only son. To make matters worse, he was a surviving twin! His brother had died at the age of four. He was struck by a car driven by a half-drunk, half-crazed gay man who had come barreling down the street after he and his lover had a fight. Mind you, there were a lot of dynamics—emotional turmoil, liquor, a broken street light—but what David's mother zeroed in on was the fact that the man who killed her son was gay. It gets worse. The drunk driver then killed himself. He left a note, the police said, not demonstrating his remorse at having killed Ms. Josephine's son, but agonizing over the fact that he could not live without his lover. Ms. Josephine was out of her mind for two years. Once the drugs wore off, she went on an all-out war against homosexuality. She even went so far as to say that if she woke up one morning to discover that her son, her brother, her husband, or any man she knew who had ever touched her was gay, she would kill herself. Ms. Josephine was a bit dramatic. The point is that this is what David heard all of his life, since the second year following the death of his brother.

SHUT THE DOORS SO THINGS WILL STAY FRESH!

Have you ever made your mind up about something, only to have someone tell you a story that flatlines your brain, making you forget everything you have made your mind up to do? Speaking for myself, this has happened to me a number of times, in a variety of situations, when I lived on the first floor. There must be something, some process of elimination in my brain that is triggered by certain information. When I am confronted with certain data, there are tiny little people who run around with erasers, wiping out my good sense. I wish it were that simple! I wish I could give myself that out. The truth of the matter is when I really don't want to do something, when I am in fear of things not going the way I want them to go, I look for any possible or plausible excuse to have things the way I want them. I had no idea that what I was seeing or hearing were clues. After I got my feelings hurt or my heart broken and was forced to do some intensive reflection, I realized that they were clues. They were signals, which at the time were too overwhelming or too inconvenient to handle, so my brain wiped them out. It was not until the clues became a big ball of energy, throwing nuts and bolts in my face, or a flashing neon sign that was all but blinding, that I would find the courage to shut the door and rewrite the script, or pull down the shades on the situation. This is what I did. Of course, I know you would never do such a thing! Unfortunately Bruce did.

Listening to the story again, Bruce calmed down. They were able to talk about it, again. Finally, David promised Bruce that he would go right home, tell Diana, and bring his things to Bruce's house. They would work it out from there. Everything happens for a reason. David practiced his speech for two hours before he got home. He was poised and ready with a mental list of all the things he would need to say, and would then pack. He opened the door of his apartment to the sound of muffled sobbing. In the living room, Diana was consoling Ms. Josephine, who was obviously beside herself with grief. "Is it Daddy?" David asked, not really wanting to know. Ms. Josephine lifted her head just high enough and long enough to blurt out,

"Davie, I told those doctors Jimmy wasn't a faggot! I told him that he couldn't have gotten the HIV virus from being with some kind of homosexual freak. He used drugs! All they told me was to calm down. Can you believe it! Calm down!"

Those words cut into David like a hot knife into a pound of butter. It was not the fact that his uncle Jimmy, who was a known intravenous drug addict, had been diagnosed with full-blown AIDS; it was his mother's reaction to the situation. To Ms. Josephine, being a drug addict was far better than being gay. Of course, his exit speech became *shhh! shhh!* and other soft-spoken words of consolation for his mother, and quiet thank you's to Diana. His packing plans became plans for taking his mother home and making sure his uncle would receive the proper treatment first thing next week. The last thing he was thinking about was Bruce, who was waiting for him with an empty closet space, a nice roast duck, and a chilled bottle of Chardonnay.

WHO ATE THE CAKE I LEFT IN THE FRIDGE?

I know you know this, but I feel compelled to remind you that the longer you put something off, the worse it will become, the harder it will be to do what you need to do, say what you need to say. I know you know this, but how many times have you let the laundry pile up to the point that you had to go out and buy underwear? How many times have you put off cleaning the refrigerator until the foul smell choked you? How many times has tomorrow taken a month to come? We know, but we don't do. We want to, but we can't. We see it, but we turn our heads. Nowhere in our lives does this kind of avoidance have a more devastating effect than in our relationships. When something goes rotten in a relationship, the smell rises pretty quickly. If we do not deal with it immediately, dealing with it becomes a difficult task, a miserable chore we would definitely rather not do. But do it we must!

David couldn't face Bruce for weeks. After receiving several calls from an obviously sobbing Bruce, he finally called just to let him know he was okay. After reassuring Bruce that he had not dumped him like garbage in the street, and against his better judgment, David broke down, agreeing to meet Bruce at his apartment. He told him the story, the entire story, which by now had a cast of many characters with Ms. Josephine acting as the director. Bruce was, of course, supporting and reassuring. He declared his understanding and forgiveness. He was searching through his AIDS services directories, which is probably why he didn't comprehend exactly what David meant when he blurted out that he was going to marry Diana and not see him anymore. Even when David was halfway down the hall Bruce still couldn't grasp that this was really happening. In Bruce's mind this was just another little challenge they would have to overcome.

Love conquers all, right? Wrong! Love cannot work through dishonesty, denial, fear, or people-pleasing. It is physically impossible for two things to occupy the same space at the same time. Where there is fear, love cannot abide. When there is overt dishonesty, out-and-out lying, hiding, and denial, love cannot be. Don't even allow yourself to think that love couldn't exist between two men in this *kind* of a relationship. Love does not discriminate! It exists wherever it is welcomed, acknowledged, and honored. Three weeks later, after many unanswered telephone calls, Bruce realized that he had been left high, dry, bitter, confused, and not quite sure where it all went wrong.

What Bruce didn't understand was that he had become a tenant on the first floor of love's house, and that David was in the basement of a meantime experience.

This is clearly a case of opening the refrigerator, detecting a foul order, and having to sift through the many things stuffed into bags, bowls, and boxes to find the culprit. As we have said before, it's a nasty job, but you sometimes have to do it. You know that everything you put into the refrigerator was good. Now, however, as a result of putting off the nasty work, you have a major problem. Now you have to try to identify what went bad, to figure out how you forgot that you had bought this, why you never served the remainder of that, and what that oozing green stuff is that's dripping down the door. You have to stick your hands into things you can no longer identify, you must clean out the soiled dishes, you must pack the trash up and put it outside. Then you remember that trash day is not until four days from now. That's what happens in our relationships. When we let things go bad, when we refuse to do the job a little at a time, when we leave things unsaid and undone, the foul smell will linger.

In the meantime, it is probably wise not to bank on your partner acting the way you expect or demand. Remember that the meantime is often a time of fear and confusion when it is difficult to predict what people will do. They can't predict it, and you certainly can't predict or know what to expect. You may also want to be a bit skeptical of a person who *promises* to do anything in the midst of the meantime. People who promise and swear they are going to do something are usually trying to convince themselves that they can or want to do what you want them to do. The minute you hear the words, "I promise . . ."

or, "I swear I will . . ." beware! Don't be lulled into collusion with your own pattern of ignoring the truth. You are being put on notice that you cannot rely on what is being said to you in this very moment. Of course you don't want to admit this to yourself, nor can you confront your partner with your suspicions. Instead, take a deep breath and retreat!

In the meantime, promising and swearing is a sure sign that the level of trust required to maintain a healthy relationship is nonexistent. Chances are that *you* have some trust issues about which you may be totally unaware. Or that this is not a trustworthy person, someone who is in fear that they are about to be discovered. Nothing is more common in the meantime than expecting or demanding that a person do what we already know they will not or are incapable of doing. It is the pattern by which we set ourselves up to be hurt. It is the pattern by which we prove to ourselves that our instincts and suspicions were correct. It is a combination pattern of passive/aggressive behavior that takes us to the meantime each and every time we engage in it. Asking someone to do what we know they are unable to do, or demanding that they do what we want them to do, knowing that they are afraid and/or confused is a very unloving and unkind thing to do to ourselves and to other people.

You must listen to what people do, not to what they say. People always demonstrate their intentions, their expectations, through their actions. They may swear to high heaven that they will do this or that, but *do* remains the operative word. The issue here is not that these were *two men* who could not have this *kind* of a relationship. The issue here is that party number one expected party number two to do what party number one wanted him to do. It's called *false expectations*. Another issue is that party number one refused to accept what party number two was doing. Instead party number one was listening to what party number two was saying. It's called denial—*not recognizing the truth*. There is yet another issue to be considered here, and that is that the party of the first part did not recognize that the party of the second part was not willing, able, or ready to sever *his family relationships* for *their relationship*. It's called being able to *know what you are looking at*, and is epitomized by knowing what to do about what you see. Now let's look at the issues one at a time.

KNOW WHAT YOU ARE LOOKING AT!

Many people enter relationships with false expectations. This is when we expect people to do what we want them to do when they are clearly indicating to us that they have other intentions. If David, who was well into his thirties, had not come out yet, why did Bruce expect him to do it now? His inability or unwillingness to do so did not mean David didn't care about Bruce, it simply meant he wasn't ready. There are times when we expect people to be able to do something that they are not ready to do. This is the very difference between those who live on the first floor and those who live on the third floor. On the third floor, love makes no demands, has no expectations. On the first floor it does. Often in relationships things don't work out because the people we are attracted to are taking another path to the summit. Each of us, from our own position, tries to convince the other to walk the path we have chosen. Nothing could be more difficult, which brings us to the use of another spiritual household cleanser—TRUTH! You must walk the path that is true for you. The path you walk doesn't have to be *the truth*, it only has to be true for you. The truth is that Bruce was out, while David was not.

You may love a person dearly, but you must also accept that they may not walk the path with you. They have chosen another way, another lesson, one which may not be complementary to yours. Which raises the second issue: Learn to face the truth. Why would Bruce, who was openly gay, want a relationship with somebody who was living with a woman and who was afraid to tell his mother the truth? Is that not a covert form of self-denial? Are you not setting yourself up to be let down? You really can't be disappointed when this person does not treat you the way you want to be treated. By participating in David's self-denial, Bruce should have expected to be denied. In fact, he was denied every night while David was snoring in Diana's face. He chose to be part of the problem, rather than being a part of the solution.

There are two big lessons for those who live on the first floor: (1) Find your center and stay grounded in it, and (2) Let people walk the path they have chosen and love them anyway. The truth of the matter is no two ears of corn grow at the same pace. No two roses blossom at exactly the same time. It could be a neck-and-neck race, but everything and everyone unfolds at their pace, according to the divine plan for their lives. It is very tempting to stunt your growth, stop your growth, or insist that someone pace themselves with you. The truth is that simultaneous growth is rare in relationships. Usually two people start out together. One pulls ahead, the other drops to the rear. In some cases, the one in the lead can reach back and pull the other one up to speed. In most cases, the one who reaches back gets slowed down, sometimes to a halt. Find your center and stay grounded in it. Know that you can still love the person who is running behind you, but if they start walking, it is *your responsibility to yourself* to keep running.

How do you find your center? There are several simple steps you can practice consistently that will help you find your center, your place of equilibrium:

1. Constantly remind yourself of the experience you want to have. (How do you want to feel?) Do not set any limits on yourself. Let your mind conjure up the best situation it can imagine.

2. Visualize yourself having that experience so that it will become a familiar feeling in your body. (This is an excellent meditation exercise.) Very often we have no idea of what it would feel like if we got exactly what we desired. Consequently if or when we get it, or get close to getting it, the body becomes uncomfortable, and we think something is wrong.

3. Acknowledge or confront and release your fears about what you want. It just seems to be a part of human nature that we want something and at the same time are afraid of having it. This is an excellent journaling opportunity. Write out what you fear, what you think could happen, what you would feel if that happened, what would happen to you if that happened, and anything else you can think of that keeps you in fear. End this exercise by writing, "I do not choose to have this experience. I choose to _____." Complete the sentence by writing out what you want.

Another excellent exercise for confronting and
releasing fear is called the Chair Exercise. Place two
chairs together facing each another. You sit in one and
visualize the person you want to talk to, or write that
person's name on a piece of paper and place it face up
in the other chair. You can also imagine that sitting in
the chair is your guardian angel, your best friend, your
minister, your mentor, Christ, or any person/spiritual
being whom you acknowledge. Talk through your fears
with this person/entity. Say anything and everything
that comes to your mind. When you are done, ask for
guidance.

4. Examine what you believe about what is true for you.
   Ask yourself: Who am I? What do I believe about me?
   What do I do to support these beliefs? What have I
   learned about myself that works to make me happy?
   What have I learned about myself that does not work to
   make me happy? Be sure to write down what comes to
   mind as answers to these questions.

The majority of challenges in our relationships come about
when we forget our goal, when we forget the lessons we have
learned in the past, when we live in fear, which in effect creates
the very thing we fear, and when we do things we subconsciously know do not work.

In response to my mother dying when I was two, I created
a very subtle and subconscious belief that the people I love will
leave me. I expect people to leave me. In my relationships, this
translated into a fear of commitment. Of course, I had no idea
it was going on. I thought I was being left because there was

something wrong with me, or that the other people, the men, were simply low-down. There was a battle going on in my mind. A part of me wanted a relationship, while the other part of me was afraid of having one. The part of me that wanted the relationship was angry with the part of me that always did something to contribute to the relationship falling apart. The part of me that expected people to leave, believed they would leave, was afraid to open up. The part of me that wanted to open up had to fight to come to the surface. In action, it looked like mood swings—I was very warm, affectionate, and loving, but just as quickly I could shift into being a real b!/**. I would swing back and forth between leave, no stay, get out, don't leave me. Eventually each of my partners called my bluff and left. Many people who live on the first floor in love's house must work through the inner conflict of wanting a relationship and believing, for whatever reason our minds cook up, that we cannot have or do not deserve to have a committed relationship. It is very akin to believing that we do not deserve love. Love is a soul attraction and a soul agreement. The people we attract love us so much on a soul level that they make an agreement, an unspoken, unconscious agreement, to spend a part of their life entwined in your life to teach you about the agreements you have made. The truth is that Bruce and David, like anyone else who engages in an intimate or sexual relationship, had such an agreement.

On the first floor, you begin to build your integrity related to relationships. You begin to develop boundaries. You must begin to get clear about what you will and will not do; how you will call people to show up and participate in your life; how much of yourself you are willing to give away; and whether or not you will keep the commitments you have made to yourself. Whenever you participate in someone else's hiding or avoidance you are not acting with integrity. You are acting from a consciousness of denial and irresponsibility. If you know someone is taking drugs and you don't say anything to that person or anybody else, you are participating in their self-destruction. You can call it helping out, being supportive, or being loyal, but you must be very clear about the effect their actions have on you. You must recognize the peril in which you are placing yourself. So very often in relationships not only do we surrender our integrity by doing things we swore we would not do, but we lose our self-respect by allowing other people to do what we would not do in our lives. When we find ourselves in situations that compromise our integrity, we must learn how to love that person from a distance until they can get it together. While this may seem like an obvious example, it is no different from Bruce and David's story. Bruce knew David was having a relationship with a heterosexual woman. By insisting on having a relationship with him, Bruce participated in something that was unprincipled.

There are times when you get into things and you don't know how to get out of them. Rather than try to figure it out, you stay. You let it fester. When you do, these things eventually rot! There was definitely something rotten in Bruce's refrigerator: the things he forgot about himself in pursuit of David, the things he told himself to justify the relationship—for example, that they loved one another. If you do not love yourself enough to live in your own integrity, if you do not have a solid sense of self-value and self-worth, loving other people is going to be difficult. You can need them or want them, which means what you are actually doing is being codependent; you are most probably involved in needs exchange, which rarely lasts or works. In the meantime, while things are molding, festering, and falling apart, you are probably very angry! If you are, you must take a little *responsibility*—it will help ease the anger. Add a little dash of *truth* to that and in just a short while you will be just fine. Just so that you can get a very good grip on the nature of living on the first floor and the efficacy of the spiritual cleansers you must use on this level of your development, let us examine another scenario.

TAKE A LITTLE SOMETHING: IT WILL HELP YOU FEEL BETTER

The *classic* first-floor story is about bringing somebody through something only to have them leave you. When this happens, chances are you will need more than a cleaning out. You will need a complete overhaul! This is a story about a woman who did not keep the agreements she made with herself, who ignored the beginning signs of trouble, who was acting out her subconscious conflict, and who did not, could not face the truth. An attractive, well-built, college-educated, professional woman who was gainfully employed, she fell in love with a high-school graduate who loved gardening. Gardening doesn't seem like such a bad thing to do with your life, but it can get pretty rough during the winter months. Although she did not realize it, the woman was looking for acceptance and companionship. The dust bunnies in her mind were doing the *"you're still not good enough"* dance because she had not snagged a permanent beau. The fungus left on her heart by past relationships led her to e that if she helped this guy, he would in return give her what she wanted and needed—completion. Poor thing! She really needed an ego cleaning! She didn't realize that she was good enough or that even if she wasn't, a man could not help her. She told all of her friends that she knew it, but as with most of us who need a thorough cleaning out, her actions inevitably proved otherwise.

He was looking for support and acceptance, with a tinge of fear and dishonesty. In some circles it is called a free ride! In all fairness, it's not that he was a bad person. It's just that he didn't believe in himself or have faith in the dream he held in his heart. He needed other people to buy into the dream, which helped him feel better about it. Actually, he wanted them to buy into the dream and pay for it. This way if it didn't work out, he had nothing to lose. Sounds pretty low-down, but we all do it in one way or another. It is the classic behavior we take into relationships, and the very behavior that gets us booted out of them. We lack faith in our dreams, so we don't say what we mean or mean what we say. It is the behavior of those who dwell in the basement of love's house. Both of these people were basement dwellers! And we all know that the basement is usually so cluttered and dusty, no one wants to clean down there!

One aspect of unconditional love is being able to give of yourself without expectation of return or reward. That's right, nothing! You must expect nothing for the love that you give, not even love. Marianne Williamson, author of the book *A Return to Love*, wrote, *"Love is giving without remembering. Receiving without forgetting."* This does not mean that you allow people to do what they want to do in your life or to you. It simply means that you live each day as an experience of sharing, with no hidden agendas or expectations of a return on your investment. Love requires an honest sharing of time, space, resources, and life for the sheer pleasure of it, while it is pleasurable. This level of conscious, unconditional love will reap many rewards in immeasurable ways. It will also magnify and expose anything that is unlike love. Unconditional love will expose dishonesty and fear. When it does and you see it, you will be able to express your concerns because you have no hidden agenda about which you are subconsciously guilty. When you have no guilt, you are empowered to choose a course of action that includes letting go of the dishonesty and fear that has entered your life, cleverly disguised as a human being. Letting go, which is a form of housecleaning, does not mean you stop loving. It means that you make a conscious choice about how to love, which can include loving someone from a distance. Unfortunately, when you live in the basement—in the clutter of being a victim, in the dust of believing that you are good enough, and in the mess of not believing in yourself—you are not yet equipped to see or handle any of this *stuff*. While you cannot see, you believe that someone else can make your dream come true for you. This blind unwillingness to clean your relationship house is the classic behavior of those who live in the basement.

During the course of their four-year, live-in courtship, she supported the household while he went to college to pursue a degree in botany and business administration. She worked during the day. He went to school at night. Banking on the returns of her investment, she spent her time, money, energy, and, of course, her *love* making life as comfortable as possible for him. He spent his days in other ways, like finding pleasure with someone else in ways that he did not find with her. He could have told her the truth, but it is hard to tell the truth to the people you are afraid of or dependent on. He also could have moved in with the *pleasure,* but she did not have the money he needed to make his dream come true. What's a fella to do in a case like this? He made the choice to love dishonestly.

Along the way she noticed a little clutter, and a few termites. They were little things that made her uncomfortable and suspicious. Things like unfamiliar numbers on the cellular telephone bill. She concluded that they were calls he made for business reasons. There were also mysterious charges on the credit card bills, which she assumed represented things he bought for himself or the business. She wanted to ask him about these things, but she chose not to. She remembered what happened the last time, in the last relationship, when she voiced her suspicions, and since she had not cleaned out her own clutter, she decided to remain in silent wonder. She also felt a bit guilty about being suspicious since she was in control of the purse strings. She concluded that because he worked hard during the summer months to build a client base, she should ignore the little *stuff,* and she accepted his half-baked explanations.

Having been raised in a single-parent household, he was accustomed to a woman being in control of his life. He didn't like it, but it was familiar, and a lot easier than doing it on his own. He had also figured out exactly what to do and say to keep her off his case. He would make her feel guilty by telling her about how hard it was on him to accept her help. How it challenged his manhood to watch her work so hard for his benefit. If you ever want to shut a woman up, tell her she is challenging your manhood. Every muscle in her body, including her tongue, will shut down. People who live in the basement always have issues with some kind of *hood*—adult*hood*, truth-*hood*, reality*hood*, or human*hood*. With her mouth shut, he knew he could talk her out of her anger by projecting her into the promise of a glorious future. It had always worked with Mom, and it worked like a charm with most women. Particularly those who were blinded in one eye by guilt and clutter!

They planned *his* business together. She taught him how to set it up and shared with him her business contacts for loans and other expertise. They talked about how the business would bloom, and how wonderful it would be for *him*. She assumed, after all she had done for him, that she was automatically included in his plans. She thought she knew, but she really didn't, because basement dwellers cannot see beyond the clutter of their own stuff. He was eager to have the chance to prove himself to her. She liked the sound of that. It would take a lot of hard work, but he was able to do anything with her by his side. She was wonderful, he said. She was his angel, he said. She concluded that she was buying all the acceptance she needed and that it was finally going to pay off. Then he said the "L" word. He said he *loved* her. With that said, followed by a few hours of wild lovemaking, she forgot about the termite inspection, and they planned to get married as soon as he graduated. He did. They did not. He wanted to get the business off the ground so he could *pay her back* for all she had done. It seemed to make sense, particularly with his manhood in question. Although she could feel the fear rising up her spine, she remained silent, agreeing to wait. Three years passed very quickly, and as they had planned, the business boomed.

At her insistence, the wedding finally took place. It was a big wedding with all the trimmings, for which she footed most of the bill. About a month after the honeymoon, she again noticed a rather large cellular telephone bill. Although he was working now, he continued to let her handle the money stuff. It's hard for basement dwellers to change their habits. One day she decided to check the most frequently dialed number. Her husband's pleasure answered the telephone. She was the mother of his children. The now Mrs. *Let-Me-Help-You-Out* was devastated. She had put so much into the relationship, only to be betrayed. She felt like a failure. She should have seen it coming. Since she had not, she was also ashamed of herself. She had supported a man, and obviously his children, for seven years. She had never felt good about what she had been doing. As a matter of fact, she had lied to her girlfriends, telling them that he was working part-time while he was in school, which is why, she said, he went to school at night. She had watched her mother support her alcoholic father for so many years that she felt justified in this "stand by your man" approach, even though it did not feel good. Now she was about to lose it all—him, her image, her companionship, and control. *He had taken advantage of her!* entered the *meantime* of her life in a great deal of anger. No, in rage. She was so stupid! No. She was so confused! No. She was enraged! No. She was in the meantime, trying to figure out what happened, how it happened, and why it had happened to her, again. She did not want to clean! She wanted to kill something!

The truth is that neither of these people was conscious of their truth and therefore could not tell it to each other. Had she known the truth about her motives, it might have been difficult, but this woman could have made life a lot easier by simply saying, "Look. I've got a good job and a decent life, but no man. I need a companion, some sex, and someone to flash around at the office parties. For half the rent and the food bill I am offering you the position." He could have honestly responded, "Look, I've got a dream and very little money. I'll pay half of the rent, offer sexual companionship with no strings attached, and I will do my own laundry. Can I stay with you for about three years?" It sounds very harsh, perhaps profane, but it would have saved them both a lot of time, money, and heartache. Now she's in therapy, he's in divorce court, and they are fighting each other to regain the pieces of their lives they gave away.

I sense great objections, such as, "People don't act like that!" Or, "You can't say those things to people!" In response to those objections I ask, Why not? Why don't we have the courage to say exactly what it is that we expect, want, or need. Have we not yet learned that by not saying these things, we create the traumatic heartbreak we swear we want to avoid? Those of us who live in the basement may not be able to tell the truth. Those of us who have been elevated to the first floor must learn how to do it. Let me share with you what I know. I know that when we learn to love and honor ourselves, there is nothing that we cannot do, say, or have unless we make the choice not to. I also know that when we have this kind of love in our hearts, the truth, as shocking as it may be, will in the end save us a lot of grief. I also know that when we learn to live from a consciousness of truth, responsibility, integrity, and unconditional love, the things we once wanted will no longer be satisfying. We will be able to go into the refrigerator, detect the slightest odor of something going rotten, and get rid of it!

HONOR YOURSELF! HONOR OTHER PEOPLE!

We do it all of the time. You find someone to whom you are attracted or with whom you are intrigued. Perhaps that person has a nice body, a gorgeous face, the right-sized body parts, or any other thing that creates ripples in your brain waves. You want that person! You pursue that person! Have you or has anyone you know ever said, *"I'm gonna make them love me?"* This is exactly the kind of situation I am referring to here. You go on an all-out campaign to catch this person's eye and capture this person's heart. In the meantime, while you are in this kind of hot pursuit, you forget who you are and what you really want. You do things you know you have absolutely no business doing. You say things that you have absolutely no business saying. You have no center, no top, and no bottom. You are on a mission. On this type of mission, you are bound to dishonor yourself.

Chances are, the person you are pursuing is being exactly who they are, doing exactly what they do. You, however, are not paying attention. You give their nasty little habits cute little names. You make excuses for them and the things they do. In the meantime, you are doing all the work, spending all the money, making all the arrangements. You are doing such a good job, you don't notice that the other person is just coming along for the ride. In addition, you have done absolutely no investigation. You have absolutely no information. You don't know the relationship history. You don't know the family history. You probably have no idea that this is the very same person whose face appears on a wanted poster in the post office! You are going your merry way, making a mess, leaving things undone and unsaid that will eventually mold or rot, leaving you with a mess to clean up. When we refuse to accept that people can walk a path different from ours, or when we attempt to drag them onto ours, we dishonor them, as well as ourselves.

There are many of us who are looking at what we need and want in relationships with eyes that have been blinded by the wrong information. What we think people can do for us or give to us, and how we think they can make us feel will shift when we accept our true identity and begin to love ourselves because of who we are—whole, complete, and perfect beings. When this happens, when we start out from a consciousness of wholeness, completion, and perfection, we will not be looking *for* the same things in relationships. We will not be looking *at* the same things as the standards for our relationships. We will not be looking *with* the same needs when we enter relationships. Consequently, we will not have the same pervading fears. In the absence of fear, love, joy, peace, and truth reign supreme. It is in order to eliminate fear that we must be willing to scrub the rings out of the tub!

THE SECOND FLOOR

it's amazing how things can pile up! You turn your head for one minute and there is stuff everywhere, covered with dust. You can't find the shoes you took off last night because they are obscured by all the junk. You know that you just put your keys down on the table, but now you can't find them because of all of the papers. You must keep the shower curtain closed in the bathroom because you have a ring in the tub. You forgot to buy trash bags again, so the trash is piling up. In the normal course of living, it is absolutely amazing how much stuff we can create and accumulate.

Yes, we can get away with it in our living environments. It is not true that we can get away with it for long in our relationships. Junk, trash, confusion, and greasy, oily buildup must be cleaned away before we can enjoy the fruits of love. It can be a messy, dirty job to clean up our love junk, but we all have to do it sooner or later.

Chapter 6
LET'S DO A LITTLE DUSTING

you are thirty thousand feet in the air, flying across country, against your better judgment. All of a sudden, just when you are about to bite the corner off your third bag of peanuts, turbulence starts! Your can of Coke goes flying in the air. The peanuts have spilled down your shirt—outside and inside. You've hit your knees on that stupid little tray, and your neighbor is screaming, "Oh, my God!!!" at the top of her lungs. The pilot is reassuring you that it's just a little turbulence, and everything is all right. As you pick the peanuts off your chest, you are trying to remember that prayer your mother taught you when you were six. The plane hits another air pocket. The prayer pops into your mind, *"Now I lay me down . . ."* No! Not that one! You would not dare go to sleep now! There is turbulence in the air! In your life! You are in the meantime, and there is not much you can do. Actually, there is nothing you can do but ride it out. You must ride it out, and think—think about all the things you will do better once you get back on the ground.

The second floor is the place that you come to learn about

the most important relationship you will ever have, the relationship you have with yourself. That relationship, which has developed almost entirely in response to your experiences in life, will serve as the model for every other love relationship you have. How do I love myself? Let me count the ways. I love myself the way I was loved the day I was born. I love myself the way my parents loved me. I love myself the way my siblings and friends loved me. I love myself the way the TV characters showed me. But wait, they changed their mind about who and how to love —again! I love myself through the perceptions of the media. I love myself with the expectations and conditions of my environment. I love myself in response to the way other people demonstrate their love for me. I love myself in so many different ways, depending on what is going on around me and what I remember from other love experiences. I love myself in confusion! I love myself in fear! I love myself in so much anger that I cannot seem to get anyone else to love me! In the meantime, however, while I am searching, yearning, waiting for love, I blame myself for the inability to find the right love or to get loved the right way!

She must have been about thirty years old when she decided that she had to learn how to love herself more. She had to love herself enough to stop—stop struggling, stop hurting, stop feeling like she couldn't stand any more. She had to learn to love herself enough to stop doing the things that caused so much struggle and pain for herself. In her silent prayers, Rhonda pleaded with God to help her change, help her feel better about herself and about life. Her children were getting older, and she wanted to be a better role model for them. She was feeling older and did not want to live the rest of her life like this. She realized that these feelings were most intense at the end of a relationship, which is exactly where she was at the time. She also realized that there are just some things you will not address until there is extreme pressure to do so. The pressure was on!

How had he gotten himself into this, again? He had promised himself that no matter how fine the woman was or how good the situation looked, he would never again find himself in a situation where he was juggling two women at the same time. "Whatever I get, I deserve!" James thought to himself. "This is just ridiculous!" Why was it that he could never say no? Why was it that when he tried to be nice to a woman, she would fall head over heels, making him feel totally obligated to stay, to help her to work through it? Why was it that when he had one woman at his apartment, trying to help her work through what she was going through, the other had to show up and make a scene? Why was it that women always knew when you were lying? Now he had Jean on one side of town crying her eyes out, and Paula on the other side threatening to flatten his tires. Here he was again, just where he did not want to be, alone.

HOW DO YOU GET RID OF
SURFACE DIRT AND GRIME?

Just where does it all start? The patterns we repeat over and over. The feelings we try to fight off over and over. Is it something that we eat? Or are we really that dumb? Dumb enough to set ourselves up over and over? There has to be an answer, and there has to be a way to save you from yourself. Perhaps we should have little lights on our foreheads like the lights on the dashboard of a car. The lights would warn us when we are running hot, idling too fast, when we need to shift into park, into neutral, or out of reverse. You definitely need to know when you are going backward over ground you have covered before. These lights would be activated by our thoughts and feelings. Your body would simply generate enough heat or energy to ignite the lights, which would in turn sound the alarms in your head and heart. When this happened, you would be required to take your overheated body to a life mechanic who would sit you down and diagnose your symptoms: You are being desperate again! You are being needy again! You are about to crash! You would then be taken in for servicing, to change your level of willingness, tune up your responsibility, readjust the truth in your consciousness.

As far-fetched as it may seem, Rhonda could have used a life mechanic. She needed some help gauging herself and her love life. Just when she thought she was getting it all together, something or someone new would pop up, forcing her into reverse, back over emotional ground she had already covered. Sometimes she escaped with only a few scrapes and scratches. Like the time before the last time. The guy was gorgeous, absolutely delicious! He pursued and subdued her. They had a great time together, but something just didn't click. He was kinda, sorta vague in his explanations about everything. He was always very busy doing something he could never quite explain. It took about three months for Rhonda to discover that he was still living with his daughter's mother (that's what they call them these days), and another six months for her to comprehend that theirs was an on-again, off-again relationship. During the weeks in which *they* were on, Rhonda found that he was vague. During the weeks in which *they* were off, he was like an ever-ready bunny!

When he finally broke down and told her the whole story, it sounded absolutely reasonable and believable—to Alice in Wonderland! By that time, Rhonda was hooked. She was trying to figure out a way to make it work. She would call late at night to see if he answered, and if he would talk to her. He always did. She started asking him to accompany her to public events. He never refused. What he would not do, ever, under any circumstances, was spend the night. He did not want his daughter to wake up to find that he was not at home. He did not want his daughter's mother to get angry and take his daughter away. He did not want to get himself involved in a serious relationship until he got a divorce. From whom? His wife lived in Texas.

There is one lesson Rhonda learned well—a married man is a married man! He could have been separated in 1902, but if his wife is alive, he is still married. She knew better than to shift into that gear. A married man who is still married can string you along forever. He can tell you anything. He will tell you anything! Rhonda had to admit that even if she had one foot in the basement and both hands on the first floor, she would not, could not, under any circumstances, involve herself with a married man— she had done that before and had gotten nowhere. The breakup was mutual. Since she did most of the calling, she just stopped. It took him two weeks to notice. When he did, he called. Rhonda was not at home. She remained away from home for a year. It made her feel a little better that it took him that long to stop calling. That helped to ease the pain, somewhat.

James, too, could have used some lights in his brain, and a life mechanic. Jean had been his steady date for the past year or so. If he wasn't so screwed up in the brain, James thought to himself, he could really settle down and spend the rest of his life with Jean. She had it all, looks, brains, a healthy sexual appetite, and a strong enough personality to keep him in check. The big thing was that Jean didn't want anything from him. She never asked for hairdresser money, car payment money, or grocery money, nor did she ever insist that he go home with her for the holidays. She was not trying to show him off to her friends, and she didn't parade him around like he was a carnival prize. She had a mind of her own, and it had a very calming effect on James. Perhaps that was it. Maybe she was too steady, too good. How many times had he told himself that he didn't deserve Jean? She was too good for him. How many times had he told her the same thing? Paula, on the other hand, was a completely different story!

Paula was a wild child! She like to party and have fun, and it was quite obvious that she was looking for a man to party and have fun with her. If it weren't for the fact that she called and chased him most of the time, he would bet that Paula would have three or four men providing for her every need— her hair, nails, feet, and, of course, the rent. He didn't mind helping a woman out if she had an emergency, but he did not want to be obligated to do so in return for sexual favors. That had become Paula's MO once they had gotten together: She was a beggar—she was always begging for money, attention, or time. Don't women know how annoying that is to a man? Don't they know that most men are barely making it on their own? Why do you have to prove yourself to a woman in terms of dollars and cents? Besides that, he never meant for it to get so serious with Paula. He was looking for a little fling, somebody to spend some time with while Jean was away on business trips. One night of a little fun and the next thing you know, your tires are being threatened. How had it gotten to this?

IS IT SOUP YET?

You can have meantime relationships. Relationships that are fun, satisfying, or fulfilling for now. You do not enter meantime relationships in need. You enter them as a choice. You know this is not the *forever one*, but it is the one for now. A meantime relationship should not deplete you. It should give you something to do, keep your spirits up, and help you prepare yourself for a greater experience. You will know that you are in a meantime relationship if you like the person, but you don't like them enough to lend them your car. If you enjoy spending time with them, but you cannot see yourself sitting in a rocking chair sharing your Jell-O with this person. In a meantime relationship, sexual activity is your call, but less is more. If you recognize that you are in a meantime relationship, relax and enjoy it. Do not invest your life's savings—meaning, you should not order the wedding rings or print the invitations. Face the truth! Know what you know! Accept the fact that the relationship you want is being prepared, like dinner. In the meantime, have a light snack!

Unfortunately, what we have a tendency to do is overindulge in the snack and ruin the dinner. We take on too much. We invest too much. We expect too much. We keep trying to make *this one the one*. The *"this is it"* syndrome is basement behavior. At that time of our development, we want so much to get away from ourselves that anyone is the one. We have a problem with ourselves, and we don't know it. We place conditions and demands on our relationships because we are preoccupied with the physical satisfaction. Don't forget your first-floor experiences! You have already cleaned up that basement mess! Train yourself to have a little light go off in your brain that flashes—WARNING! WARNING! WATCH YOUR STEP! YOU ARE GOING TOO FAR!

Rhonda was an independent consultant. She had an excellent reputation in her field. However, things were very slow. She had not worked in months. As a result, there were money pressures. She had accepted a long-term project that was way overdue. If she could just get it finished, she would have some money. Some real money. Money to pay bills, to get the children a few things they needed. And perhaps there would be enough left over for her to take a short trip somewhere, anywhere, just to give her mind a break. Fat chance of that happening! She knew the pattern—money comes in, money goes out before you can do what you need to do. It was just about the same with the men in her life. They came in, they left. Rhonda had some very important lessons to learn.

Then there was the little issue of the house. She needed to move. She had been putting the search off for quite some time because the money just wasn't there. Rhonda had held her landlord off for as long as she could, but now he was getting a little weird and very threatening. Threatening to put her belongings in the street. Threatening to sue her. It was more pressure. If only she could finish the work, she would have the money to move and the pressure would be off. That was another pattern.

It seemed that whenever she had something very important to do, there was always some kind of pressure. It's hard to plan, to work, to look for a house when you are being pressured by bill collectors and your landlord. Needless to say, she was doing it all alone. Her last relationship had recently ended, but at least that had been different. This time she was the one to do the leaving. At thirty years old, Rhonda had left her first man. Hallelujah! At least something was changing! Unfortunately, the fact that she was alone *again* was a very familiar scenario. When you are alone in the meantime and you do not want to be, how you came to be alone is of little or no consequence. For a brief while, you may feel good about the fact that your heart is not battered or bruised. When, however, you realize that the one who took so long to come is now gone, *how* he left does not seem as important as the reality *that* he left.

Rhonda was cruising along at a nice steady pace, doing her work, making pretty decent money, enjoying herself. She had just begun studying spiritual things. She wasn't a new age fanatic, but she was interested in the mind/body/spirit stuff she kept hearing so much about. Spirit had her attention when the man caught her eye. It was one of those chance meetings. She was on a business trip the first time she met him. He struck up a conversation with her. They went out to dinner, where they had a wonderful time. They went their separate ways without even exchanging telephone numbers. Back in her hotel room Rhonda was elated. This is it! This is the life! Find a man who will feed you without asking you for a telephone number—I've died and gone to heaven!

Although he knew exactly how, James retraced his steps, thinking, *"If it wasn't so pathetic, it would be funny."* He should have followed his first thought, which was to never go back to Paula's for a second dip in the pool. He almost made it, but then she promised him a home-cooked meal. He was a sucker for a home-cooked meal, and he had to admit that Paula could cook her tight little buns off. Jean, as much as he loved her—scratch that, liked to be with her—could not cook worth a damn! In addition to the wild nights, Paula was good for the best breakfast a man could ask for—ham, home fries, grits, pancakes, waffles with strawberries, on a weekday morning! It beat a bagel and coffee any day. After one of those breakfasts, the next thing he knew, six months had gone by and Paula was offering him a key. It was almost worth it. Almost, but not quite.

Jean had come home early, eager to see him. She had presents and wanted to bring them by the house. He had figured out very early that it was dangerous to bring Paula to his house, so he usually went to hers and prayed to God that she had forgotten his address, having only been there once. Then there was the policy. He had a policy that no matter how much he fooled around, his primary woman was his primary woman! All others had to wait! When the primary called you, drop everything. He hung up from Jean, called Paula, and told her he had to cancel the movies. Something had come up. They would do it in a few days. That's when she started whining. He reminded her that he had just left her house. He told her that everything was fine, and that he would call her later. He should have followed his first thought! Something told him to call Paula in the middle of the day, just to check in, to make sure she wasn't suspicious, but he got busy at work and forgot. He had also gotten very excited at the thought of seeing Jean.

When he got home, Jean was waiting. After the preliminary welcome, they ordered Chinese food. He opened his gifts, they talked and ate, and were just about to head for the shower when the doorbell rang. It was Paula! She was downstairs at the front door! When he heard her voice on the intercom, he thought he would have a stroke. "Thought you had something to do, M—— F——!" He released the button. Too late! Jean heard the venom that spewed through the system. "Who's that?" "I don't know!" James snapped as he walked toward the bathroom. Bad move. The minute you get defensive, women know something is up. The bell was ringing again. Which way do you go? Which way do you go? "Start the shower," James told Jean as he walked back toward the intercom. Jean started toward the bathroom. Stopped. Headed toward him with that look in her eyes, the look that lets you know you are in deep doo-doo. "Let her in, James. Just let her in! I'll leave!" *Oh, Jesus!* he thought, *this is a mess!* He couldn't think fast enough. His mouth opened involuntarily. The words fell across his lips from a place he did not want to go. "Let who in?" Dumb question!

TIME IS ON YOUR SIDE!

There is no simple path to discovering the truth about love. There is, however, *the meantime:* the experiences during our search for love that teach us to understand what we do. Relationships are the experiences in which we work out our false notions, skewed perceptions, fears, and judgments about love. For some of us, *the meantime* lasts for what seems like forever. We can't find the right person. We can't be the right person. We can't capture the right feelings. When we do, they don't last long enough to make us feel good enough. *The meantime*, there-fore, is not a *learning process*, it is *an unlearning process*. It is the time we are given by life to reflect, reevaluate, and remember the truth about who we are and what love lends to our identity. The goal is to provide you with some new things to reflect upon and to provide you with some new tools with which to evaluate and reflect. In the meantime, your experiences are meant to jar your memory back to your first experience of true love. With that in mind, you will have a pretty good idea of how close to or far away from the reality of love you are. Hopefully you will be able to keep that memory alive long enough to recapture it in your soul and activate it in all of your relationships.

In the process of doing this work, you may discover that it will be necessary for you to start all over again from scratch, from the bottom of the pile, building new, more loving relation-ships. That is real work! In *the meantime*, there are always rela-tionships going on. What will you do about them? What will you do about the relationships that have been built on mold, fungus, outdated fashions, and *meantime* hysteria? Hopefully you will be willing to love yourself through them. Some of these relationships will survive. Others will not. There is hope, how-ever, that once you remember the truth about love, you will so shower yourself and those around you with it, that you will be empowered to go out and find more love, give more love.

The dinner remained a pleasant memory that Rhonda had just about forgotten a month later when she went on another business trip. She had checked into her room, changed, and was going downstairs to check out the conference happenings when she heard the voice. When she turned around, he was standing there, the dinner man. He spoke as if their date had taken place only a few days ago. "Hey, what's happening? How are you?" Rhonda was pleasantly surprised. Could this represent another round of crab cakes tonight? "Hey! Look at you? Are you here for the conference?" It was on, again. They walked, talked, and previewed the conference weekend together.

As a matter of fact, they spent the entire conference walking and talking. On the final day, they went out for Greek food. He knew the city and exactly where to go. Since neither of them was leaving until the next day, they made plans for an early breakfast and sightseeing. He walked her to her room door and kissed her on the cheek, with a quick about-face as he headed toward the elevator. Rhonda was beginning to waver. Maybe something is wrong with him? Maybe something is wrong with me? It was beginning to feel very weird. She knew she was doing exactly what she wanted to be doing, having fun, taking it slow, not getting overly involved, but it was new, too new to feel comfortable. You would think if the guy was interested he would at least ask to come in, or kiss her on the lips. The minute she had the thought, a little bell started ringing in her head. "DO A NEW THING! DO A NEW THING! If you want new results, do a new thing."

Paula must have put a piece of adhesive tape across the doorbell—it was ringing nonstop now. Jean was gathering up her things. "What are you doing? What are you doing?!!!" He couldn't read her. Was she mad? Was she hurt? Jean was so steady, so calm, he simply could not read what was going on with her. "Look, it's nothing. I'll take care of it. Go start the shower. It's nothing! Okay, nothing!" James could hear himself rambling. In fact, he was almost pleading. Jean was beginning to tremble. *"Okay, she's mad. No, she's hurt!"* She was headed toward the door. The bell was still ringing. "You've got more nerve than a bad tooth!" Jean told him. That's why he loved her —scratch that, *liked* being with her so much. Any other woman would have called him every kind of foul and indecent name known to man. Here was Jean, a beautiful, sensible woman, talking about his teeth. How could he be so stupid? He reached out to grab her, hold her, stop her. Dumb move!

When you live on the second floor of love's house, you will cry a lot. You will cry because you will think you will never get it right. You will cry because it will seem as if you still have so very much to do. You will cry because you will be so very grateful to be on a healing path. When you are not crying, you will be trying to *fix* yourself. You will watch your every word. You will focus on your every thought. You will want to lose twenty pounds and cut your hair in an attempt to make it look like you know what you are doing. One day, at the height of your second-floor experience, you will realize that you really don't know what you are doing, and that there is a big chance you are doing it all wrong. In response to this miraculous revelation, you will cry some more. You will cry because things will be better but they won't be great. You will cry because you will feel better, but you won't be completely *fixed*. You will want so much to do great and be fixed, but you just won't know what to do. You will be confused. In response to your confusion, you will throw yourself on the floor and utter the ultimate prayer, *"Dear God, Please help me!"* In a relatively short span of time, you will get the help and answers you need.

I remember the day someone told me, *"God loves you just as you are."* I was shocked! I was also relieved that I had in fact done it *right*. But it was frightening to think I had no conscious understanding of what I had in fact done. More to the point, I was so grateful to hear that God loved me, I cried in relief and for release. In a second-floor meantime experience, you too will remember that you are love embodied, that you are the essence of love. If you do not remember it on your own, you will either read it in a book or hear it at a workshop. It does not matter how you get it. The point is that you will get it. Hopefully at that point you too will cry. Crying is a very helpful and meaningful experience when you live on the second floor of love's house.

When we forget that God loves us, we strike out in search of a human lover to fulfill our need to be loved. On the second floor you can surrender that need and forgive yourself for having it. You have been elevated to the second floor of love's house by the power of God's love for you. Now you must learn to actively apply surrender and forgiveness to everything to do. You must surrender hiding. How do you do that? You must feel what you feel and express what you feel. You must surrender your judgments about what you feel—*I shouldn't feel this way! Maybe what I feel is wrong!* Give that up in favor of, *"I forgive myself if my perception is inaccurate, but right now I am feeling _____."* You will be shocked! You will be shocked at your willingness and ability to tell your truth and risk looking bad, weak, or stupid. Good! You have now changed your mind about not telling the truth, which means you are willing to tell it—on the spot.

SING NO VICTIM SONG!

Rhonda went to bed after laying out her clothes for the next day's date, which turned out to be great. They rode around in his car. They had lunch on the waterfront. They laughed. They talked. They exchanged telephone numbers, and he took her to the airport. All the way home, she tried not to work herself up into a frenzy. She forced her mind to think about other things. She tried to read. She promised herself she would not call first. A month later, she had not called. She didn't have to call, because in another city, at another conference, she walked through the revolving door into the lobby of another hotel. When she looked over at the registration counter, he was standing there, registering in the same hotel, for the same conference she was about to attend. This time she walked up to him and tapped him on the shoulder. He turned around with shock, surprise, pleasure all over his face. Rhonda smiled. He spoke first, "Okay. Who are you? Who are you in my life?"

This was a divine union! There was no way either of them could resist being together after this series of divine chance meetings! We will use anything we can to convince ourselves that what we are doing is the right thing to do! Rhonda reflected on how quickly things moved after that. They called each other every day, two or three times a day, because they lived five states apart. They saw each other every two or three months, which helped the three and a half years to pass very quickly. He was nice. It was nice. When you have a lover who lives so far away, you believe him when he says he misses you every day. As a woman, it just makes you feel good to know that a man is going to call you, or that if you are having a problem you can pick up the phone and call a man. You must, however, be clear about what you want and what you are doing. Rhonda realized that she had stopped being clear and had started playing the game. The game of trying to hold on to another relationship that just didn't click. A relationship that wasn't giving her what she wanted.

Now she realized that instead of being patient, she had settled. She was frighteningly aware of the fact that he was nice, but she could not see them sharing Jell-O. She had convinced herself that since this was the one who had shown up, she would have to deal with it. In dealing with it, she had tried to make it work, knowing full well that it was not going to work. But, thank God, he wouldn't commit. He was real clear that he wasn't ready. He kept saying it. He had a million excuses, and although she hated to admit it even to herself, she had tried to convince him that he was ready. She had retreated to first-floor behavior, badgering him, insisting, and doing all kinds of craziness to get him up to her speed. She became a part of her own problem. She was lying to herself again. On the second floor of love's house, the lies you tell will grow feet and claws and scratch your brain. They will scratch until you ask yourself, "What's the matter with you?!!!" Rhonda now realized that when she asked herself that question, the answer was that she did not want to be wrong, again. She did not want to admit to herself or her friends that she had been wrong, again. Now, when something itches, keeps on itching, you will either keep scratching until you draw blood or you will find the cause of the itch. Rhonda realized that in her case, the cause of the itch that was scratching in her brain was a lack of self-love.

Jean turned, twisted, heaved her body away from his reach.

Without thinking, James heard himself saying, "I'm sorry! I'm sorry!" Now he knew for sure Jean was hurt because she was crying. She was crying, trying to hit him, and push him away all at the same time. It doesn't get much worse than this! It doesn't get much worse than standing in front of the woman you love, realizing you have never told her you loved her. It doesn't feel any worse than when you are watching her cry, as she tries to gouge your eyes out because some lunatic you really don't care about is ringing the doorbell. It doesn't get much worse than this! It does, however, get better! The doorbell stopped ringing. Then it got worse! Jean dropped to her knees, put her face in her hands, and began to wail. James stood there, watching Jean, feeling himself grow more helpless, powerless, and inadequate each time Jean screamed "Why?" Slowly he knelt next to her, collected her in his arms, and quietly whispered, "I don't know. I just don't know! Please forgive me. Please help me! I'm so sorry." For the first time in a long time, James wanted to cry. He wanted to, but he resisted.

You must learn to surrender avoidance. How do you do that? You learn to listen, you learn to communicate. You surrender the judgments that what you say doesn't matter, what you feel doesn't matter, and that people do not care about what you say or feel. Change your mind by surrendering that garbage. While you are at it, you may also want to change your mind about the way you react to what other people say. Remember, what is true for you may not be true for everyone else. Every living person has the right to their own experience. That experience determines what they do and how they do it, what they say and how they say it. This is their right. People have a right to express how they feel. Most important, you must realize that because someone exercises their right to express their truth, it does not mean you must take it on or do anything about it. Learn to listen. Learn to forgive. Learn to surrender. That is about as much as you can do right now.

HAVE COURAGE UNDER FIRE!

Jean was sobbing into his shoulder now. "I knew it! I knew you were messing around, but I thought you would get over it. I figured you were just getting it together, trying to make sure. I knew it!" James figured this would be the only chance he would get to tell his side of the story. "I don't know why, Jean. She doesn't mean anything to me. She's a good cook and a quick lay. It doesn't have anything to do with you. It's like every time I get something good going, I have to do something to mess it up." Thinking back on it now, James realized the truth of that statement. When things were going well at work, he would start staying out late, oversleeping, and going in to work late. When things were going well financially, he would buy some expensive thing he didn't need and run his credit card bill up. It seemed as if he could only be happy when there was something going on in his life that made him feel bad. That was so sick! That was absolutely neurotic! Did he hate himself that much? James was thinking now about what he had been thinking then, realizing that he had some work to do before he could even go back and ask Jean for a second chance. Then he thought about what had happened next and realized a second chance with Jean was probably, almost assuredly, out of the question.

Healing anything takes time. If you cut your arm and it's bleeding, gushing, you can nurse it, dress it up, put a Band-Aid on to avoid infection, but you know the wound needs time to heal. For the next few days, maybe even weeks, you must treat the wounded appendage very gently. You must be careful about where you put it, what you do, and how you do everything while the wound is healing. You are waiting for a new layer of skin to grow. Our relationships need the same healing time because we do bring wounds to the relationship. When we do not allow ourselves the opportunity, either in relationships or between relationships, to heal, we are prone to stick our fingers in the wound or rip the Band-Aid off too soon. As with most things in life, we want an immediate fix. We forget that there is a process involved in healing.

One reason we do not honor our own healing process is that we hate ourselves. We criticize, we believe we are wrong, we get caught up in trying to fix every little thing, which ultimately leads to exhaustion. You hate yourself for making yourself do such exhausting work. Exhaustion and self-hatred lead to feelings of inadequacy. We believe we are inadequate because we can't stop doing the things that make us hurt. We can't figure out how we started doing these things in the first place. That inadequacy then leads to fear. Fear that we are running out of time, fear that we will never get it together, fear that if we get really close to someone, they will find out just how inadequate we actually are. We are not inadequate at all! We are wounded. We are wounded soldiers because we have made love a battlefield. When a soldier is wounded, s/he must leave the battlefield. S/he must go away in order to heal.

Every individual who has encountered the normal occurrences of everyday living on the planet has something they need to heal. It doesn't have to be a serious gash or oozing wound, but there is always something we need time to get in touch with. There also comes a time in every relationship, whether it is good or bad, that the partners may need to go away to heal. Unfortunately, fear of losing prohibits us from taking the time to go away for a few days or a few hours, each to our own place, to do the healing, so that we can come back and address the wounds together. When partners do not take the time individually to heal, there is an even greater chance that they will create all of the chaos and confusion they work so diligently to avoid. It is not the relationship itself, it's the wounds that we bring and keep reopening because we don't take healing time. Self-love will enable you to take the healing time, the healing space, without the fear. Sexual compatibility will not do it. The need to be needed will not give you the strength. The desire to be taken care of will not give you the courage. You've got to know how to love yourself whether you are in or out of a relationship. If there is no self-love you will have no choice but to do the hellish and idiotic things in your relationships that make you crazy.

DON'T GO LOOKING FOR TROUBLE!

Rhonda knew that she was headed for a brick wall with this guy. It wasn't just the fact that she knew he wasn't the one. It was her neurosis raising its ugly head again! She knew that once sex came into the picture, she became a neurotic! Then she would start making demands. She would get her feelings hurt by every little thing. She would begin laying out conditions and demands and having expectations. Damn! She had done it again! Before she took one more step into or out of the relationship, she had to figure out a few things. Okay, why are you expecting this? What did he say? What did you do? What is going on? She realized that this was not something she needed to discuss with him yet. She needed to do this work *on herself with herself.* She knew that she had to take sex out of it long enough to look at what she was feeling and where she was headed. She needed to assess and possibly redesign her agenda. She realized that the other part of her neurosis was always allowing the guy to set the agenda and then getting angry about what he was doing.

He was just about to spill his guts to Jean when the door came tumbling in. Wood was flying everywhere! Jean was screaming. James was scrambling around on the floor trying to pull Jean out of harm's way. Paula had stuck her hand through the hole in the door and was trying to get the lock opened. *Damn she had a good memory!* Certain events in life will force you to take action that you think you are not willing to take. In doing so, they teach you to be responsible. James ran to the door, opened it, and pulled Paula inside. The neighbors were asking if everything was all right. *Oh yes! Everything is just fine! A manic kicks my door in at least once a month!* Paula was screaming, swearing, and moving toward Jean. James had Paula by the arm with no intention of letting her go.

Jean was no wuss. She was not going to let Paula bully her, but at the same time, it was obvious that she was not going to slink around in the mud with her either. "You have absolutely nothing to say to me!" Jean told Paula, which shut her mouth for a moment. It was definitely a girl thing that James knew he did not understand. "If he wanted you in, he would have let you in. Since you forced yourself in, have a good time, I'm outta here!" She didn't run. She didn't back away. With all the class and dignity a woman in her position could muster, Jean picked up her things, including the presents she had brought with her, and left. Paula was sitting on the sofa, arms folded, crossed legs swinging, saying some of the most inappropriate things, which James thought made absolutely no sense. Things like, *"You used me! You lied to me! You owe me!"*

It can be very hard to make a decision you know you must make when you do not love yourself. When there is a lack of love, a lack of respect, a lack of self-trust, you waver back and forth before deciding to undertake a process of healing, or that you can live through your sickness just a little longer. If you really hate yourself, you will lie, telling yourself, "It's really not that bad!" That's when the scratching will begin. If, however, you are willing to do the work, determining that you can finally face the truth, you will instantly assume responsibility for the agenda you have set and act accordingly. You will take a deep breath, stick out your wounded chest, and apply the only spiritual cleanser that can help you begin the healing process: surrender. On the second floor, surrender is not giving in; it's giving up the things that are not working. The bad habits, the things that are not helping you to learn to love yourself. You overcome self-deception on the second floor. One of the biggest self-deceptive things that we do is saying we can do something when we know we can't. We know we cannot fix, change, help, heal, or save ourselves. We want to, but we can't. That is why God created love. Love is the only thing that can heal. When we really want to be healed, we must surrender to love. When we don't know what love is, God sends us to the meantime to find out what we need to know about it.

THE WAY YOU DO THE THINGS YOU DO

It's a time of waiting, the meantime is. You are waiting for further instructions, more guidance, additional support, mental or emotional clearance. As it relates to love and relationships, you can enter the meantime willing to wait or unwillingly to wait. A willing meantime experience is the experience of those people who walk or run into the meantime, willing to do the work. The work required to establish a better relationship with yourself. A willing meantime means recognizing that you are not by yourself but that you are with yourself, and you don't mind keeping company with you. Finding somebody, being in love, having a relationship—these are not the motivating factors of your life right now. You are still very much interested in these things, just not right now. Now you want to get *you* in order. You want to shed some weight, physical and emotional weight. You want to get in shape, mental and spiritual shape. You want to take care of some unfinished business, healing business, growing business, and you recognize the meantime as a prime opportunity to get your business taken care of.

A willing meantime dweller is someone who is headed for big things—big revelations, big understanding, big development projects. This is a person who realizes that it ain't working! While they may be upset about it, it being the history of their relationships, they are not willing to give up. They want to know what it is and why it is that they cannot do, have not done the very thing they want to do so badly, establish a loving, committed relationship. They realize that all of the past relationships have been meantime experiences in which they missed something. A lesson perhaps. A pattern unfolding. An insecurity being fed. Now that they have been left or left unsatisfied, been cheated on or done a little cheating of their own, acted the part with all their mind, body, soul, and still did not get picked, they want to know why. The meantime is an excellent time to ask yourself why. More important, it is an excellent time to get youself ready to receive an answer.

On the other hand, we have unwilling waiting. This is the experience of those people who get pushed or fall into the meantime and are quite angry about it. They are blaming someone else for their predicament. *"He left me!" "She couldn't get it together!" "They didn't make me happy!"* These people just don't get it—the meantime is a growing and healing time. It is regrouping and recoup time. Unwilling waiters want to fight and complain. They continue to reach back, trying to hold on, or look back, in an attempt to figure it out, and place the blame on the appropriate shoulders. In the meantime, you must be willing to let go and admit you don't know so that you will remember what you do know. You always know what you did and did not do to create your present circumstance. Admitting what you know is the hard part. If you enter the meantime unwilling to admit, holding on, looking back, blaming, complaining, and feeling bad, the time you spend out of a relationship will become more than a brief course in memory improvement. It will be shock therapy!

It can be quite shocking to see, learn, and remember the truth about yourself. The more unwilling you are to see, the more shocking the revelations will be. In the meantime, you are alone. There is no one for you to look at but yourself. There is no one for you to complain about but yourself. There is no one for you to fight or hold on to but you, and that is a good thing.

In the meantime, an unwilling wait can seem to last forever. The harder you reach out, the longer the wait becomes. The more you look at others, the more desperate the wait will seem. Not until you surrender the anger, resentment, desperation, insecurities, and fear can the meantime become a meaningful experience.

There is no prescribed period or length of time you can spend in the meantime. It is not a matter of *"If I do this, I'll get out quicker."* Or, *"If I do it this way, I'll never come back again."* The meantime is not like that at all. You will stay in the meantime for as long as it takes, not only for you to get ready, but for the other side to get ready. In other words, you may be ready, but your divine mate may not be ready. You may be healed of your insecurities, but your perfect partner may not be quite healed yet. You may have done all the forgiving you need to do, but the person you are waiting for may have not even begun to do forgiving and releasing work. Consequently, you will be in the meantime until the divine person is prepared and ready for you. The meantime is protective as well as preparatory.

Now, this is not to suggest that you must sit around waiting and twiddling your thumbs. It means that even while you are in the meantime, waiting for the divine experience, you can and will have meantime experiences, meantime relationships that are valuable and meaningful. Do not believe that what you do in the meantime is useless. Everything you do, every relationship you have, prepares and brings you closer to the grand experience of total, unconditional self-love and love for others. Many meantime experiences are designed to do just that, bring you closer, not take you all the way there. Your job is to avoid the temptation and the trap of thinking *every* relationship has to be the relationship that lasts forever and ever amen. Every relationship is *the* relationship you need at that time. When the divine reason for the union has been fulfilled, or the divine season for the union comes to an end, a relationship will end, and you will enter the meantime, until next time.

I'M OKAY! YOU'RE OKAY!
NOW LET'S GET TO WORK!

He finally had to call the police to get Paula out of his apartment. When he got to the police station, he decided not to press charges but got an order of protection just as an insurance policy. That was three days ago. He had only spoken to Jean once in that time. When he did, he told her nothing but the truth about everything, including the others about whom she never knew. He also told her that he was ready to get himself together, to settle down and build a life with her. He also told her that he loved her, to the best of his ability, admitting that he had a lot to learn. Also acknowledging that he had to first master the art of loving himself. Jean, in her own steady, calming way had thanked him for being honest, and for loving her, but said that she needed some time to get herself back on track. She even went so far as to express concern for Paula, wondering how a woman could let herself sink to that level. James told her that it was easy when you had a man willing to sink with you. It was all in the name of having fun. Sick fun, but fun nonetheless. Jean suggested counseling. He said he was willing. He had called the numbers that Jean had given him and was waiting for some return calls. He was frightened about the prospect of some shrink probing his mind, but the minute he felt the slightest bit of resistance to the idea, he surrendered. Jean had taught him how to do it.

Rhonda realized that it was all a distraction. The relationships, the rent, the challenges that kept cropping up, were all distractions she was creating in her own mind through her own actions, as an escape for not sticking to the agenda she had set for herself. Learn to love yourself more! Learn to feel better about yourself! Learn to stop doing the things that make you miserable, crazy, and more distracted than you already are! She was learning not to make life an either/or proposition. Either you do this, or you don't. Either you have this, or you don't. How about taking in a little bit at a time? How about doing a little bit at a time? That would make life so much easier to handle.

She had to learn how to work on her life, work on herself, work with the children, a little bit at a time. Right now, she could not move, so she would work. When the work was finished, she would move. Once she moved, she would resume spiritual classes as the means by which she would work on herself. When she felt a bit more stable in her spirit, she would once again open herself to a relationship. She finally realized that loving herself meant giving up the either/or stance, replacing it with choice. She realized that the most self-loving thing she could do was to take time to heal herself, without beating up on herself for the things she could not do, had not done. It served absolutely no purpose to hash, and re-hash, the error of her ways. She would not do that anymore. If she found herself engaged in that self-abusive activity, she would simply stop. That's what surrender is all about: simply stop doing the things that make you miserable, crazy, unhappy, self-hating, and neurotic. When you stop abusing yourself in these ways, love moves in, and the healing process begins.

Chapter 7
GET THE RING OUT OF YOUR TUB

the crowd in the parking lot of the mall was growing. What is it about adversity that attracts human beings like moths to a flame? Joe was trying his best to assure the growing crowd that everything was just fine. Marie would calm down long enough for him to make the statement, and then she would start screaming again. In the distance, he could hear the siren of the approaching police car. The crowd parted just enough to allow the two officers, one male, one female, to approach Joe and Marie. Marie was quiet again. Joe was in tears. The female officer asked the first stupid question, "Is everything all right here?" Just for a second, Joe thought about the number of times and the number of places he had been asked that same question. He said, as he always did, "Yes. I mean, no, officer. My wife has Alzheimer's, and she is having an episode of dementia." God, how he hated those words. The officer, like the crowd, just stared at him. Marie was screaming again, flinging her arms to ward off the imaginary attackers she was seeing more and more lately.

It was the male officer's turn. "Is there anything we can do? Do you want to go to the hospital?" Joe heard himself scream, *"NO! No hospital!"* in his mind before he turned to the officer to say, "I'd like to try to calm her down first. If you could move the crowd away that would help." That would keep them busy just long enough for him to get Marie in the car so that he could take her home. Once he got her home, gave her the medication, put her to bed, he knew he would have to seriously consider the hospital question again. Marie was really getting much worse, and he didn't know how much longer he could care for her. The mere thought of it brought tears to his eyes. He didn't know how he was going to live without his Marie.

Joe and Marie had been married for thirty-seven years. Their union had produced five children. Joe, a postal worker, and Marie, a teacher, had enjoyed a wonderful life together until six years ago. Six years ago, their lives fell apart in the span of two weeks. Their oldest daughter, June, was diagnosed with breast cancer. They discovered that their oldest son, Joe Junior, was in the midst of a raging cocaine addiction. Their youngest son, George, was moving his wife and family to Italy where he would be a military chaplain. Marie was diagnosed as having Alzheimer's. Two years later, June passed away. Three years later, Joe Junior was virtually living in the streets. Four years later, George's wife refused to come back to help care for his mother. Nicole and Natalie, the twins, did the best they could to help, but they both had children of their own. Besides that, it was too hard on them to watch what their mother was becoming. On this Saturday morning, standing in the parking lot of the mall, Joe knew he was going to have to do what he did not know how to do. He was going to have to put Marie away again.

He had done it once before. When he realized that George wasn't coming back, and that the twins really couldn't take it, he had put Marie in a nursing home. She was only fifty-nine, but she had succumbed to the deteriorating effects of the disease quite rapidly. The doctors couldn't explain it, and he didn't understand it. Marie, his lovely vibrant wife, had lost her memory and most of her mind. Joe would go to work, leaving a perfectly normal Marie in the house, but would return to find her half-naked in the street, doing any number of things. The neighbors started complaining. They offered no help, but they complained about her walking in their yards, frightening their children, coming into their homes. At first he was embarrassed. Then Joe got angry. He changed all the locks so that he could lock Marie in the house. It worked for a while. One day he came home and found her bleeding. She had broken three windows, cutting her hands to the tune of twenty-three stitches. Joe had a porch built onto the back of the house. This way he could leave the back door open so that Marie could at least sit on the porch during the day. That was an excellent idea that almost worked. It did not, however, prevent Marie from setting the house on fire trying to cook. She had done that twice.

Joe was at his wits' end. He had spent their entire savings on home attendants, people who would stay with Marie during the day until he got home. He wasn't eligible for any government assistance because of his income. When the money ran out and he could no longer afford to hire help, he put Marie in a day center with other Alzheimer's patients. That went well for a while, but then the dementia became so profound that the doctors at the center recommended putting her in a nursing home. They too were amazed at how quickly Marie had deteriorated. Perhaps it was because she was so sweet, so gentle in her right mind. Perhaps it was because mental illness ran in her family. Maybe it was because the stupid doctors simply didn't know what they were doing.

Joe had listened to the doctors the first time they told him Marie would be better off in a nursing home. He had eighteen months before retiring with a full pension. Joe thought that if Marie could stay in the home just that long, he could work double shifts, save some more money, and take her out when he retired. Sounded like a pretty good idea. Worked pretty good too. The problem was that he couldn't visit Marie as often as he liked, and he missed her. In addition to missing her, he started noticing little marks on her body, face, legs, and back, which no one could explain to him. Is it possible that someone was beating his sweet Marie? Or was she really falling down, like they said? The pressure started getting to Joe—the pressure of missing his wife; the pressure of working eighteen, sometimes twenty-four hours a day; the pressure of trying to visit Marie between shifts; the pressure of trying to convince the twins that they needed to visit their mother more often. The day he went to the home to find that Marie had a black eye that no one could explain was three months short of his retirement date. By the time all the paperwork was complete, he had retired. That was a year ago. Since then Joe had taken care of Marie to the best of his ability, but now it looked like his best simply wasn't enough.

Joe could not bear the thought of living without Marie. What would he do? He couldn't bear the thought of being with another woman. In thirty-nine years of marriage, he had never been with one, not even once! Marie's illness had put such a strain on his relationship with the children, most of them were no longer speaking to him. He felt that they had abandoned him; they felt like he was in denial about Marie's condition. *In sickness and in health* . . . Joe kept reminding them. He wasn't in denial, he was fulfilling his commitment, but where was the money going to come from? Money for medication, for care, for the home, if he really had to put her back in there. It was all too much for him to think about in the mall parking lot. As the crowd thinned out, Marie settled down. He looked up at the heavens, and silently whispered his favorite prayer, "He leads me beside the still water. He restores my soul." Then he looked at Marie. She was lucid again. She raised her hand to Joe's face, touched his cheek, looked him dead in the eye, and said, "He really is a shepherd, you know!"

THE LOOK OF LOVE

Love is an inward and very personal experience. It is not, however, a personal possession. Love does not, cannot, belong to anyone, because love is a universal concept, an experience to be shared by all. The concept of *universal love* refers to the love that God has for all of God's creations. It is the love that life is, the manifestation of God's energy. It is the love extended by life to us all. Universal love, God's love, is the only real love that exists. It is the love our soul longs to experience and comes to life to experience. Universal love transcends the self and the needs of self, moving us into communion with the energies of the universe and the love of all living things. Universal love has no conditions. It accepts all as is, because All is the true identity of God. The experience of universal love is not what most of us are consciously seeking in our relationships. It is, however, what we have all come to life to learn through our relationships.

On the more earthly, human level, what most of us seek and desire to experience is the caring, sharing, communion, and experience of love that relationships can offer. The experience is just that, an experience created in response to our limited human knowledge. We must understand that what we know and want does not fully define the true essence of love, nor does it limit it. With this understanding comes the realization that we cannot make people love us the way we want them to love us. Nor is there any way to ensure that they will be in love with us for as long as we are in love with them. This does not mean that there is not enough love to go around or that we will never have a deeper experience of love. It is to say that we may not have it with a particular person, at a particular time, or for as long as we want it to last.

In our development as human beings, our minds and souls will evolve, and our vision will expand. This evolutionary expansion will provide us with a greater awareness of ourselves, the world in which we live, and the mysteries of life. In order to ensure that the trip is worthwhile, the journey remains meaningful, and the insights we gain can lead to even greater insights, we must keep our hearts open to greater experiences of love. We must be willing to give up old notions, incorporate new information, change the direction in which we are traveling, and most of all take the strings off love. You can never love anyone to your own detriment. That is not love, that is possession, control, fear, or a combination of them all. Yes, we make commitments. Yes, we have responsibilities. Yes, we want to keep our loved ones near to us. However, when loving someone is causing you pain or putting your own life in jeopardy, you must learn to surrender. If you are not willing to surrender, if you insist on struggling in the name of love, love will let you struggle.

Lisa was in college full-time, working full-time, had two small kids she was raising alone, when her grandmother refused to be treated for stomach cancer. Lisa tried to explain to her that if she didn't get treated she would die. Nanny wasn't interested in the horror stories. She had lived her life, and if this is the way she was going out, then she was going out without being poked and prodded. When the pain got to be too intense, however, Nanny was hospitalized so she could be fed intravenously. Every day between the time she left work in Manhattan and before her classes began in Brooklyn, Lisa would go uptown to the Bronx to visit and take care of Nanny. Lisa had to make sure Nanny had her paper and her butterscotch nuggets (what the hell difference does it make if I eat candy now? Nanny asked) and that her hair was combed. Nanny had lots of hair that easily became matted. This went on for more than seven months before Nanny was sent home to die. Lisa was exhausted, but she was Nanny's favorite. Besides that, no one else could stand Nanny. She was very feisty.

Nanny was hanging on, sometimes just to make people miserable, Lisa thought. Then, quickly, she would retract the thought, replacing it with memories of all the fun times she had had with Nanny. When Lisa's father and mother divorced, it was Nanny who held Lisa together. The breakup was nasty— Mom had a boyfriend, Daddy's ego was hurt, there was a child on the way whose paternity was in question. It was quite a mess. Lisa had always been closer to her dad and wanted to go with him. Mom wouldn't hear of it. Lisa, her two sisters, and her brother ended up with Mom and Mr. Webb, who saw them all as reminders that Lisa's mom had been with other men. Lisa and her siblings were the proof. Mr. Webb made a habit of reminding them that he was not their father, but as long as they were eating his food, they would do what he said. He didn't say much because he was usually drunk. As the oldest, Lisa was the most rebellious and most vocal, which is probably why she and Mr. Webb fought like cats and dogs. Of course, that meant that Lisa would usually have to run away to save herself from his wrath. Whenever running became necessary, Nanny, her father's mother, always had a good meal and the right words.

At seventeen, Lisa left home to live with Nanny. It was great. They did everything together. They shopped. They talked. They cooked. Nanny was just like a girlfriend, an older girlfriend, who let you do all the things your mother wouldn't let you do, within reason of course. At age nineteen, when Lisa told Nanny that she was pregnant, things changed—drastically. Nanny told her she was too old to take care of a baby and that it was time for Lisa to be on her own. She was devastated! How could Nanny do this to her? Lisa had thought they would be together forever, or at least until she got married. Nanny said that Lisa needed to learn how to be responsible. If she had missed the lesson before she had the baby, she would need to catch it after she had it. Lisa got a small apartment with her boyfriend and refused to speak to Nanny for two years. It was only after she had her second baby that she understood what Nanny was actually trying to teach her. Humbly she went to Nanny. She told her about the new baby, her rotten boyfriend, and her fear, and she apologized. As though two years were just a yesterday away, she and Nanny were right back where they started, talking, laughing, raising Lisa's two boys.

That was just two and a half short years ago. In that time, Lisa had lived a lifetime. She had been in and out of two or three bad relationships that Nanny warned her about. How is it that everyone can see what you can't see about the person you think you love? Lisa had landed a great job that Nanny said she *prayed up* for her. She had reconciled with her mother, or at least they were speaking. Lisa had kind of cooled out on relationships, at Nanny's advice, until she could get herself a little more together. Then Nanny got sick. Not all at once, but little by little. She wouldn't eat. She had no energy. She was spitting up blood. It had taken Lisa almost three months to convince Nanny that she could go to the doctor and that she would not become a guinea pig. Then came the diagnosis. It was hard for Lisa to believe that Nanny was going to die. Why didn't she want to fight for her life? Nanny was such a fighter about everything. She fought with Lisa to get her life together. It was Nanny who encouraged Lisa to go back to college. It was Nanny who took her social security check money to buy little things for the boys that Lisa could not afford. It was Nanny who gave Lisa all the advice she needed about men and love and other, as Nanny called them, "womanly things." All of that was about to end, and Lisa was beside herself.

Lisa's dad and his mom hadn't spoken to each other in years. They were just alike, strong-willed, hard-headed, and very opinionated. It was like mixing oil and water trying to get those two to agree about anything. When Nanny got real sick, Lisa told her father that if he couldn't make her feel better, he should stay away. That was the only invitation he needed. Rather than keeping his big mouth shut so he could spend time with his mother, he put the responsibility on Lisa. He would call Lisa to see how she was doing or to find out if she needed anything. He would call Lisa to tell her how he felt about his mother dying. During one of Nanny's hospital stays when it looked like she was really going to check out, Lisa called her dad. He came rushing to the hospital, took one look at his mother, broke down crying, and never came back again. Lisa was furious! She reminded her father that her mother was not his wife, and that he needed to assume responsibility for his mother. He said that he simply couldn't do it.

Lisa's brothers and sisters had never been as close to Nanny as Lisa. They were too afraid to do anything that would upset Mr. Webb. Every now and then they would call, and they always sent birthday, Mother's Day, and Christmas cards. Nanny called them a sorry lot. She couldn't understand how they or their father could ignore their blood relation. Your relatives are the fabric of your life's quilt, Nanny always said. "If you start pulling the squares out of your quilt, you are going to freeze to death!" Nanny was so wise. She was also very hurt. She didn't talk about it, but Lisa felt her pain whenever she talked about her son or his children. Lisa decided it was a battle she was not going to fight. She had her Nanny, and that was good enough for her.

It was spring. Nanny had been in and out of the hospital six times in three months. Each time they all but pronounced her dead. Each time Nanny fooled them and bounced right back. Finally they sent Nanny home to spend her last days in a familiar environment. She had a home attendant, and her neighbors came to keep an eye on her. This took some of the pressure off, but Lisa still felt obligated to make it over to the house to see Nanny. It wasn't bad until midterms rolled around. Lisa had tests all week, so she called Nanny to say that she couldn't come up. Lisa promised she would get someone to bring her a newspaper and candy. Nanny wouldn't let anyone but Lisa comb her hair. Nanny told Lisa not to bother. She would read yesterday's paper and be fine. That was on Monday. Lisa was so exhausted that she slept late on Tuesday, and went to work and school without calling Nanny. She called after class on Tuesday, but got no answer. She called her Wednesday afternoon, and got no answer. Thursday she went to Nanny's between work and class. Nanny was sleeping. She had been medicated into Zion. Lisa kissed her, promising she would be back on Friday. Friday was hellish. She called Nanny, but now she knew why she wasn't getting an answer. That weekend she studied, took the boys to the movies, and washed ten loads of laundry without calling Nanny. Nanny died Monday morning.

Lisa was riddled with guilt. She was so guilty that she did not go back to school the following semester. For weeks, she walked around beating up on herself. When she found out that her father saw his mother before she died, it didn't make matters any better. *"I should have been there! I should have fixed her hair, read her the paper. There was so much I should have done."* It was like a song in Lisa's mind. She couldn't shake the feelings of guilt and irresponsibility. Eventually she shifted from the guilt song to the anger chant: *"Well, how much is a person supposed to do?!!! From New Jersey to Manhattan, to Brooklyn, to the Bronx, every day for three months! How much is a person expected to do?!!!"* When she wasn't guilty she was angry. When she wasn't angry, she was depressed. Lisa was trying to remember all the things

Nanny had told her, so that she could put them to use. She wasn't doing very well. She wanted to surrender. She needed to surrender, but she couldn't do it until she learned how to detach.

YOU'VE GOT TO KNOW WHEN TO LET GO

All relationships have the same basic components: people, needs, and expectations. Try as we may to keep the needs and the expectations stuff in order, we usually get so caught up in them that the pure essence of the relationship is lost to what we think we should be doing and what we expect should be done. Sometimes the needs are very real. Other times they are not. Sometimes the expectations are based in solid reality. In most cases, they are not. Sometimes the expectations of having needs met are placed upon us. At other times we place them upon ourselves. What we fail to realize before it is much too late is that when love is the foundation of the relationships, all needs and expectations are met without any effort on our part.

No matter how horrible you have been told you are, don't believe it! No matter how bad you think you are, have courage. No matter what is going on around you, stand your ground. No matter what happens in your relationships, take hold of yourself. No matter what you get in return for the love you give, know that you are protected. Divinely protected. As long as you stand for love, with love, refusing to allow your "self" to be lost in the search for love, you will be just fine. You cannot lose in love. Nothing you do can make someone who loves you, really loves you, stop loving you. They may get angry with you. They may be disappointed with or in you. That's about *their* needs and expectations. It is not about love. The more love you give, the more love you will receive. It may not always look like that, but it is the absolute truth. You may not get it from those to whom you give it—just know that you will, no, you must get it. Love is always returned to those who give it freely and courageously, without strings or expectations.

Guilt, shame, fear, anger, and resentment are not the outgrowths of a loving relationship. They are a function of the conditions we place on ourselves and the people we love. When you find yourself in either of these places as a result of your love experiences, you are being provided with the opportunity to make the shift from conditional to unconditional love. Your level of mental, emotional, and spiritual development in response to your love relationships can serve as a springboard to even greater development and the unfolding of a grander, greater, more noble you. Making the shift enables you to realize that you don't have to be guilty or hurt, you don't have to be ashamed or angry, you don't have to be resentful or alone, all you have to do is love you and all others the best you know how. You do not have to prove your love, nor should you ask others to prove theirs. When you do, you are asking to relive the same experiences, learn the same lessons, walk through the same terrain you have already traveled. Until we grasp the concept that love asks for nothing, we will do the same thing over and over. This is not a very spiritually enlightening thing to do!

Surrender and detachment are two spiritual household cleansers that bring us closer to the experience of love. Surrender, the act of consciously admitting what we can and cannot do, keeps us from assuming false responsibilities and from doing those things which are detrimental to our own well-being. So often in relationships, we want to be all, do all, give all, when we know full well it is impossible. We are trying to prove our love. We are making a desperate attempt to prove we are worthy to be loved. The key here is to surrender every thought, every belief, every idea that leads you to the conclusion that you are unlovable. If you can get to the point where you no longer believe that you are unlovable, you will instantly become lovable! When you are lovable, you are required to do *nothing*. Just be. The path to this realization is detachment. Detach from all of the conditions you have placed on yourself. There is nothing you must do. There is nothing you must have. There is nothing you must be. You are *all* right now. Anything you think you must be, do, or have to make yourself more deserving of love is like a ring in the bathtub—it must be removed.

EXPRESS YOURSELF!

She couldn't figure out when or how it began. It just sort of happened all of a sudden, overnight, in the course of the first thirteen years of her life. One minute, Daddy was going to work, teaching Sunday school, playing with her and her sisters, while Mommy was taking care of the household duties. The next minute, Daddy was sitting in the living room, having been fired from his job and exiled from the church because he had been drunk one time too many. One minute Mommy was screaming and running because Daddy was fighting her. The next minute Mommy was crying because Daddy had fallen down and she couldn't pick him up. One minute your life as a child is just fine. The next minute Daddy is dead and things really start to fall apart. In the midst of this moment-by-moment, thirteen-year-long saga, Iris felt absolutely helpless. She couldn't help Daddy or Mommy, and she sure as hell couldn't help herself!

Intelligent people do not drink themselves to death! So he had to be an idiot. She had to work with that one for a while. Iris had concluded that her father was an idiot! She loved her father, but now she was angry with him for dying and leaving her alone with her mother. Her mother, her smothering, worrying, frightened mother, who wouldn't let her do anything. Her mother, as sweet as she was, was weak, whiny, and totally out of touch. Her mother, who had never worked and could not for the life of her figure out how she was going to raise six children alone. Her mother, whom she loved and hated at the same time because she was everything that Iris did not want to be. How could her daddy die—scratch that, kill himself—leaving her home alone with her mother?

When life gives you lemons, you must make lemonade. If you are allergic to lemons, you drink water! Water may be bland, unexciting, and uninteresting, but it gives you energy! She couldn't get out of high school fast enough. She couldn't go away to college fast enough. She couldn't get a degree or a job fast enough to wash away the conflicting feelings she had lived with since she was thirteen. Her father had taught her how beautiful, brilliant, and gifted she was. Her mother had taught her how frail, helpless, and vulnerable she was. She didn't believe what Daddy told her. She couldn't believe what Mommy had told her. She made it through school, she got a job, she bought a house, all because she was angry. There are some types of anger that are like fuel in the furnace! Although she was angry, she never said a word. Anger upset Mommy and made her cry. Everything upset Mommy! Iris learned at a very young age that no matter what she felt, she'd better keep it bottled up in her head. Especially her father's death, because it was just so bizarre. How can you be angry at someone you love for dying? How can you hate your mother? How can you express what you feel when you don't understand it? For twenty-seven years, Iris had this train wreck going on inside her head and her body. When it all got to be too much, she simply shut down.

It can be hard to find a decent relationship when you are shut down, but hey! who wants to go through life without some kind of relationship? Iris decided that she was not under any circumstances going to have a relationship like the one her parents had. She was not going to be dependent on her mate. She was not going to have anything to do with a man who drank. She was not going to be a whiner, complainer, or crier. As a matter of fact, she was too angry to say anything. Men have radar, you know! They can pick up on an angry woman from ten miles away. Rather than run the risk of having her anger detected, Iris became quiet, very quiet. Everyone commented on just how quiet she was. She was always referred to as sweet, quiet Iris. And because she was so quiet, people believed she was helpless. People were always trying to do things for her and help her do things because they mistakenly concluded that her quietness was a coverup for weakness.

Iris had three memorable relationships. She remembered them because they were such disasters! The first one, when she was in college, was with a guy who began and ended his day with marijuana. Iris didn't know it was marijuana because he put it in his cigarettes. He was high most of the time, and by the time she found out what he was doing, he thought he owned her. He thought that because she had never told him that he didn't. It took her three months to get rid of that idiot. The next guy she met at a party. He seemed nice enough, but he turned out to be a fighter. He had the very unpleasant habit of slapping Iris around when she didn't do what he wanted her to do. Her mistake was staying more than five minutes after the first slap. Although the second one didn't come until six months later, Iris was real clear that this was not what she had in mind.

The third relationship was the most serious of all. Serious in terms of length of time and emotional commitment. She and Buddy moved in together and were seriously talking about marriage. Buddy was all that she could ask for, if she had been doing a lot of asking, but she wasn't, and neither was he. It took two years for the signs to manifest—his possessiveness, his jealousy, his demands. It seemed that just when Iris felt comfortable to start coming out, to start talking and expressing herself, Buddy lost his mind. He would tell her how stupid she was, how weak she was. He found very creative ways to demean her and, in any way he could, undermine her confidence. Iris didn't want to believe him, but there was so much damage caused by the train wreck in her brain when she was younger that the residue was still lingering in her heart. Perhaps Mommy had been right all along. Maybe she was too weak and vulnerable to stand on her own. Or Daddy could have been right. Maybe she should just walk out on this guy, stand on her own, and do what needed to be done for herself. *"I just don't want to be lonely!"* Iris thought. She and Buddy would have to work it out.

Iris had so little experience with relationships and such poor models to emulate, that she was in total confusion. Buddy wasn't unbearable, but he was quite a lot to handle. He didn't respect her opinions. He didn't honor her judgment. He didn't value her input. Iris didn't talk enough or to enough people to know any different, so she stayed, keeping her mouth shut for five and a half long, passive years. It was when the women started calling the house that she knew it was time to leave. In her own inimitable way, without ever saying a word to Buddy, she came home from work one day, packed her clothes, took a few items of sentimental value, and left. She went right home to Mommy, who spent the first few days singing, "I told you so!" She probably would have continued singing that song, but Buddy was calling so often she barely had time to talk. She was too busy answering the telephone!

When Iris refused to talk to him, Buddy started coming to the house. Iris took to working two and three shifts at the hospital. Buddy, who would not be outdone, took to coming to the hospital. He had made three visits before he started to make a scene, but it was such a big scene, Iris was glad he had not done it before. Buddy not only threatened to kill her, he brought the gun. By the time the police arrived he was gone. Then he decided to wait for her in the parking lot. Being as wise as she was, Iris would have one of the *big* orderlies walk her to her car. Buddy would sit in his car, wait for her to pull off, and follow her home. There were days when she was too afraid to get out of the car once she got home, so the two of them would drive around for hours, until he got tired, or she became too tired to care what he did to her. After three months, he went away. By then the damage was done. Iris was so afraid, so beat down, so confused that she retreated even further into herself. She retreated so far that she took a bottle of scotch to keep her company. Eighteen months later, she was suspended from her job and advised to get counseling.

SAY IT WITH FEELING!

One of the most powerful things I have learned through relationships is just how painful *emotional dishonesty* can be. Emotional dishonesty is the state we enter when we fail to acknowledge what we feel. It is the conscious attempt to deny an emotion. We sometimes do it in fear. Fear that what we feel is somehow not right. More often than not, we do it when we are confused and unsure of ourselves or of our emotional experience. I believe that the greatest catalyst of emotional dishonesty is our learned response to what we have been told about the *rightness* or *wrongness* of what we feel.

Where are we taught that it is okay to feel or that what we feel is okay? I imagine there are very few families that have open, frank discussions about the emotional side of life. I do not mean what happens in life, but what we feel in response to what happens. As children, we are taught everything about almost everything, except what we feel. We are definitely taught what not to feel, and told why not to feel it. When, however, we take a risk and feel something, we also run the risk of expressing what we feel. Nine times out of ten, when we do we make someone angry. This is where the confusion begins. Few of us are taught the difference between the acknowledgment and the expression of our emotions.

For some strange reason, while adults believe they are at

liberty to feel and express their emotions, they also believe children are not. Very early in life, the little people receive the subliminal message, "What I feel must be in alignment with what others think I should feel or want me to feel." Nothing could be further from the truth, and nothing gets us into more trouble in relationships than this kind of censoring of our feelings. In response to childhood messages, we miss two very important lessons: (1) how to identify what we are feeling, and (2) how to express what we feel appropriately. In order to eliminate the barrage of toxic emotions that generally spills forth in relationships, you must be able to identify what you are feeling and allow yourself to feel it. It is called *acknowledgment*. Once acknowledgment occurs, you can choose or decide what, if anything, you would like to do about the feeling. What you do in response is called *expression*. The confusion most of us have is around the appropriate way to express what we feel. Our parents and caretakers were trying to curtail inappropriate expressions, and in doing so they unwittingly taught us to suppress the feeling. Feeling and expression can be risky, but they are the only sure way to stay emotionally healthy. They are also the foundation of emotional health, which is pivotal in the development of lasting and fulfilling relationships.

As an outgrowth of our childhood experiences, we sometimes deny what we feel or that we feel anything at all. How do you express anger appropriately? Anger, which is the flip side of unexpressed passion, is probably the biggest no-no in our emotional repertoire. You are not supposed to get angry, and if in response to some human weaknesses you do get angry, you better not show it! How do you move through emotional confusion? When you feel what you are not supposed to feel, people will get mad at you. They may talk badly about you or call you names. In the meantime, you will become even more confused about why no one understands why you feel the way you feel, when you are not sure what you feel. How do you distinguish between the rumblings in your stomach that are caused by indigestion and those caused by fear? Fear can cause you to double over in pain. So will lack of lunch! Both will make you moody, indecisive, and short-tempered. A slice of pizza will cure one of these problems. How do you know what will cure the fear, if it is fear? It is one thing to be an adult and ask these questions. It is another thing to be a child who is afraid to ask them. In the meantime, most adults carry their childhood questions right into adulthood with them.

FEEL WHAT YOU FEEL!

I must have been about seven or eight years old when my grandmother took my brother and me to Virginia to what is now fashionably called a family reunion. At the time I thought it was a big picnic with a lot of strangers. Although my grandmother kept asking me, "Don't you remember so and so?" and telling me, "You remember so and so, go play with them!" I had no idea who any of these people were, and there were hundreds of them. They were loud. Some of them were drunk, and most of them kept pinching my chubby cheeks with their barbecue-drenched fingers. In an attempt to protect myself from insult and bodily harm, I clung to Grandma's skirt. She kept pushing me off, telling me to go play with the other children. I would not hear of it! They were playing with frogs and wallowing in mud that they called clay. It was more than my

New York City, apartment-dwelling, diva mentality could handle. Divas do not, under any circumstances, play with frogs!

Grandma kept swatting at me like I was a fly. She must have forgotten that the more you swat at flies, the more persistent they become. My brother, traitor that he was, had been lured away by a group of frog inspectors. As for me, where Granny went, I went. Suddenly someone announced that the boat was ready for the first trip. What boat? What trip? Someone else suggested that the children should go first with Uncle Somebody. Go where? With who? Slowly we were all ushered down to the waterfront like sheep being led to the slaughter. I was now hanging on to the elastic of Grandma's panties. As we approached the dock, I was trying to figure out how I was going to get out of the slaughter. My brother became my salvation. He took one look at that tiny little boat sitting in all that water and freaked out! He was screaming, "No! No! I'm scared! I can't go! I don't wanna go!" As he turned to hightail it off the dock, Grandma caught him by the arm and told him to, *"Shut up!"* because, *"You're not scared!"* A few of the children started laughing about him being a city kid and a fraidy-cat. Some of the drunken adults were trying to cajole him into the boat. He looked like he was having a seizure of some sort, jerking, shaking, screaming, and foaming at the mouth. Grandma told him if he didn't shut up she was going to take his pants down and whip his behind. He didn't. She did. In the meantime, while I was thanking the boat fairy and my brother was getting his whipping, the boat left without us.

Emotional honesty begins with being able to acknowledge what you feel. It is the way by which we honor the fact that we are emotional beings and that we do have feelings. This is something adults often fail to realize about children, that they are emotional beings. Consequently, as adults, we fail to recognize it about ourselves. It is not always necessary for you to announce to others what you feel. You must, however, allow yourself to feel it. Only through the experience of what you feel are you able to stay in touch with your inner self. Once you are in touch you will realize that all feelings are neutral, and that they derive their meaning from the energy that we give them. In essence, there are no good or bad feelings unless we tell ourselves they are good or bad. The actual conflict or confusion we experience is knowing the difference between acknowledging what we feel and the appropriate expression of that knowledge. Being able to identify and acknowledge what you feel is a sign of emotional health and stability. It empowers you to choose the appropriate response. When, on the other hand, you get stuck judging the right or wrong of your emotional experiences, to the degree that you deny having them you are painting yourself into a very tight corner, an emotional tight spot that can often lead to inappropriate expressions.

Whether or not you are involved in a love relationship, emotional suppression, which is a form of self-deception, does not honor you, nor does it honor those with whom you interact in any way. Self-deception is failure to acknowledge the truth about yourself or others. If you cannot accept truth, you are in denial. When you are involved in something as powerful as loving yourself or others, the attempt to deny the depths of your experience creates what you know as pain. In the meantime, while you don't have this figured out, you are prone to do everything in your power to deny what you feel, believing that denial will keep you from speaking the painful truth. Important love rule here: acknowledgment and expression are not the same thing! Acknowledgment means having the courage to admit to yourself what you are feeling. Expression means having the presence of mind and the courage to let someone else know. They are two active reminders that love does not strip you of your decision-making faculties or the power to make a choice.

No life experience invokes more feelings than relationships, yet all too often in relationships we do not allow ourselves to feel. Don't say "I love you" first. Don't ask too many questions too soon. We remember what happened before, the first time or the last time we acted on a feeling. Learned responses often make us lose sight of the difference between the acknowledgment and the expression of emotions. Acknowledgment also means being able to have an emotional experience without judgment. It is called *detachment*. It means giving yourself permission to have an experience without anticipating the results of the experience. In the struggle to determine *emotional rightness*, we remember that in voicing our concerns, suspicions, or anxieties *the last time* we were criticized or told that we should not feel that way. In response, you conclude that the feeling, not the expression, is inappropriate. The key is to detach from or surrender all of the judgments you have made about what you feel.

All feelings are appropriate. It is often our response to or expression of the feelings that get us into trouble. This is why emotional honesty is critical. A mentor once told me, "Allow yourself to feel what you are feeling, and know that you don't have to do anything about it." Let me tell you, it was the hardest thing I have ever learned to do! For a very long time it seemed to me that my tongue was attached to my heart. If I felt something strongly enough, I had to say something about it. As a child, it kept me sitting in the corner. As a student, it got me sent to the principal's office. In relationships, it resulted in my being left broken-hearted! Expressing my feelings had its most devastating effect when I did not acknowledge what I was feeling. The things I said that were attached to unacknowledged emotions usually got me into a lot of trouble.

There is another aspect of acknowledgment that bears mentioning at this point. It's called *dwelling*. Well-meaning friends will be the first to tell you, "Don't dwell on it," meaning do not stay focused on negative emotions or experiences. Of course, they never tell you not to dwell on the good things. Consequently, if you are dwelling, chances are it is about something not so pleasant. When we hear *don't dwell* we interpret it to mean *don't feel,* don't acknowledge. Dwelling has more to do with expression than acknowledgment. Chances are, the person who has said "Don't dwell" has heard your sad story ninety-nine times. Rather than saying, "Darling, stop expressing your drama in my life!" they will say "Don't dwell." Dwelling means you are stuck. You are trying to figure out what happened, why it happened, and what you can do to make it better. You are thinking or talking about the events, not the feelings. Remember, acknowledgment of what you feel gives you the freedom to choose how to express. It also gives you the power to release, heal, or transform the experience in a way that will make you and your friends feel better.

YOU MUST TAKE GOOD NOTES

In relationships, emotional dishonesty is a self-defense mechanism we adopt as a protective measure against having our hearts broken. We do it so often it seems like a natural response. On the other hand, life will not hear of it! You cannot get away with emotional dishonesty for long! You must honor your feelings, and eventually you will be called upon by life to make your feelings known. In response to this calling, you must learn how to express yourself to one other living person. If it is the right person and your acknowledgment is sincere, all will be well. If you are not lucky enough or courageous enough to acknowledge what you feel, you will be confused when the call is issued. You will find yourself in a very tight corner. You will be stuck trying to figure out what you feel and what to say. In the midst of confusion and in the process of trying to get unstuck, you will say the wrong thing to the wrong person. That person will tell the very person that you would not want to know, and they will stop speaking to you. Now you are more than confused or stuck. You are mad, embarrassed, and friendless.

Relationships bring up your stuff, and feelings are the stuff we are made of. Whether it is a relationship with your parents, an employer, or a loved one, the interaction is going to evoke deep and powerful emotions. Very important love rule: You must learn to be as honest as possible about what you feel. A simple mental sentence should do the trick: "Right now I am feeling _____." Once you acknowledge what you feel, you have a choice whether or not to express it. If you choose to express it, people may get upset with you. Being upset is not life-threatening! People have a right to be upset if they choose to be. Your job in the presence of upset people is to resist the temptation to label yourself as the cause of the upset. Stay with your feeling. Notice the sensations it creates in your body. Notice the thoughts or memories it brings up for you. You have a prime opportunity for healing at this very moment. If you can remember the circumstances and situations that evoked the same or a similar feeling, you can ask to be healed.

At the precise moment of an emotional response, you can train yourself to stop and take a deep breath. This is how you can reconnect with the love that life is. Along with the breath, I always find it helpful to take a quick inventory of my body with the breath. That means asking yourself, "What do I feel? Where do I feel it?" Once you have located the feeling, ask, "What is this?" It may sound like this would take a long time. It doesn't. I have found that fifteen to twenty seconds is usually sufficient. Probably just enough time to catch yourself or another person in midsentence, having uttered the words that will push your emotional buttons. Emotional buttons are often triggered by unconscious, learned responses to mental or emotional stimulation. How many times have you said, "I don't know why I got so mad." It is very likely that you were responding to an unconscious memory for which you have learned a response. Anger is the natural response to feeling powerless. Fear is the natural response to not knowing what to do about feeling powerless. We all learn, through pre- and postbirth experiences, how to respond to both of these emotional experiences.

The mind and body are very cooperative. They will respond immediately to your slightest request. If you asked to be healed, you will be healed. You must, however, be willing to surrender control of the healing. You must also be willing to do a new thing to facilitate the healing. Deep breathing at the onset of an upset. Resisting the urge to judge what you feel. Asking yourself questions about learned emotional responses. Learning to detach from what you think might happen when you express yourself. Allowing yourself to feel what you feel and express what you feel. These are all new things that you can do to facilitate emotional and spiritual healing. They are boosters to the spiritual cleansers of surrender and detachment. They help to facilitate being able to stay in touch with yourself, acknowledge what you are feeling, and express feelings in appropriate ways. In any relationships, these keys will help you stay emotionally healthy. They are acts of kindness and self-love.

WEEP NO MORE

Joe put Marie in a nursing home very close to their home. It was very difficult at first. He spent most of his day running back and forth between the house and the home, bringing Marie the things he thought she needed to be comfortable. He missed her so much, and he could not bear the thought of her being unhappy. He also thought she was angry at him for what he had done. Joe joined the local church, thinking he might find some comfort. He found friends with whom he could play cards during the evenings. Books that he could read to Marie when he went to visit. And, yes, he found a lady friend who knew all about Marie and was still happy to accompany Joe to the movies and out to dinner every now and then. Everyone knew that Joe loved Marie and would continue loving her even after she died. They knew because he told them so every chance he got. What he finally figured out was that he could love Marie and live his life in a way that was best for them both. It was called surrender.

Lisa never did resume her classes, but she did finally get over Nanny's death. For her the key was forgiveness. She started by forgiving her father for dumping his responsibilities on her. She forgave herself for accepting them as her own. She forgave her mother for abandoning her for the company of Mr. Webb. She forgave herself for being angry at her mother. She forgave all of her ex-boyfriends for preying on her weaknesses. Then she forgave herself for not loving herself enough to work on herself. For Lisa, forgiveness was the path to surrender. Surrender helped her to detach from the conditions she had placed on herself. She recently got a really big promotion on her job, and she is involved in a pretty decent relationship.

Iris isn't ready yet. She still has a lot of pain to deal with. She made it through the alcohol detox program, but she still isn't talking. There are some experiences in our lives that have such an impact on us that the emotional toll seems overwhelming. When this happens, the road to recovery is long, narrow, and very steep. Processing through some emotions is akin to dying. You must die to the old before you can be reborn or enlightened. Iris isn't ready. The pain of her father's death, the years of silence, the ambivalence about her mother, the hatred of herself is still too great. We do know, however, that the moment Iris becomes willing to surrender, the moment she finds the courage to allow herself to feel, the instant she utters the ultimate prayer *"Help me!"* the healing will begin. Love never fails to answer a request made in its name.

Chapter 8
TAKE OUT THE TRASH

robert was married. joan knew he was because he told her he was. Joan was attractive, well-educated, an up-and-coming lawyer, the daughter of a prominent politician, but was seemingly unable to snare the love of her life. When she met Robert she had a need to fill—she just didn't want to be lonely anymore. Robert, who was nine years older than Joan, offered a prime opportunity to enjoy an occasional dinner, good company, and sex. The fact that he was a married man didn't seem as unattractive as being by herself. Besides that, she was very busy, and a casual relationship meant that she did not have to make a commitment and that she could continue searching and exploring other relationship possibilities. An added benefit was that she would ease her father's mind about her being an old maid. It also made her feel better that her father always spoke so highly of Robert.

Joan kept telling herself that she wasn't doing anything wrong—she wasn't the one who was married! It's called denial, but Joan didn't know that. Perhaps it was because she had already walked the married man path with some reasonable measure of success—never got caught, got in and out of the relationship with little or no drama. She was looking for a decent man with whom she could occupy her time until the right one came along. Joan had yet to understand that when you are hanging on to the wrong thing, the right thing can't get in! Then there was the fact that she was at an emotional low and she wanted something to do. Something fun, something exciting. Looking for excitement in a relationship will get you every time!

Joan wasn't sure exactly when it happened, maybe year two, no, it was the middle of year four, that she realized she was thinking about Robert day and night. They were so compatible, it was amazing! He loved seafood, she loved seafood. He loved the opera, she loved the opera. The best part about it was they were both lawyers and could share their day-to-day experiences. Especially because they shared one person in common. Joan's father. Robert was Joan's father's legal counsel, his personal attorney. As hard as she tried to fight it, Joan couldn't help but think about how wonderful it would be to spend the rest of her life with Robert. He was so generous! The tennis bracelet he had given her for her birthday and the diamond heart pendant she got for Valentine's Day were what he considered only tiny tokens of his affection. Best of all, he was so discreet. He had a uniquely discreet way of cheating on his wife. Joan admired that about him, that he was so responsible and thoughtful.

Robert wasn't like the other married men with whom Joan had been involved. After a few home-cooked meals and a few months of sex (which was why she was in it), each of them had fallen off the deep end. They wanted to leave their wives for her. No strings attached, remember, she would tell them as she gently pushed them out the door. This time it was Joan. She realized that she was totally in love with Robert and wondered whether he was in love with her. She didn't dare ask him and he never mentioned it. What she knew was that he was very much *in like* and *respect*ful of his wife. They were pillars in the community. Everybody who knew Robert knew his wife. They were that kind of couple. There wasn't an inkling that Robert and Joan had been an item, even after four years. Daddy was a little concerned that Joan had stopped bringing guys home, but she would always remind him that lunch dates were as good as dinner dates.

Joan let her mind wander in fantasyland about her and Robert because she could not talk about him to anyone. She could not run the risk of disgracing her family, particularly her father, who was about to run for office again. Besides that, Robert had made it perfectly clear that he would not, under any circumstances, leave his wife. She was his best friend and the mother of his children. Joan was tempted to ask him what that made her but usually decided against it. In all of the years they had been together, they had never had an argument. A cross word had never passed between them. She was not about to start picking a fight now, not after almost four years. She did, however, wish she had someone to talk to about her plight. She had tried to talk to friends, but when she told them that the guy was *"seeing someone else"* everyone gave her the same advice, dump him! Particularly her daddy. Daddy said that she was headed for disgrace and scandal and that she better watch her step.

It was in the eighth month of the eighth year of the relationship that Joan and Robert were forced to deal with the realities of their lives. Joan was pregnant. She had never, in her entire life, been pregnant before, but she was now. Joan was in her late thirties, which had great significance on the biological clock. The truth of the matter is that she had been secretly praying for a baby and might have missed a pill or two to help it along. Along with the baby prayer, she had also prayed for a husband. Joan finally confided in a friend that she was four months pregnant by a married man and did not know what to do about it. Together they thought through the whole mess, only to realize that Joan had gotten everything she requested. *"You asked for a baby, you got that. You asked for a husband, you got that too,"* her friend declared. Joan retorted, "I don't have the slightest prospect for a husband. I've been with Robert for the past eight years!" Her friend calmly explained, "You weren't that specific. You didn't make it clear that you wanted your *own* husband. You got exactly what you wanted and expected—a husband and a baby."

There are dilemmas, and there are DILEMMAS! Guess which one Joan was having? Does a single woman in a small town have a baby, disgrace her father, ruin her career, and tie herself to this married man? Or does she slink off to the big city to have an abortion, thereby staining her mortal soul and running the risk of burning in hell? These were the questions Joan and her friend pondered. Isn't it funny how absolutely pious we become when we are in trouble? Joan never once considered the fate of her soul during the eight years she was with Robert, but that's another book. Right now, the trash was piling up and Joan had to make a decision.

Let us take a quick review of this very delicate second-floor meantime DILEMMA to be sure that we do not miss anything. A single woman has an eight-year relationship with a married man who happens to be her very prominent father's legal counsel. During the course of this relationship, although the woman swears she is waiting for Mr. Right to come along, she has unprotected sex with the married man, the result of which is pregnancy. When this thirty-something-year-old single woman discovers that she is pregnant by her married lover, she confides in her girlfriend that she is four and a half months pregnant and that she has in fact been praying for a husband and a baby. However, since the baby's father is not *her* husband, she must now decide whether she should have the baby—the result of which could be family scandal and disgrace—or risk burning in hell for an eternity as a result of committing the mortal sin of abortion. Realizing how challenging some meantime experiences can be, you want to give the people the benefit of the doubt. In a story like this one, however, you realize that everything and everyone is up for grabs!

When we have hidden agendas, unclear motives, unachievable fantasies, dishonesty, and false responsibilities as the basis of a relationship, it is a safe bet that there is no love present. What is present may look like love, it may feel like love, but it is not, in any way, shape, form, or fashion, even closely related to the essence of love. You cannot do what makes absolutely no sense and call it love! When love is present, everyone wins. In this scenario, no one can win. When you are willing to tell one lie after another lie after another lie, when you sneak or hide, when you do to someone the very thing you would not want done to you, you are not in pursuit of love. You are acting out your garbage! Mental and emotional trash! The thing about trash is that you know exactly what it is! You know that it is what you do not want, what you no longer have use for, what has been cluttering your environment. There's another thing about trash: There are times when you throw things into the trash that you do not mean to throw into the trash. Once you do, you run around the house in a panic looking for the items. Suddenly it hits you, *"I must have put it in the trash!"* Slowly, methodically, you must wade through the old useless stuff, the gook, the foul-smelling stuff in the trash, to find what you are looking for. When you find it, it is covered with trash. Now you have to clean it off, and hopefully it will still be useful.

Robert was dumbfounded. He was supportive, but he was also horrified. His first instinct was to run away. Instead he asked Joan what she wanted to do. She admitted that she did not know. She wanted the baby, but she did not want to disappoint her father. She particularly wanted to have Robert's child, but she did not want to cause him any trouble. Robert told her it was her decision, and that he would accept his part of the responsibility, no matter what she decided to do. Three weeks later, when Joan was still fumbling around, Robert, being the honorable person that he was, told Joan's father. Well, let's get real—he wasn't actually being all that honorable! He was scared! He told because he didn't want Joan's powerful father to find out from other channels—namely Joan. Robert wanted to explain himself. He wanted to save his skin! Joan's father was not in the least bit pleased, but he was supportive. He suggested to Robert that he tell his wife immediately, because women are very funny about hearing things like this from other people. He knew, because it had happened to him many years ago after Joan was born. Robert was shocked! With what he knew about this man, and with all that Joan had told him, he expected to be fired and then shot. Instead, this *gentleman* was talking to him as if he were a son, a friend, a colleague in trouble who needed his help.

If you don't take the trash out when you first get a whiff of it, it will pollute your entire environment! Or you could get maggots, nasty little things that can crawl into the most private places. If or when that happens, you will have to deal with it— head-on. Joan's father went to his daughter and told her that he knew. He also told her that he would support her regardless of her decision. He reminded her that he wanted grandchildren, and that he could not control how he got them. His concern was for her happiness.

There is some trash that is heaped upon us. It is the result of how we are raised and the experiences we have in life. We can call this *outdoor trash,* that which comes from external sources. Then there is the trash we collect. We pick it up, we bring it home, we make a place for it in our environment, and more often than not we then complain about the smell. We call this *indoor trash,* the conclusions we draw in response to the experiences we have in life. Often our response to the combination of outdoor and indoor trash is to find a way to move the trash around so that it will match our picture. Very often we ignore the smell and make the necessary adjustments to live with the trash. All the things Joan feared that her father would say and do were in response to her own trash, which she eventually had to wade through and deal with. Joan projected that image onto him, adjusting her actions accordingly. Joan decided to leave home and have the baby. It didn't matter, because everyone in town found out. They usually do when something in your trash smells very bad.

When we have a desire to have a thing or an experience, the first images of the desire are pure. They emanate from the essence of our being, which is love. What we do is put all of our trash on top of the desire, determining that it has to look this way or that way. Yet quite often we act in ways that are totally inconsistent with both the desire and the picture we want to see. When you want to get married but only married men show up in your life, there is something wrong with the projector (you), not the picture (what shows up). There may be some trash in the way that is clouding the intent or the expectation. What you may need to do is release the picture and stay focused on the experience you desire. If you stay focused on the experience, the proper picture will show up.

What do you want to feel like? Because our human knowledge is so limited, we respond to what we see rather than what we want. We believe that we must take what shows up and fit it into the picture we have created. This is often because we think we know the end of the story. We think we have the entire script at every moment. Just when we begin to adjust what we have to fit what we want, a new character will show up, a new story line will be introduced and throw the picture out of whack. When this happens we usually go into fear. This is what the meantime is all about, learning how to adjust the projector —ourselves—through the power and the presence of love. When love is added to the projector, the picture becomes a

clearer representation of the desire. The intent falls into alignment with the expectations. The character becomes an honorable representation of the intent that is not polluted by the
trash. Remove the fear, remove the conditions, and the experience will show up.

In life and in relationships, we must be very clear about
what we are looking for, what we expect, what we want to
experience, and what we are willing to do to get it. On the
second floor of love's house you will learn a great deal about
this. Learning on the second floor centers on vision (getting it
clear), integrity (what you are willing to do in pursuit of your
vision), intent (what it is that you are trying to accomplish), and
expectations (what you believe about what you are trying to
accomplish), all of which can be obscured or polluted by the
trash we hold in our minds. *"I never get what I want! All the good
folks are married! I am running out of time! I better grab the first
thing that comes along!"* These are the things we project, yet we
wonder why the picture doesn't match what we say we want to
experience.

You can get into big trouble on the second floor, because it
is very easy and tempting to want one thing and not follow a
course of action that will produce the thing or the experience
you are after. It is dangerous to believe that everything that
shows up in your life is the path to what you want. Some things
show up to help you get clearer vision. Other things show up
to help you clarify or heal your intent. Then there are those
frequent occasions when things on their way to some place
else show up, and you mistakenly believe they are yours. Your
expectations were not clear, so you begin to adjust the picture.

1. *What is my vision of love? What am I looking for? What am I looking at? What am I looking with?* Your vision of love is the sum total of your experience, added to your expectations, divided by your desire. That's a lot of stuff, and it may take you a while to sift through it all. Answering this question is the tool for spring cleaning in love's house.

2. *What do I really expect from love?* When you start pulling blocks out of the foundation, the entire building will shake. The old habits, old ideas, old expectations were the blocks in your foundation. You have begun to pull them out of your consciousness. Unfortunately, you did not replace them with new ideas, new habits, or new expectations. As a result, you may want something new, but you must realize you will not get it using the same old modus operandi. There may be some garbage here that you want to clean up.

3. *Do I really believe that I deserve love?* Expectations equal results. What you believe in the deepest recesses of your being will manifest as your experience. If you miss some of this stuff along the way, you will find yourself asking for one thing and experiencing something else.

These are all second-floor questions, which, when we are searching for answers, will manifest as meantime experiences.

Remember that when you are on the second floor, you know what the problem is, but you do not know what to do about it. You know what you want, but you do not know how to bring it into your life. The first step is to examine your expectations and intent. What are you trying to accomplish?

What is the experience you desire to have? When you are in the meantime on the second floor of love's house you must learn to trust. Trust yourself, trust the process, and most of all trust love. Love will always bring you the highest repre-sentation of your intentions and expectations. Fear will bring your worst nightmare to life! Trust grows from willingness, the lesson you learned in the basement. In order to master trust, you must be willing to give up everything you now believe and think you know in order to learn something else. This learning will adjust the project. It will help you to clarify your intent.

By now, you must know that the voice of Spirit is talking to you. That voice is your Spirit, your *Self.* Your job, through all of your meantime experiences, on all the floors of love's house, has been to listen, and to trust what you hear. It is this self-trust that enables you to make clear and conscious choices about the experiences you are having and those that you desire to have. Some of us have been told that this is selfish—it is selfish to think about yourself and what you want. In response, we be-lieved in the necessity to always concern ourselves with the good of those around us. Trusting yourself and honoring what you feel is not selfish. It is the most self-loving thing you can do. This does not mean that you become insensitive to others or that you use others to get what you need and want. Trusting, honoring, and loving yourself means recognizing that you have a right to be happy. At the same time, honoring yourself enables you to support and assist others without anger, resentment, or obligation. You do it in love because you want to do it. This is what relationships are meant to do, provide us with a structure in which we support and assist one another in finding and sharing happiness. It is a mutual support system, not a crutch. It was in the basement that you learned how dangerous it can be to use relationships like crutches.

WHERE AM I?

It is quite normal that during a meantime experience on the second floor of love's house you will become confused about where you are in life. Perhaps your past has been so fraught with pain and confusion that you will allow yourself to believe you are doing the best you can do. If you come to this conclusion, you are both right and wrong. You are right that you are doing exactly what you need to be doing. Not because you can't do any better, but because there is still more for you to learn. You are wrong because where you are is a function of choice. The things you have done, the decisions you have made, the vision that you have, and how you are pursuing that vision are all a function of choice. While it may be quite true that the odor of your indoor and outdoor trash has influenced your choice, it is not true that the choices you have made are the only choices that were available to you. If you desire to have a new experience, are ready to take out the trash, and are willing to trust the process, an accurate assessment of exactly where you are is in order.

This meantime process of assessment, evaluation, and reflection requires that you ask yourself certain very probing questions, and that you be ready to hear the answers. This is a powerful spiritual house cleaner that brings the many ingredients of all the other cleaners to the boiling point. When the boiling begins you will find that you have shifted from a posture of getting ready to a position of being set. Question one: Where are you? Not geographically, but where are you in your heart and mind? Are you feeling fine, needing nothing, but wanting something you seem unable to get? Are you willing to learn and attempting to grow? Are you tired, frustrated, or angry? Are you lonely, confused, and horny? Are you working hard but getting nowhere? Are you hardly working and watching the blessings unfold? You may think of a few more questions to ask yourself, but these will provide you with a good place to begin. Now here's how to ask:

1. Get still. Focus on your breath. Find its rhythm and listen to yourself breathing for three to five minutes.
2. Call forth the presence of light, love, and Spirit by reciting a prayer or repeating an affirmation.
3. Ask all voices in your head to be silent so that you can hear the voice of Spirit.
4. Ask one question.
5. Listen for the answer. You may want to write the answer—that means write what comes into your mind. Do not censor it, write it. Once you have written, read the response.
6. Begin the process again and ask another question.

If nothing comes into your mind, do not ask another question. Move into your day or evening in a receptive posture because the answer will come. Someone may say, "You sure look/ sound _____." That's the answer! A song may arouse certain feelings or memories. That's the answer! It can happen in any number of ways, but over the course of the day or the next few days, the answer will show up. When you get the answer, you are ready for the next question.

HOW DID I GET HERE?

Armed with the answer from the first question, you can receive the clarity you probably desperately need with the second question: How did I get here? Follow the same process you used for question one to get this answer. One word of caution: You must avoid the temptation of blaming anyone else for where you are in your own life. If the answer you get begins with, "Because s/he did _____," you have not breathed deeply enough. You have not silenced the voices. You are in fear. You are hiding. Spirit never blames anyone for anything that happens to us because Spirit knows *there are no victims.* Spirit only recognizes choice, the commanding force of life. Take a few more breaths and ask the question again, adding, "What were the choices I made or failed to make?" Now you are ready to hear the truth. When it comes up for you, write it down. Study it. Read and reread it. When you are ready, move on to the next question.

WHAT WAS I TRYING TO ACCOMPLISH
BY MAKING THAT CHOICE?

I was once asked in a workshop, "If you could have anything you wanted in the world, something that would make your life all that you want it to be, what would you ask for?" This was long before I became spiritually enlightened, so I said, "Money." As it rolled off my tongue, I could feel the whole room cringe. Without batting an eye, the facilitator asked, "Do you want the money, or do you want the experience you believe the money will bring?" Talk about fry your brain! I started stuttering. Finally I said, "I want the freedom that the money would give me." To which the wise facilitator responded, "So why not ask for freedom and let the universe bring it to you in the divine and right way?" I had never in my whole life thought of it from that perspective.

Very often in our lives, we will do things or not do things, ask for things or resist asking for things, because we believe that the action or inaction will create an expected outcome. The truth of the matter is, if we focus on the experience, the appropriate way to achieve it will be provided. In relationships, even the relationship with ourselves, we want a certain experience, and we devise the means we believe will create the experience. We buy things to get acknowledgment. We say things to feel accepted. We don't say certain things in order to avoid rejection. In most cases, we focus on the very thing we do not want, which in effect creates more of that experience. This question will help us to identify what we have been focusing on and the experience we were attempting to create. Follow the same process. Write the answer. Study it. It is helpful to ask yourself this question several times because if you are anything like the rest of the world, you were probably trying to accomplish more than one thing at a time. Take your time. This process could last for several weeks, but it is worth it to get clear.

WHAT DO I REALLY WANT?

This is an easy question, one for which the preceding question has provided your answer(s). The process is simple. Make a list. Write down all of the answers you received or realized from the previous question, turning each response into the statement: "What I really want is _____." Limit your response to three to five words. Example: What I really want is to experience freedom of movement. What I really want is to be accepted. What I really want is to be acknowledged. Study the list very carefully to make sure that you have not made anyone responsible for what you want. By this I mean avoid statements such as, "What I really want is to be acknowledged by my father." Or, "What I really want is to be loved by _____." You can avoid making these statements by cutting them off at the word "by." The key is to remember that no one can give you what you cannot give yourself. Once your list is complete, giving you total responsibility for creating what you want, you may move on to the next question.

HOW CAN I CREATE THIS EXPERIENCE?

If you have used the proper amounts of this cleanser you are set! You are willing and prepared to move to a new level of loving and being loved by yourself and everyone else in the world. You have cause to celebrate because this has been no small feat. You have eliminated a lot of trash! In coming this far, you should have a clear vision of what you want and the experience you are after. You have demonstrated your ability to accept the truth and a willingness to trust. You have learned a great deal about yourself and how you interact with others. You can now delineate your weaknesses and your strengths, your fears, and foibles. You are open to new experiences and are willing to assume the responsibility for creating them. You are set to make better choices with a clear intent. Your knees are bent, your tush is in the air, your feet are planted firmly, and you are ready to run this race like the champion you are. Next move, forgive!

You cannot move forward with a heart or mind full of shoulda's, coulda's, or woulda's. The only way to lighten your load so that you can move up to the third floor is to forgive. You have scrutinized yourself and are now well aware of the things you did not do so well. I know this process works, but I also know that you are a human being. Because you are a human being, you are going to beat up on yourself. Stop it! You are going to analyze yourself. Remember, you cannot fix you! You want to know why you did or didn't do, what you did or didn't do. You didn't know what to do, that's why you did what you did! You want to know what is the *right* thing to do next. You were supposed to give up the need to be right in the basement! You want to know why he got away or she got away scot-free (according to your perception), and why you were left here to suffer and struggle. Be careful! If you are blaming and pointing fingers, you can be sent back to the basement!

I too am a human being, and these are the things I always want to know! After wading through my own trash, I have discovered that no matter how much of an experience or how much of my trash I try to toss onto another person, in the end there is no one to deal with other than myself. That's right, me! I made the choice or failed to make the choice. I was not clear. I was not honest or willing. I went out there with strange expectations, looking for trouble, and I got it! When I find myself in these kinds of dilemmas, second-floor meantime dilemmas, forgiveness always helps me. If you are willing to admit that you are anything like the rest of us human beings, then perhaps you too must forgive.

Forgive yourself, not because you did anything wrong, but because you *thought* you were wrong in the first place. That's right, you human being you! You probably thought there was something wrong with you. Something you did not want anyone else to know about. So you hid yourself. You covered yourself with nice words, cute gestures, and strange excuses when deep inside you were probably thinking, "I hope they don't find out that I'm _____." Feeling this way in your heart of hearts obscured your vision and governed your actions, which probably took you out of alignment with the experience you were going after. Forgive yourself, not because of all the signs you failed to acknowledge or all the things you did not ask for, but because you did not understand that the only way to discover what you want is to spend some time in what you do not want.

This is a very simple exercise. Every morning and evening for seven consecutive days, write the following statement thirty-five times:

"I forgive myself for thinking I ever did anything wrong."

In making the statement, you are shouldering the responsibility for yourself and your life. No matter what or who pops into your mind, write this statement. If you simply cannot shake the urge to consider how someone else has contributed, use the following statement:

"I forgive myself for thinking _____ ever did anything wrong."

This is how you will eliminate the temptation to blame. Whoever they may be, they did not do anything wrong. They, like you, were simply discovering what they did not want in order to get clear about what they did want.

GO!

Getting clear, examining intent and expectations, honestly acknowledging the experience you want, and forgiving yourself for carrying so much trash is like having a wisdom tooth taken out—it may take a while to heal! The good news is that this healing process will work regardless of the issues confronting you in the meantime. It could be a family matter, a work- or job-related issue, or it could very well be a relationship issue. Going through the process will bring you clarity regardless of the issue. If you are alone, not in a relationship, you will probably have a very easy go of it—when you are alone there is plenty of time to work on yourself.

For those who are in a relationship, there is an additional requirement. You will have to make time to be alone. You will have to make the space to complete the breathing and writing exercises. In the meantime, the relationship is progressing. Issues are still coming up. Things are being said, and you feel the need to respond. Your job is to use any of the spiritual cleansers you feel will work. That is, what can you apply to the situation as it is right now to establish peace? A quick review of the previous floors will help you determine what to do. Remember, begin within! Ask all questions and make all statements from your own perspective. Do not point your finger outward! Do not blame anyone, including you! Do not accuse: Instead accept responsibility. Ask your partner to give you the time and opportunity to get clear. In the meantime, don't pout, don't stomp your feet, do not stop speaking, and above all else, do not shut down on the process.

Everything must happen in the invisible before it can become visible. The meantime is an active time. Even if you are hurt and angry, you must believe that you are shifting and growing. There is healing going on! That you cannot see it does not mean it is not happening. Use a little willingness, wrap yourself in trust, remember the truth, do a little dusting, and take responsibility. Finding yourself and finding loves requires work—and you must be willing to do the work in a patient and responsible manner. You can accomplish this by keeping your vision clear, with an honorable intent. If you are hurt, what cleanser must you use? If you are angry, what cleanser should you apply? If you are becoming impatient, remind yourself of how far you have come, how much you have healed.

In the meantime, always remember that you are climbing up the steps of love's house. Know that you are being guided and that the people or information you need are just a prayer away. At times you will take baby steps and feel that the journey is too long to attempt to make it alone. You are never alone! There are, at all times, angels watching over you. You will also have the experience of making giant strides for which you will be tempted to pat yourself on the back. Don't be so quick to take the credit for your growth and evolution. Give God the credit, because it was God who never, not even for one second, gave up on you. You may find yourself in situations where you will be tempted by basement behavior and attitudes. Fear not! Keep in mind who walks beside you. Know that you cannot fail. Know that you need not lose your way or your footing. You need not fall into the mode of negative thinking and dysfunctional relationships.

BETWEEN THE SECOND AND THIRD FLOORS

you want to ignore it, but you can't—it's a disgrace! If your mother saw it, she would have a fit, and you would be grounded—forever. There are piles of papers. Some of them could be important, but how would you know? You haven't sifted through the pile in weeks! Oh! I see! Perhaps you couldn't see the papers because they were hidden by the socks, the mismatched socks that you rescued from the dryer monster. That's right, those socks are clean, but who would know it, since they're draped over that dirty glass, sitting on the dirty cake plate. That *was* cake on that plate, wasn't it? But what does that matter! What are a few clean socks in a pile of dirty T-shirts!

Now, you know that if your mother saw that dresser she would lie on the railroad track and drink scotch straight out of the bottle! You also know that she taught you better than that! Clean up that dresser! Clean out that closet! Get your act together! There may be something you want but cannot find because you've got so much stuff lying around!

Chapter 9
CLEANING OFF THE DRESSER

you are going to be a fool, period! The thing you've got to decide is how many times you're gonna be a fool. Two times? Six times? Ten times? Give yourself a limit, but don't say you're not going to be a fool, because you are going to be one, at least once. People who avoid relationships in fear of being a fool need to get over it. Give yourself a prescribed number of times, and just go for it! I know your mother told you, *"Don't be no fool!"* Actually, she was telling you to choose the kind of fool you want to be, be that kind of a fool, and get it over with! I don't know how many people I've talked to whose big thing is, *I don't want to be hurt! I don't want to be a fool! I don't want to look weak! I don't want to look stupid!* That's going to happen no matter what you do, so make some choices. Once you realize that you've been a fool for the prescribed number of times, that's when you gotta start getting yourself together. When you hit your limit, one of two things will happen: Either you'll stop being a fool, or you will give yourself a few more chances.

Carol's limit was three. She was going to be a fool three

times. She increased her limit to six, but decided to stop at five. It was just too damn painful! It was embarrassing, too. She was always attracted to the same kind of guy, for the same reason, and it always ended in the same way. It wasn't just the money, it was the way they made her feel. The thing was, in order to get them to make her feel that way, she could not be herself. She had to be someone else. She had to be cute, witty, passionate, and submissive. That's not who she was! That is who she thought she needed to be to get the kind of guy who made her feel good. But you know what? It was tiring! It was tiring and she was tired, and she decided to stop before she got into any more trouble—before she reached her limit and could not stop.

John had no limits. He was on the rebound. He met her at a restaurant. They started talking about music and beer. They talked for eight hours that night. It's hard to find a woman who really appreciates beer, and when you do find one, you want to take full advantage of the situation. She was outgoing, funny as hell, and she had a *really* nice body. He was a fool for a nice body. It lent to the sexual mystique. He knew he was about to be a fool again, but he needed a relationship with some energy. His marriage, which was just ending, had grown stale. Come home. How was the day? Fine. Watch television. Go to sleep. He was looking for someone who was ambitious, on the move, and doing some positive things. He knew he had always been attracted to women who were like that, although he didn't marry one like that. That was a foolish thing to do. Chance one down the drain. Chance number two on the horizon.

Faye was not a lustaholic, she was just very, very needy. She wanted to be somebody's special somebody. She wanted to be loved by someone. In her mind, sex was the one thing that could make her special and get her the love she so desperately needed. Even with this as her MO, she was picky. She didn't just go with anybody. She had a very carefully orchestrated selection process. There were very specific things a potential candidate had to do in order to get a chance to be with her. These were the things that made her feel special. They were the things she had convinced herself that no man would do for a woman unless he loved her. It is absolutely amazing the things you can get a person to do when you use sex as the carrot and lust as the string! Faye had it down to a science, but even scientists fail at some experiments. There were those times when she forgot what she was doing, or forgot the goal, and changed the rules of the game. It was on those occasions, when she forgot and fell head over heels, that she really got knocked for a loop. It was on those seven or eight occasions, over the past twelve years, that she had used up all of her chances for being a fool.

WHAT'S IT ALL FOR?!!!

That's it! That's what we all want! We want to be loved the way we are—totally and unconditionally. Unfortunately, we keep trying to get an "A" in the love course. You don't have to get an "A" or a perfect score! All you have to do is pass! This, unfortunately, is not good enough for most of us. We want to do the forever thing with somebody. In the quest to get the "A," to do it right, to be in it forever, we pick up a lot of stuff that we believe will take us straight to the heart of the matter. When, however, we enter the meantime, we come face to face with that stuff, all the things we do and have done in the search for love. And you know what? We don't like it! We don't like what we see! We don't like what we see ourselves doing for love. We don't like what we hear ourselves saying to get love. It makes us look and feel foolish.

Even when we recognize that it was our choice to do or to say these foolish things, we blame *them,* the people we thought we loved. When that doesn't work, we try comparison, comparing what we have done to what others have done to determine which was worse. When you are in the meantime, you must figure out why—why did you do it? Why did you allow it to be done? Why do you keep doing it? Why can't you stop doing it? This is the *stuff,* these are the questions you must answer on this, the final leg of your journey through love's house. You have done a lot! Your progress has been phenomenal! You have looked at a great deal of stuff, but there is just a little more you must do.

Love is the grandest emotion a living being can experience, and it is not limited to the experience of human beings. After watching hundreds of hours on the Discovery Channel, I have concluded that animals love their young and each other. I have also witnessed in the animal and human kingdom the vast devastation caused by the lack of love. Love is the spiritual extension cord that connects each of us to all of us. We are not always consciously aware of the connection or of the fact that every life experience is designed to make us aware. In the meantime, while we are reconnecting to and through the miracle of love, we spend a great deal of time in fear and anger. This is the stuff that leads to the devastation we call heartbreak in our relationships. This is the stuff you must clear before you can find your way to the third floor.

DO ONE THING AT A TIME!

To master some *stuff* does not mean you have mastered it all. Nor does it mean you cannot move ahead in the learning, healing process with the *stuff* you still have. Can I tell you something? Unless your name is Jesus, Buddha, Gandhi, or Mother Teresa, you are going to die with some *stuff!* You must understand this. You must learn how to leave some *stuff* hanging. You know it's there, you know it needs work, but you must also know there is no need to do it all in this lifetime. Do some, leave some, grow some. Do a little more, grow a little more. If we just do what we can do, it will be more than enough to propel us forward. We keep working on ourselves because we believe that we must do it all, right now! This is the same thing we do in our relationships. We convince ourselves that something is wrong and that it must be fixed immediately. It has to be perfect, right now! Things will fall into and out of alignment as the world turns. Relax! Learn how to choose to leave some things hanging. They won't bite you. They won't kill you. Leave them right where they are, knowing you can come back to them later.

As a matter of fact, some of your *stuff* may come in handy as you are learning the major lesson of giving unconditional love. That is why you are moving to the third floor. You want to be able to give and receive unconditional love at all times. When you look back at the pieces of your life, tattered and torn in relationships, unconditional love is the spiritual cleanser that will help you realize that it really wasn't *that bad*. With love, you come to understand that life thus far has been a self-authored script, and that those who played in your *stuff-show* were in fact those that you asked to play. It's always been about you and your *stuff*, that is what has made the love *stuff* so confusing and sometimes difficult to figure out—because you were looking at their stuff! Choose how you are going to respond to *stuff*! Your *stuff* and other folks' *stuff*. Get clear about what is really going on, and choose what you are going to do in response. Heretofore, most of the stuff that has been going on in your life has been quite normal. Your life has been unfolding, you have been growing—it has all been quite normal. It is usually our response to stuff that creates the problem. We must learn that just because something is going on or not going on, we do not have to respond.

There is some other *stuff* worth mentioning here because it is so easy to miss these things in the healing process. Without a good grasp on this *stuff*, you could lose your way or get stuck in some deep dark closet. It's hard to find your way out of a closet when you have unfinished or undetected *stuff* in your way. As you climb the steps from the second to the third floor, moving closer to unconditional love, you will have to use some heavy-duty cleansers to eliminate the built-up stuff that has resulted in your bad-luck love affairs: *Choice* is one cleanser, *clarity* is the other.

STOP PICKING ON YOURSELF!

When you are already thinking that you're not doing it right or that you're not doing enough in the right way, delineation will make you crazy! Delineation is when you start saying, *"I've got to fix this!" "I've got to do that!" "I've got to change this!"* When you start delineating, you also run the risk of thinking that you have to do it all, fix everything at once. If you get stuck in this level of picking on yourself, you will never get clear. Invariably you will get to the point where you think, *"It will never work out for me!"* Delineation is the reason we say, "I've done so much work and it's still not working." What you have done or are doing is not the problem. The problem is that before you were clear, *you* delineated what the work should be and how it should be done. You responded to your experiences, your fears, your feelings of inadequacy. The truth of the matter is, you really don't know what to do or how to do it. Yes, there are some things, some of your stuff about which you are very clear. This is the stuff you can work on. You can apply the principles. You can adjust the attitudes. You can alter the behavior. The bottom line still remains that there are just some things that are not going to work out the way you think they should. You must be clear about this.

You must also remain open and willing to do whatever is necessary, as it becomes necessary, one thing at a time. When you see your stuff come up, put everything you know, everything that supports you in cleaning it up into practice. Do not resist! Do not suppress! Let it all come up in your conscious mind so that you will at least be aware of what is going on. Once it is up in your consciousness and you are aware of it, choose what you are going to address, and address it. Choice is important here. If you are working through your fears, but you know you have some self-worth issues, choose one, fear or worth—and work on it. If you know you want a relationship, but you also know you have some adequacy issues, choose one to work on—and work on that. If you choose to work on one thing and something else comes up for you, you can always change your mind. But if you try to work on one thing while you are cleaning up another, you are going to make yourself sick! You will be sick of you! Sick of working! Sick of cleaning up stuff! Focus on the experience that you want to have. Let the feeling of the experience come up in your body without judging it right or wrong. Resist the temptation to delineate by saying it *has to be* this way or that way. Learn how to express the feeling you are going for so that the universe can respond to you. Keep in mind that whatever you think you want is only a fraction of what God wants to give you.

Love does not ask that you deny or abuse your "self" to embrace love. Quite the contrary: Love asks that you bring every part of you—those broken and mangled parts, those polished and shining parts, those you acquired, and those you were given—to the third floor of its house. Love welcomes you and all that you bring to be healed through its presence. Love wants to make you one again. One with the One who loved you then, now, and always in whatever shape you are in. Love does not ask you to give of yourself more than you have to give. If you can just give love to yourself, that will be enough. When you can give love to you, it opens your heart to receive the love held in store for you by others.

ANY MISTAKE CAN BE CORRECTED!

I met a young woman who was so convinced that so much was wrong with her that she was resigned to living alone for the rest of her life. She had lost the one man she thought she would love forever. She had lost the job that she really loved. She was about to lose her car because she no longer had a job. She was a mess! Miraculously, in the midst of it all, she decided she was going to work on herself. This is what happens when you really master the lessons of the first and second floors. You may lose your footing, but you don't get lost! Having worked in the field of marketing, she decided to apply what she had learned in her career life to her personal and love life. She called it the Four P's: product, price, packaging, and promotion. After determining that she was the product, she recognized the need for development. She had to get really clear about who she really was and what she wanted. She understood that she was a multi-faceted human being. Like an onion, she was unfolding layer by layer, piece by piece. She had done a great deal of work, but she realized that each time a new layer unfolded, she had to do some more of the same work, at a deeper level.

If you want your product to be well received in the market-place, she thought, you must be able to describe it, define it, and articulate to others, those who will buy it, exactly what it is and what it can do. This is a vital element of self-esteem and self-confidence. Knowing who you are, the good and the not so good, is the first step. Learning to recognize your addictive and destructive behavior patterns in order to dismantle them is the big second step. A pattern is a pattern. We all have them. When, however, we have the courage to admit that the pattern is an addiction or that it is destructive, this is a major developmental coup! In order to do this, you cannot be in judgment of, nor can you criticize, yourself. You must instead become consciously aware of the choices you are making, moment by moment. You do this by listening to your self-talk and by interrupting the negative messages. You do this by replacing need with desire, desperation with receptivity. You do it by replacing obsessions with determination. The receptive determination must not be to find somebody. Instead, it must be to love you. Time spent alone in the meantime will help you get clear about who you are and about the behavior patterns that conflict with your identity.

Be willing to share your product information openly and honestly, first with yourself and then with others. Too many people on the mission to find love engage in false advertising! Sometimes we simply don't know the truth. In other situations, we know but choose not to disclose. In the end, when we get *"taken home,"* and the buyer discovers the truth, we are promptly returned to the shelf. If you do not want your product to have a short shelf life, product development is critical. Your internal, emotional, spiritual growth, the ability to acknowledge, accept, and love yourself, is essential to finding the love you want. It is paramount in learning to love yourself, whether or not a lover ever shows up.

It was through your relationship experiences in the basement and on the first and second floors that you got the first hint that love can be a win/win situation. As you journey toward the third floor, this is your goal. You must now work to understand that you can give love, or anything else, without losing a thing. You can consciously choose to share your time, resources, or life with someone because survival is not an issue. When you make this conscious choice, you cannot lose. You grow. A relationship can end without depleting you. You have learned what works and what does not work for you. You now realize that the benefit of each and every one of your past experiences is total self-acceptance. You can now accept yourself as you are, and you accept the choices you make because you know that you can choose and choose again until you are satisfied. This is a major discovery! The compass is now in good working order. Your exploratory journey through love's house, which brought you to this point, may not have been easy, but you made it!

YOU GET WHAT YOU HAVE PAID FOR!

Price. What is your product worth? What will the market bear? Once you have a very definite idea about what or whom your product is, you must decide how to price it. In the realm of self-development, pricing refers to being able to clearly articulate what it is that you want. It is a function of self-worth. It is knowing that you do not have to settle for whatever comes along because of your age or background or because of the number of hairs sprouting from your chin. You have set standards for how you want to be treated and what you expect from yourself and for yourself. Of course, some of these standards are negotiable, while others are not.

Now that you know your product, your strengths and weaknesses, and are not afraid to acknowledge them, your value has increased tremendously. The things you have done are no longer a secret you must struggle to keep hidden. Your slips, falls, or missteps cannot be a crutch, things you fall back on when things do not go the way you planned. No more feeling sorry for yourself! No more beating up on yourself! You are a valuable and worthwhile product, full of love, consciously making choices. You have full confidence in your product. So are you going to price it for bargain hunters? Or are you going to price it like a designer item? The value and worth you place on yourself will determine the people you attract. Those who shop in the high-priced markets know exactly what they want and how to treat it once they get it. They know a masterpiece when they see one, and they are not afraid to pull out all the stops to be in its company. Basement bargain hunters are not as clear or conscientious. A bargain hunter could have a rare piece of art and not even recognize it. As you dust the last few fragments of self-doubt from your consciousness, you will be able to price your product according to its true value and worth.

You are moving from the second to the third floor of love's house. This is the best meantime of all! You have learned to listen to yourself and to trust what you hear. You now realize that trouble comes to pass, not to stay! You understand that a delay is not a denial! You are fully aware that all of life's experiences are temporary. You also understand that while a temporary meantime experience could last for one, ten, or twenty years, you are willing to keep moving, keep doing, keep growing to the best of your ability. You have a bucket full of principles —willingness, trust, truth, responsibility, choice, surrender, and detachment—that you can use to dust off any of life's temporary, although challenging, situations. You should also realize now that even when you know there is something going on, something that requires a little work, you have the stamina to take enough time to get clear about what it is before you move forward and do something foolish.

How will you distribute your product? In what markets will you place it? This can be a difficult call to make. I am a firm believer that when you are ready, love will find you. The self-love, self-worth, and self-confidence that you have developed will magnetize your soul and attract more of its likeness. On the other hand, I realize that it is very easy for a magnet to attract metal fragments or things cleverly disguised as silver and gold. Not to worry! You have standards. You are clear. You will easily recognize those things that are not pure or solid. That is your blessing for all you have been through on this journey. You have picked up skills and abilities that will kick in when you need them. The key here is not to convince yourself that you can make platinum from tin fibers! That is an old pattern, calling a thing something that it is not. You have been healed of that affliction.

Place yourself in loving, nurturing environments, even when there is not a great deal of excitement going on. A word of caution: Do not go to these places looking for love—go to enjoy yourself. Go to places and do things for the sheer fun of it. Having fun is an excellent way to distribute your product. When you are in pursuit of fun, joy finds you. When you are not looking for ways to ward off loneliness, pleasant experiences occupy your mind. When you eliminate the essence of desperation that has been clogging your aura, you will find many pleasant and joyful activities with which you can occupy your time. Nurturing the soul, mind, or body, as well as enlivening the spirit, is an outgrowth of having fun. In the meantime, while growth, learning, and healing are taking place, be sure to place your product in a joy-filled, loving, supportive, and fun-filled market.

Promotion of the product includes packaging and advertising. Packaging is essential in the meantime. There is always the temptation, in the absence of a relationship or when there is trouble in the relationship, to overindulge in other things—

food, sweets, alcohol, and a host of sedentary endeavors. Beware! You can ruin your packaging in the meantime! Effective product promotion means keeping the product in good shape. Meditate. Exercise. Pray. Keep a journal of your thoughts. Each of these activities, done individually or in consistent combination, help to create and maintain a well-defined mind and body. Attend a class, join a community service organization, engage in volunteer work. These are great methods for advertising the product and promoting its availability in appropriate markets. It is also a great way to avoid meantime eating and other forms of self-pity.

Another critical aspect of promotion is knowing how you are going to reach those you wish to attract to your product. This is not so much the result of where you go as it is a response to who you are, how you feel, and what you are thinking. Clearing, releasing, and strengthening exercises do more than prevent package destruction. They also enhance package presentation. People know when you feel bad, when you are angry or frustrated. People have a sensory perception that will pick up your vibes of emotional distress. We humans really do have emotional radar. Besides that, people are bound to notice the pounds piling up, the frizzies in your hair, and the dark circles under your eyes. When they mention it to you, you become annoyed. They are, however, warning you that you are falling down on package promotion and advertising.

Sarah, the young woman who told me about the Four P's, did it all. She stopped looking for and fretting about not being in a relationship in order to do some work on herself. She moved from one city to another. She changed jobs. She bought a house. She joined a church, and she had only one goal in mind—to find and get herself in order. Yes, she wanted to be in a relationship. Yes, she dated in the meantime. Yes, she spent some days and nights being lonely, depressed, and questioning whether or not she had done the right thing. Wondering if she would ever get it together. What she did not do was stop working on herself, one thing at a time, one day at a time. She did not use Oreos as a replacement for sex. She did not call her ex trying to make herself, or him, believe that it could work. One day, all the work, all the tears finally paid off. A gentleman suitor sent her a note from the opposite end of the church pew. That's right! He passed the note down the line of twenty or more people. He gave his name and telephone number, asking her to call if she would like to go to dinner. She took two weeks to respond. She has not been disappointed yet.

The Four P's are an excellent way to elevate yourself from the first floor, where you don't know what's wrong, to the second floor, where you don't know what to do about what's wrong. They are a valuable tool that will help you work through all of the stuff that keeps you from getting from the second floor to the third floor. If you earnestly apply the Four P's to yourself and your life, all of the spiritual cleansers you have picked up along the way will be increased in their potency. You will learn to take even greater responsibility for yourself and the experiences you desire to have in your life. You will learn to surrender even more of the past so that you can live fully in the moment. These four principles are like an antibacterial cleanser that helps you to sift and sort through your stuff so quickly that your ascension to the third floor is a guarantee.

Using these tools in a meantime experience is like hiring a housekeeper, one who knows what to do and does it with overwhelmingly satisfying results.

Can I tell you a secret? We all have the same problem. We all believe that we are separate from each other. We also believe that we are separate from God. As long as we are in bodies we will have the belief that you're over there, and I'm over here. You've got your stuff over there, and this is my stuff over here. Because of our bodies, we cannot see the interaction of the soul. We are not aware of the commonality in Spirit. Our experiences have been varied and different. Life has unfolded in different ways for each of us because of our experiences. We may not have experienced the same exact things, but we have all heard the same things, said by different people, in different ways. We have all heard, *"It's me and you against the world,"* and *"It's us or them."* We have all heard, *"It doesn't have anything to do with me!"* These are the minor details that support the belief in separation.

Our souls, however, know the truth. Souls long to be joined, which is why we keep trying to get the relationship stuff right. In relationships, we are called by the higher forces to come together, to learn how to be one. By the time we reach the third floor of love's house, we will be ready to fulfill the urge in our souls, the urge to be one in love. By now, we are so clear about what to do and what not to do, we no longer have to think about it. That is an essential ingredient most of us miss. People always ask, "How will I know? How will I know when it's right? How will I know when I'm right?" If you have to ask, then you are not clear, and you cannot know. This is a lesson we learned down on the first floor! The best way to describe the blessing of mastering your stuff to the degree that you will know love when you see it is to say, *"The sheep always know the voice of the shepherd."*

As you get closer to the third floor, love will speak to you. It will whisper gently into your heart, reminding you of God's grandest vision of you and for you. Love will sing soft, melodic songs into your mind. The baseline lyric will ask, "How does the lover speak to the beloved?" The choral refrain will be, "I will find a way to honor us both. I will find a way to honor our identity and equality." When love is speaking or singing, you must be listening; otherwise you will not hear its gentle voice. Once you miss it, your thoughts will become preoccupied with the many things you think love is not and does not offer. Love wants you to know and hear its voice above the clamor of your own fearful thoughts about it. You must realize, however, that love will not argue with you. You must learn to listen, to recognize and trust its voice. In the meantime, while you are learning to listen, do not waste time being afraid, lonely, or doubtful.

Chapter 10
CLEANING OUT THE CLOSET

theirs had been a long-term relationship, thirty-two years to be exact. Those years, while sometimes testing and challenging, had been fairly good years. They had accomplished quite a bit together—a nice home, two children who were now grown and were doing reasonably well. They also had an up-and-coming business in which they shared equally. Jeri had gotten two advanced degrees. Willie kept threatening to go back to school but had never quite made it. Together they were like sightseers, cruising along in life, doing what they could do, the way they knew how, taking the ups, downs, and in-between times, the meantimes, in stride. Like any two people who had lived together so long, they knew each other fairly well, got on each other's nerves sometimes, and one was always there for the other in a pinch. Something happened, though. Sometime around the end of the thirty-second year, Jeri began to change.

People develop habits. They do certain things, in certain ways, not because that is the only way they can be done. Rather they act in certain ways because human beings are habitual.

Let's face it, we are easily trained, habitual creatures who become comfortable doing certain things in a particular way. If we want to be honest, we would have to admit that the way we do the things we do is more often than not an attempt to avoid pain, discomfort, and unfamiliarity, not necessarily in pursuit of doing things the best way or the right way—if there is such a thing. Taking this into consideration, we can honestly say that as human beings, we don't always do the right thing. We cut corners. We tell little fibs. We do what we think we must do to save ourselves. We react to many life situations in fear, with a fear response. This is normal and true for most human beings. It was normal and true for Jeri and Willie.

Jeri had been playing around with spirituality and spiritual issues for a long time. Willie watched from the sidelines. Whenever Jeri came up with some information or a practice that appeared to be helpful, Willie went along with it. When the outcome was favorable, Willie would be just a little more swayed, not convinced, just swayed. Jeri, on the other hand, was becoming more and more swayed to a spiritual way of living. We are not talking here just about meditation, prayer, or some kind of phase Jeri was passing through. We are talking about using the principles and concepts of spiritual law, which in effect will alter the way you view yourself and the way you view life. Jeri began to question life, its meaning, and her role in it. Jeri began searching for a purpose and how that purpose could be applicable to every single phase of living. Willie, still watching from the sidelines, was supportive, but skeptical. When, however, the changes became so profound as to affect the way they did things, Willie became concerned. More than concerned— Willie was afraid.

Jeri, who loved Willie dearly, talked openly about a new approach to life, pointing out that they had lived through a great deal of chaos, crisis, and drama as a result of their decisions and choices. While admitting that they had made out "okay," Jeri was convinced that it did not have to be that way. Life is a function of your desires, multiplied by your expectations, divided by your choices. Obviously something Jeri had read in a spiritual book, Willie thought. Jeri insisted it was the voice of inner guidance urging them to explore a new path. Jeri wanted to support Willie in moving through the fear to, as Jeri said, "a higher level of being and consciousness." Willie, who liked the old way, the old way of living and doing things, saw no need for change. They had come this far together, Willie reasoned. They weren't criminals. They had never hurt anyone, so why did things have to change? Jeri couldn't explain why. "They just do" became the usual response, and as Jeri used this response more and more, the real trouble started.

Jeri began to do everything in a new way, a way that was in no way familiar. In fact, the new way was so new, Jeri kept saying, "It has to come from within me." Jeri began to spend more time reading books on spiritual matters, going to classes, workshops, seminars, listening within, and following her *inner* guidance. Willie was always welcome to attend, but Jeri went alone when Willie refused. After about a year of this, Willie began to act up and act out, fighting Jeri about everything, at every turn of their lives. Jeri began moving slower, wanting to take a closer look at all decisions, examining all choices, refusing to give in to fear by looking for a new way to do the very things they had always done. Willie went berserk! This was life-threatening! When the life you have built is confronted with the possibilities of change, in effect it means the old life, the old way must die. Willie went into a high-gear fight for life!

MASTERING SOME MORE STUFF

This was not about love. There was no doubt, no question, that these people loved each other. This was not about infidelity, outside family members, or even just a difference in opinion. Those are the normal things people face in relationships. This was about a powerful shift in consciousness, how to make it happen, what you will be required to do in response to that shift, and how the people around you will respond to your shift. This was about identity, who you are, and how you behave in response to that knowledge. This was about self-love, self-realization, and self-actualization. As the United States Army puts it, this was about being all that you can be! This was about trying to find out who you are when someone else is telling you who you should be.

Jeri and Willie were facing some pretty pressing issues about themselves and their relationship. These are the same issues we must all face as we move from the second to the third floor of love's house. Whether or not you are in a relationship, if you are serious about growing spiritually, you must work through this stuff—birth stuff, learned stuff, the stuff you perceive to be holding you back, keeping you down. You will be forced to examine where you are limited in your thinking and your life, in order to determine whether the limitations in your life are real or fictional, and whether you choose to keep them. As you move through your stuff, making decisions and choices, you will be learning how to stand your own ground, on your own two feet. This will mean you must believe in yourself and in what you are doing. If you are in a relationship, this will not be about trusting your partner; it will be about learning to trust yourself. There's only one small challenge here for which you must be prepared. There is no guarantee that what you are doing will work for the relationship. You must face the fact that as you move forward, growing spiritually, shifting in your consciousness, there is no guarantee that your partner will be there on the other side, the other side of the way it is right now. Jeri understood that, and so did Willie.

If you ever want to test the strength of a relationship, drop a heavy money issue into the mix! Money brings out the worst in people. It activates their stuff to such a degree that the person with whom you have been living for most of your life can become unrecognizable! What people do with money, how they respond to money issues, what they will do for money, is more a function of their stuff than any other issue in life. Our notions about money are in direct correlation to our notions about self-worth and self-value. Life was ready to test Jeri and Willie and did so through a money matter. Under normal circumstances, the old way of doing things, Jeri and Willie would have sat together and come up with the most expedient means of moving through the situation with as little damage as possible. If that meant borrowing the money, they would have borrowed it. If that meant telling a little fib to buy themselves more time, they would have agreed on what fib to tell, and they would have told it. If getting out of the situation meant hiding, not answering the telephone, having other people tell fibs for them, they would have done that and more to save themselves from the perceived crisis.

In the midst of it all, the normal procedure would have been to run around like two chickens without heads, each one blaming the other, then feeling bad. They would have made promises to change, plans to change, which would have lasted only as long as the crisis. They would have called their friends, told them the long sad story, made excuses for themselves, and accepted whatever help was offered them. This also meant they would have gotten angry if help wasn't offered. In the end they would apologize to each other and keep moving ahead, with few changes being made. In the thirty-two years they had been together, they had developed an unconscious laundry list of what they would have done under normal circumstances to alleviate the pain of a financial crisis. These, however, were not normal circumstances.

Jeri had slowed almost to a halt, wanting to investigate the situation from every angle. Willie wanted to move ahead, attacking the problem by any means necessary. Jeri began to pray—before a telephone call was made, Jeri prayed; before a question was answered, Jeri prayed. Willie, in the meantime, was absolutely hysterical! It made absolutely no sense to stop thinking in order to pray! Willie said. No prayer could stop your world from falling apart, or the bill collectors from calling, or the repo man from taking your stuff back! Jeri had a good answer to Willie's objections. "Things are just a little out of sync. That does not mean you must lose yourself." Willie thought that was the most ridiculous thing anyone could say and told Jeri so in a few choice words. In response, Jeri prayed.

The more Jeri prayed, the worse things seemed to get. People were stopping by the business office with legal documents demanding this, that, or the other thing. Willie had retreated to the office, refusing to come out to speak to anyone. Jeri told everyone the same thing, "There is nothing we can do right now. Can we please get back to you in a few days?" Willie was too freaked out to even notice that everyone did just as Jeri asked—they went away without a fight. "What are you going to do in a few days?!!! What are you going to tell them when they come back?!!!" Jeri admitted that there was no answer available at the moment but felt pretty confident that when one was needed, it would be provided. "By whom?" Willie demanded. "By Spirit," Jeri responded. "I have surrendered my life, and this situation, to *Spirit*."

KNOW THAT YOU KNOW!

Let us do a quick review. In the basement, you did not know you had a problem. On the first floor, you knew you had a problem, and you learned the nature of the problem. On the second floor, you knew the nature of the problem, but you did not know what to do about it. On the second floor, you learned what to do about the problem. Now, in order to be elevated to the third floor, you must learn how to do what you know. How do you learn to be responsible? That was the first-floor lesson. You take responsibility for yourself by telling the absolute truth. Once you tell the truth, what do you do? You surrender. You stop fighting, stop trying to figure it out. Stop acting like you don't feel what you feel. It's called detachment. You detach from the outcome, allow yourself to feel what you feel, and figure out an appropriate way to express what you feel. In order to express your feelings, you must be clear. You must have a vision you can articulate. You must also have expectations, not of others but for yourself. You must always expect that you will survive. You must know you will make it through whatever the situation is that confronts you at the time. Jeri had learned these things on the journey through love's house. When you are armed with this theoretical data, life will present you with situations, experiences, in which you can practice what you have learned.

Practice what you know! This is the major challenge, the empowering challenge of moving from the second to the third floor in love's house. Here's the theory. When you *know* a thing you do it. When you *know of* a thing, you try to figure it out. To know a thing means you must have practice in doing it. You have firsthand knowledge of putting what you know into practice and getting the desired results. When you know of a thing, which is the same thing as knowing about it, that means you have intellectual knowledge. You've been reading about it, hearing about it, all that you know is locked in place in your mind. You do not, however, have the experience of putting what you know into practice. You are, excuse the term, an armchair spiritualist! You can talk the talk but have never actually walked the walk! In our relationships, as with all other aspects of life, this is what drives us crazy! We know what we should do, but when the time comes, when the meantime is upon us, we cannot seem to practice what we know. We know we should always be loving and supportive to our partner in a relationship. However, when we are afraid, when it seems as if things or people are out of control, doing things that we do not understand, it is hard to be supportive. It is hard to practice all the theory we have studied.

Jeri was putting the theory into practice in the midst of a financial crisis. She was practicing how to be true to herself. She was honoring what she felt and what she knew. She was not being insensitive to Willie; she was simply not allowing Willie to sway her from her own truth. She was not trying to force Willie to see things the way she saw them. Whatever Willie chose to do was fine. Jeri kept moving along the course that she had chosen for herself. That is a very hard thing to do—particularly after thirty-two years of doing things in a certain way. Jeri was just as frightened, just as unsure as Willie. The difference was that Jeri had made a commitment to change within and change without. She was also willing to give up the relationship in order to make the change. Willie, on the other hand, was holding on for dear life to what was—what was familiar, comfortable, expedient, and not always the best or the right thing to do.

Willie began to sabotage Jeri's actions. I mean, consciously sabotage things by making commitments Jeri would have to keep. By saying things to people that Jeri would then have to clean up. Of course, this put a terrible strain on their relationship. It was a battle of wills, a tug of war. Willie did not want to change. It was too frightening, too new, too unfamiliar. Perhaps things had not always gone well, but they had always managed to struggle along and get by. Even Willie had to admit that perhaps there was a better way, an easier way for them to live, but it meant work—hard, frightening work. Besides that, who is to say that things would get any better? They had no proof, only theory, spiritual theory. Willie was well aware that this theory was causing pieces and parts of Jeri to disappear. Jeri was becoming distant, less willing to listen to reason, Willie's reason for keeping things the same. Jeri wasn't even willing to fight or argue any more. She would make a statement, ask for support, and no matter what Willie said, Jeri would smile, pray, and keep on moving. It was all a bit much. There had to be a showdown. A final showdown. If Jeri would not at least take Willie's point of view into consideration, the end was inevitable.

THINK ABOUT IT, IT'S DONE!

Be careful of what you ask for! More important, be careful what you think! If you even think that you need to change, the forces of the universe will hear your request and put the wheels of change into motion. Before Willie could say a word, Jeri handed Willie a letter. Thinking it had something to do with the financial problem, Willie opened and read the letter. It said:

Dear Willie:

I write this letter to thank you for all that you have been to me. I thank you for all that you have been in my life and for the many ways you have served and supported me. We have had many great times together, and while our relationship was loving and healthy at one time, I find that it no longer serves me, what I desire, or the purpose which I believe God intends for my life. I find that we now have an unholy relationship which I no longer choose to continue. I now, therefore, release you from any conscious and unconscious agreements we have made in the past to continue our relationship. I now forgive you totally and unconditionally for any acts committed by you which have had an unloving, unsupportive, or unhealthy impact on my life. I now ask for and claim your forgiveness for any of these roles I have played in your life. You are now free to pursue your higher and greater good. I am now free to pursue my higher and greater good. I wish for you love, light, peace, and an abundance of every good thing in God's kingdom. I release you. I surrender your energy from my being, and I ask that any remnants of you be transformed into productive and useful energy according to God's perfect plan for my life. I thank you. I love you. Jeri.

Once Willie read the letter, Jeri took an old picture of herself, put it in a shoebox, and took it outside to the backyard of her house, where she said a short prayer before burying the box. You see, Willie and Jeri were the same person. Wilhelmina Jermaine Johnson, almost thirty-three years of age, was on a path of self-discovery. She was on the path to self-love. She realized that the old her and the new her, the person she once was and the person she wanted to be, both existed in the same body. The old her, the frightened her, had been programmed to do things in a particular way. It did not matter how outlandish or nonproductive those things turned out to be, Willie kept doing the same thing over and over. She kept attracting the same kinds of relationships, unsatisfying and noncommittal. She kept attracting the same kinds of crises and chaos in her life. Whenever the new her, the conscious her, tried to make a change, the old her would sabotage her efforts by reverting to the old ways of doing things, the old ways of thinking about things.

Willie was Wilhelmina, the frightened little girl who grew up in a dysfunctional home where love looked confusing, and proved to be very painful. Jeri was Jermaine, the brilliant young woman who was willing to break old patterns, family patterns, in order to love and honor herself. Like most of us, she was having an intense battle with herself—wanting to change, not knowing how. Needing to do things in a different way, afraid they would not work. Expecting more from herself, wanting more for herself, realizing her old ways did not get her what she wanted, all the while afraid that she could not handle a new way. Needing the approval and support of the people she loved while realizing they were comfortable with the older her and afraid of the new her. There came for Jeri, as there comes for all of us, the moment in time when we have to decide to stay or go, to stay the same or risk becoming someone new. It is a soul-altering experience, through which the only thing you can depend on is love. God's love.

Jeri decided to change. She changed her name, indicating that a shift in her consciousness had taken place. She was going for love, realizing it meant giving up everything she knew, everything with which she was familiar, even her name. These were her patterns, her unconscious responses to life. You must know your patterns and be able to recognize when you are actively participating in them before you can hope to change them. Jeri recognized her patterns in relationships, when she attracted men, where she attracted them, how she was feeling when they showed up, and most important, what she was willing to do to keep them. She realized that what she was doing had not made her happy. She became conscious of her patterns with money: how she used money, what she thought about money, how she felt when she had money, how not having money readily available, influenced her feelings about herself. Why love and money? Because they are both ruled by the same planetary vibration. Love and money are both influenced by the same universal law, the law of cause and effect, which says that what you put in is the cause, what you get out is the effect. When you give love, you get love, and what you think about yourself, the cause, manifests as your bank balance, the effect!

Jeri wanted a loving, committed marriage into which she

wanted to bring and raise children, her own children. She wanted a loving, spiritual partner who was willing to grow. She also realized that until she could *be* the love that she wanted, she would never receive it. Jeri had been through the "what love is not" process so many times that she was an expert. One day in the midst of a very broken heart, a very difficult meantime, she realized that there was one key and consistent element in all of her relationships. It showed up no matter what she was doing or who she was doing it with. Jeri was the element.

That element is you. You are the key ingredient of every relationship in your life. Now here comes the hard part, the part we always have difficulty accepting. What we struggle with in our relationships, particularly our love relationships, reflects —very clearly, I might add—our own inner conflict. The why and who in your home, family, and job is always the same. Unfortunately, we do not often realize that the issues we confront in life are ours. We do not realize it because we are looking out rather than within.

STARTING ALL OVER!

It is all rooted in the misunderstanding of and the belief in a lack of love. The issues and challenges we face in life, and particularly in our relationships, are created from our misunderstanding of the purpose of love, from a lack of love for ourselves, which ultimately determines how intensely we suppress parts of ourselves. The frightened part. The part we believe is unworthy. The part that has been rejected, abandoned, abused in the past. The energy that we suppress—in the form of thoughts, feelings, and beliefs—comes back at us with great force through people and experiences. We can mask ourselves and dress our issues up in any way we choose, but they will keep pounding at the door asking, "What is it going to take for you to deal with this? What is it going to take to get you to deal with this part of me?"

I have personally been involved in relationships with people who had never hurt a fly, yet their lives were in a constant state of disruption and chaos. As a matter of fact, I have been one of those people! I was one of the people who always said, "I never have good luck with relationships." I thought all the good people were married or dead! I have been picked on, shunned, dishonored, and abused for what seemed to me to be no good reason. I thought the who and what of my dilemmas were pretty clear. They were mean. They were crazy. They had a problem with me for some unknown reason. I made myself content to just muddle along, deflecting the blows, smiling in the face of it all. Until one day, a friend said to me, "There's nothing in your world, your experience, except you and God. If it is not God acting up, it is you!"

Jeri realized that she had been acting up again. Being neurotic again. She realized that she didn't feel good about herself or her life. She realized that she didn't feel good about the way she acted in relationships. She had made her love partners responsible for providing her with all of the things she had not done for or given to herself. She had spent far too much time setting conditions about what love should look like when in fact she had to admit that she really did not know. Jeri had no idea of what pure, divine, unconditional love would look like or feel like because she had not given it to herself. Now she was ready. She was ready to see things differently and receive things differently. She had learned from her experiences and was now ready to apply what she had learned. In order to do that, she had to bury Willie. Once that was done, Jeri entered the meantime. It was a meantime that lasted three and a half years.

When you start talking about killing off pieces and parts of your consciousness, you are entertaining radical change. This is not for the faint of heart. It takes more than commitment, more than dedication. It takes absolute and total self-trust. There will be no guidelines for you to follow. There may be help or support from those who have walked the path before you, but they have not walked in your shoes. They may not know the intricate little details of your modus operandi. They don't know the depths of your pain, confusion, or desire. Only you know, which is why you must stand by you throughout the entire process. And only you know whether you can be trusted. The old you is going to pop up in your brain and say, "Oh, no! Not again! Are we going through another one of those phases again?!!! Why bother? What's the point?" You will be tempted, I mean really tempted, to turn back to your old ways of thinking and feeling. You must trust yourself enough to hold your own hand throughout the entire process, no matter what happens.

Jeri was so absolutely committed, it was unbelievable. She went on an all-out campaign to find herself, love herself, and attract her divine mate. She was doing very, very well. Breaking down old pattens. Trying new things. Responding to her life in a very different way. Then came the test. It was a two-legged test. You see, she knew of self-love. The time came, however, when she had to test her knowledge of self-love. She met her test one hot day in Washington, D.C. She was walking down the street, minding her own business, thinking loving thoughts, and all the rest. She passed the test and admired, to herself, his wonderful face and physical composition. She had strolled about ten feet past the test when it called out to her. "Hello. What's your name?" Jeri responded by not calling herself Wilhelmina. He smiled and shook his head, saying, "I am so glad to meet you, because you are my wife." Jeri was shocked! She was elated! This was a very direct approach. Interesting, to say the least. Jeri was very curious.

He had it all! The looks, the personality, the philosophy, the line, the body to die for—scratch that, to live for. He had it all! They started talking, going for walks, eating out; they were doing it all—except sex. Jeri was real tempted, and he was very eager, but Jeri was very clear about what she was doing and what she wanted. No sex! Nada! Zippo! Now what do you think this man asked of Jeri at least 53 zillion times in the first three months of their meeting? You've got it! Sex. He wasn't pushy, but he was very persistent. "Come spend the night with me. Let me take you away for the weekend. Can I come spend the night with you? Is something wrong with me? Is something wrong with you? How do you expect me to marry you if I don't know you like that, intimately?" It got very hot, very heavy, but Jeri, bless her heart, wasn't giving up anything but the time!

When you start working on yourself, your spiritual self, you are going to attract a corresponding energy. Not the same energy, but a corresponding energy. The spiritual person is going to attract a nonspiritual person. The person who thinks that spirituality is a bunch of hogwash. The person on a diet is going to attract the mate who likes large people. They will tell you how good you look, how they love to eat the meat off from the bones! You are on a quest to build your spiritual muscles, and what builds muscles is resistance. The thing to remember is not to get caught up in the other person's program. Stand your ground! Stay your course! Accept and embrace the other person, but remember what you are doing. Pray while they are watching television. Let them take you out to dinner, but have a salad. The fact that this person is not walking the path you are walking does not mean you two cannot be togther. It is learning to work through the resistance that will build your muscles.

THE ENEMY IS IN ME!

While she was building her physical resistance, she was fighting a mental temptation. Willie was screaming in her head, "Give him some! Give him some! Show him how much you like him!" Jeri bent, but she did not break. Willie changed tactics, *"This is the first nice guy you've met in a long time. See, he's willing to wait. He's offering to take you on a trip. He's buying all the food. Don't you want to try it out?"* NO! Jeri thought to herself. As a matter of fact, just stop it. Shut your mouth, and stop it right now! Sometimes you've just got to talk to yourself! You must talk yourself through the fear and the weakness. You have to remind yourself of the vision and the goal. You must work through the resistance of the old you. You have to keep your expectations of yourself and for yourself in mind. You must stand vigilant watch for the resurgence of the patterns, the patterns of the past that failed to yield the results that you desired.

Let us be very clear: We are not talking about punishing yourself or the other person. We are talking about taking your time, staying in touch with your body, feeling what you feel, and appropriately expressing what you feel. You cannot do that if you move too fast. Step by step by step is the best way to move through any process. There's one thing you can always do that will give you the opportunity to get clear about what's happening with you and another person, and that is to slow down. Time reveals all things, and you really do have as much time as you need to be sure. Not *think* that you are sure, but *feel* that you are sure. Your body will never lie to you unless you are moving too fast. When you slow down and feel what you feel, you stand a greater chance of not falling into the trap of your patterns.

We do not like to move slowly. We live in a world of instant everything, and we want instant love. We get damaged and bruised in relationships because we move too fast. You meet the person, and within two weeks you are having sex, they have a key to your house, you lend them your car, they've got your PIN number, and before you know if this person has a middle name, your heart is broken. Even when bells and whistles are going off in our heads, we keep moving. You don't know if these bells and whistles are a response to old patterns, old suspicions, old neuroses, or if they are genuine warning signs. Always listen to the bells and whistles, for they are your internal protective devices! It's called intuition. In order to hear them, you must take the time to identify what you feel. If you identify that the bells are old suspicions coming up, then you need to work through them. You need to work on trust. You need to take a little step and then another little step until you feel peaceful again. If you identify that this is part of your neurosis, you can work on the neurosis.

What am I thinking here? What am I doing? What is it that I want? Take time to get some answers before you proceed. Make sure you feel that what you are doing will get you what you want. The worst thing that can happen when you take your time is that you discover that this person really is a lowlife who slinks around in the swamp mud. Time, however, has given you the opportunity to back up before getting emotionally battered or bruised.

Mind you, you will not be in such situations alone. Relationships are about two people, so chances are that your test, or your true love, is going to show up with two legs, two feet, and a name. If you find that the other person is moving too fast, you simply say, *"There are some bells and whistles going off in my head that have absolutely nothing to do with you. I have to move slowly. I have to honor what I'm feeling so that I can be sure I'm doing what is right for me."* Do not put your stuff on the other person. Set your own agenda, and accept responsibility for yourself. If this person is not a truly loving teacher who has come into your life to help you heal, laying the truth on them like that will make them disappear. They will be gone so fast you will think it was all a dream. If that happens, you can say, "Oh well, here's another one that didn't work." You can also say, "Thank you, God! I know you will send me the appropriate teacher and a relationship that will help me work on myself." In order to do that work, you must be willing to move slowly and throw back some of the sharks who get caught on your hook. Jeri was willing. She told him about the bells and whistles. He laughed.

PAY ATTENTION TO THE SIGNS!

Laughing is not quite the same thing as disappearing, but some tests can be confusing. Jeri kept moving forward—slowly. They continued seeing each other, and one day she went a little too far. She let him kiss her. That's right, four and half months without so much as a kiss! The girl was doing some serious healing work, and he seemed to be a cooperative doctor. They were sitting in the car when suddenly, but gently, he reached over, took her in his arms, and planted a big, long, hot kiss on her lips. The moment their lips met, her brain flatlined! There was no sign of life in her body. Her breath was gone. Her name was gone. Mind you, this was after thirty-nine months of not being kissed! In the process of the kiss, bells and whistles were going off in her head. Warning! Danger! Shift into reverse! Get out now! Those were the bells and whistles going off in her brain. It was only by the grace of God that she did not slither away and head out the window because opening the door would take too much time. She knew in a place deep in her soul that she was headed for deep trouble.

As quickly as he kissed her, Jeri said, "No! I'm not going there yet." He laughed at her again, but he also started the car. The minute she said that, she realized that she had kept the covenant with herself. He didn't *feel* right, and she was trusting her intuition. It was a risk, a big risk, but Jeri was willing. Do you know what happened? Every ugliness that could exist in a human being started to manifest in this man. He had every nasty attitude and habit a human being could possibly possess! How he was allowed to take oxygen from the atmosphere was a mystery to Jeri. The rest of the relationship lasted three weeks. He was just that horrible. And you know what else? When Jeri said to herself, not to him, but to herself, "I'm outta here!" he disappeared. He stopped calling, and she never heard from him again.

When it was all said and done, Jeri had broken another

pattern. She had stopped allowing the fear of being alone to run her life. She did not talk to her girlfriends, she did not moan and groan at night, she did not go out and buy the biggest, richest chocolate cake she could find. Instead she worked with herself. She let herself feel sad, but she felt good about what she had done. She did not blame him. She didn't even talk about him. She reflected, retraced her steps, and was very, very grateful. She realized that had she not given in to the kiss, it might have taken longer for the ugliness to manifest. She also realized that if she had gone further than the kiss, she might have been in too deep to get out. Jeri kept working on her neuroses— the feelings of inadequacy, the neediness, the self-criticism, the self-judgment. She worked on her career. She finally came to the conclusion that by taking her time, staying in her body, and honoring her feelings she could not lose! If you work the process and the principles, you cannot lose, and you feel a lot better off in the end.

IF YOU WANT TO KNOW THE END, LOOK AT THE BEGINNING!

It is such a shame that we do not start out in life with the consciousness, "I am whole. I am complete. I am perfect." We are all of this and more. Unfortunately, however, we do not remember all that we are once we are born. The memory lapse turns into myriad insecurities: fear of abandonment, fear of rejection, fear that we are not enough. An insecurity is an unremembered piece of information. That's all it is. When the insecurity is fear, it is actually the fear that you have forgotten something very important. When the insecurity is a suspicion, you suspect that you will make the same poor choice or bad decision you made in the past. Since we have forgotten the truth, we believe that we are messed up in some way or in many ways. This, more than anything else, is what we take into relationships. In relationships, we call to mind everything we think is wrong with us to support the belief that we are not lovable. We call forth the people, the situations, the experiences that are meant to help us remember. Unfortunately, what we do is get mad at them and miss the healing possibilities.

The things that are hidden in the closets of your mind and heart will keep showing up in your life, because love wants to heal you. It will show up in your loving relationships or any time you invoke the power or presence of love. You may call them tests, but they are actually the things in your conscious-ness that require healing. These are the things that keep you from the fullest experience of love. Why do we make the same mistakes over and over in our relationships? Because we keep responding to the people trying to help us remember that we are whole, healthy, and perfect. They are the answer to our cry to remember all there is to know about love. The moment you begin to remember, new people and new situations show up, providing you with an opportunity to demonstrate that you are doing much better, that you are remembering a little more. This is why it is so important that we do not become angry with or resentful of the people who come to play in our healing dramas. God does not always send you what you think you want. God will send you what you need in order to heal. It's going to come up at different levels, with different characters, and each time it is going to evoke a different feeling. Your task is to remember the truth.

We go into a relationship in search of somebody who wants the same things we want. We want somebody who likes the same things we like. We want somebody who is going in the same direction we are going. Someplace in the back of our minds, we believe if there is someone else out there like me, that means I can't be all that bad. Without realizing it, we go out looking for ourselves, believing that if we can find ourselves we will be happy. The thing is, we don't always like who we are because we have forgotten the truth. We think we need to be fixed—not healed, but fixed. There is a big difference. Consequently, when we see ourselves in other people, in our partners, in our family members, in our friends, we get busy fixing them rather than healing ourselves. There is also the issue of balance. Love wants us to heal our concept of balance and wholeness.

The universal principle of polarity that explains the concept of balance states that everything is dual. Everything has poles. Everything has its pair of complementary opposites. Like and unlike are identical in nature, different in degree. Extremes meet. Balance is having two different things on opposite sides of the scale that look different and act different, but are in fact extremes of the same thing. The extremes are necessary for wholeness. For example, if you are always on time, you will most probably attract somebody who doesn't own a watch, who can never get anywhere on time. We are talking here about a person who cannot pee on time! That's balance. If you look at the universal laws, what you have is light and dark, up and down, good and bad, male and female. They are all complementary. They all lend to wholeness and completion.

If you have somebody on one end of the scale who wants to make love three times a day, and somebody on the other end of the scale who wants to make love three times a day, these two people could kill themselves! They would never get anything done. Balance requires that a person on one side of the scale is going to be the person who loves sex, wants it three times a day, and on the opposite end of the scale will be somebody who thinks that sex is horrifying and that you should use it only for the purpose of procreation. The lesson here is acceptance, tolerance, and harmony. Don't believe that because you like sex or don't like sex there is something wrong with you. Clean out your closet of inadequacy and fear. Learn to work together. That is what love is about. Do not attempt to create a carbon copy of yourself. That is not balance.

We keep looking for sameness when healing requires tolerance, acceptance, and unconditional love of complementary difference. If the on-time person marries a person who is always late, they get an opportunity to teach and heal each other. The on-time person gets an opportunity to teach, *"Hey, you gotta be responsible! You gotta be accountable! You have to be honorable and respectful of other people's time!"* The person who is always late teaches, *"Look, you've gotta be loose because life is too short! Don't make yourself crazy! You'll get there when you get there!"* The two of them working together can come up with some reasonable facsimile of, *"We are gonna make an effort to get there on time, but if we don't we're not gonna kill each other! I'm not gonna beat you up! You're not gonna be angry! I'm not gonna stop speaking to you! You're not gonna sell my firstborn!"* Both sides teaching, both sides learning create the healing and balance required for unconditional love. Sameness does not heal. It allows us to hide the things we think and feel about ourselves in the closet.

Somewhere between the second and third floors in love's

house, you must learn to love people no matter what they do. Stop banging your head on the table and screaming that you can't do it. You can do it! You must do it! You must learn to accept and forgive people in order to heal yourself. This is a big, big, big step. It requires a willingness to see people as God sees them—as innocent little children trying to find their way home. It means that you must look at what you do, not what's been done to you. It means examining what makes you respond to people and situations the way you do—that is, what you feel and why you feel it. With that information you realize that every experience, and the outcome of every experience, was simply an opportunity to re-create the way you respond. This revelation is your healing. This revelation will begin the burial ceremony of the old you.

With the old you gone and the new you emerging, when you find yourself in a situation similar to one you faced in the past, you can create a new response. That's what Jeri did. She created a self-loving response because she realized that no matter how ugly people act, they were acting out her stuff. People will do the same for you in an attempt to help you clean it up and clear it out of the closet. You must love them for that. Love those who come to wallow in your stuff with you. As you are loving them, you can forgive you. Forgive you for making it so difficult on yourself. Forgive you for having such bad feelings about the people who have been trying to help you. Forgive you for asking and allowing other people to help you hurt yourself. This is the ultimate demonstration of responsibility and just about all you will need to propel you up to the third floor. P.S.: Jeri married a minister. They now have two children and are living on the third floor.

THE THIRD FLOOR

you did not have to do it all at once, you know! You did not have to empty all the drawers and the closets; put all of the blinds in the tub; turn the refrigerator off so that it would defrost, leaving puddles of water everywhere; dump all of the dirty clothes into the middle of the floor; set off a roach bomb! You didn't have to make it so hard on yourself, but you did. Not only did you do it, you did it! You made it! You have cleaned up the entire house. Done the laundry. Evacuated all of the dust bunnies. Hung up the freshly washed curtains. Put all of the clothes away and thrown away about twenty bags of trash. Congratulations! You should be very proud of yourself! But before you sit down to rest, let us take one more run through, just to make sure everything is in place.

Chapter 11
PULL UP THE SHADES
AND LET SOME SUN IN

they had been sweethearts since they were teenagers. They grew up together. Karen and Stan probably should have stayed just friends, but once you put sex in a relationship, it just takes off in another direction. Karen was like a daughter to his family, and Stan was like a son to her family. Although the two families never met, they knew all about each other. They were all involved with one another. As Karen and Stan's relationship grew, the family entanglements grew. After high school Karen went off to college. Stan went off to work. When Karen's family moved across the country, Stan moved with them. When Karen came home from college, Stan was there waiting for her—living in her mother's house. It didn't seem unusual that they were living together in her mother's home because everybody thought that any day now they would be getting married.

Not too long after her return from college, Karen became pregnant with their first child. It was then that Karen told her mother, "I will never marry Stan because I'm not in love with him. I love him, but I'm not *in* love with him. I know he's a good person, but he just isn't motivated. He makes promises that he does not keep. He thinks that everyone has a problem except him. He is so talented and gifted, but he refuses to apply himself. I thought it would be different when I came back from school, but it isn't." Mother was hysterical! Living with a man to whom you are not married, having the child of a man with whom you are not in love was more than an old-fashioned mother could handle. She tried to handle it by asking, *"If he's not good enough to marry, how can he be good enough to father your children?!"* Karen never answered that question. She couldn't answer it. It made too much sense.

The child was born, a lovely little girl for whom Karen did everything. She took care of the baby, she paid the bills, she did it all. She never asked for Stan's help, and he never offered it. Now, don't get me wrong; he adored his daughter. He would do anything in the world for her. The thing is, if you wanted Stan to do something you had to ask. Once you asked, he usually did it. If you did not ask, he would not move. The man had no get up and go. Right around the time their daughter turned two, Karen decided that she didn't want to be in the relationship anymore. She wasn't exactly tired of Stan, she was just plain old tired! Besides that, it increasingly seemed to Karen as if she was in the relationship alone anyway. Stan always promised he was going to get a better job, but he didn't. He always talked about the things he wanted to do to build a better life for himself. He never did any of it.

What he did do was complain about people and how he never got a decent break. He talked about wanting to be a better father, but he rarely volunteered to do what was required. Most of all, Stan was very temperamental. Actually moody is a much better description. From one day to the next, Karen didn't know what to say, how to act, or what to think; she didn't want to hurt Stan's feelings or set him off on a not-speaking tirade that would last for days. Karen and Stan lived together more like brother and sister raising their younger sister than like husband and wife raising their daughter. Perhaps that's because they weren't married. Perhaps it was because although both were present, they were both absent from the relationship.

SAY WHAT YOU MEAN TO SAY!

Karen thought that she had made it real clear to Stan that she was through and ready to move on. Stan was very clear that he wanted the relationship and wanted to do everything in his power to keep it—like all the other times he said he was going to do something. All Karen could think was, "Yeah, right!" Suddenly, there was a burst of light! Much to Karen's surprise and pleasure, Stan began to help a little more around the house. He was helping a little more with the baby. He was doing all of the things that he thought would please her. In a moment of weakness—yes, you do still get weak on the third floor—Karen broke down, saying she would try it again. It lasted three weeks, culminating with Karen's announcement that she and the baby were moving out of her mother's house. "What about me?" Stan asked. "What about you?" Karen replied. As gently and lovingly as possible, Karen let Stan know that what he did from that point on was none of her business and none of her concern. Needless to say, Stan was not too pleased about the announcement or the situation. Did he tell Karen what he was feeling? No. Did he ask how they were going to manage child care, visitations, and so forth? No. What Stan did was lose his job! He got himself fired for mouthing off to a supervisor.

Now their problem became another family problem—he had no money. He couldn't move. They were living in her mother's house. She was getting ready to move, and her mother was getting ready to lose her mind! But, like a good mother, she kept her mouth shut! Karen was ready to move out on her own, but how could she leave Stan behind in her mother's house? If nothing else, Stan was her friend, and friends always help each other out. Karen told Stan he could come with her just until he got himself together, got a new job, and was on his feet. Stan told her he didn't want to be a burden. Karen felt torn about being responsible for Stan. Karen wanted to move and start a new life. Stan didn't seem very interested in making a move in that direction. As a result, Karen tried to move around him. She began saving money and house hunting. She put a deposit down on one place, but then changed her mind about it. All the while, Stan sat there, which made her feel guilty. In fact, it made Karen feel so guilty that she took Stan with her without any further discussion of their plans or their relationship.

When you do not allow people to be responsible for themselves, they will not assume the responsibility. If you do for them what they should do for themselves, trust me, they will let you do it. If you make a decision and do not follow through on it, what you have decided to do will not get done. If you do not honor yourself, others will not honor you. If you do not honor other people, their choices and decisions, you will have a pretty difficult time honoring yourself. Assuming responsibility for others, not following through on decisions, not honoring yourself, not presenting yourself in a way in which others can or will honor you, leads to emotional paralysis—you know what to do, but you don't know how to do it. This is what you have come to the third floor to learn and practice.

You have worked very hard to get where you are, and you have done an excellent job. You are probably tired, very tired. This is to be expected. However, if you remember your second-floor lessons, you know that in order to have come this far, you must be a good student. Therefore, you must know that the good students always get the hardest tests. On this floor of love's house, your assignment is to practice what you know, to do what you know how to do, all of the time, in every situation, under all circumstances. You are working toward mastery. You have mastered the knowledge, now you must master the practice of that knowledge. You must put all of the cleansers in the pot, your mind, and allow them to be the guiding force of your life. Yes, you have done most of this work on the lower floors before. Now, however, you will do it on a different level, from a higher state of consciousness. You will do it from a consciousness of love—self-love and unconditional love.

YOU'VE GOT WHAT IT TAKES!

Living on the third floor will be a cakewalk because you've got all the information you could possibly need to move yourself through almost any situation. You know that love heals anything and while you are here on the third floor, your work will consist of mastering how to apply love to every situation—first self-love and then unconditional love for everyone involved. If for any reason at any time you fail to apply love, you will find yourself emotionally paralyzed. You will not be able to move forward. You will not be able to make a decision, or you will not be able to follow up on the decisions that you make. Why? Because you can't fool love anymore! When you really love yourself and love other people, you honor your word.

Being on the third floor does not mean that you will no longer have the natural, normal, emotional responses to life and its often nerve-wracking situations. What it means is that you will quickly recover from an emotional upheaval because you will apply love to the situation. What would love do here? That is the third-floor mantra, the prayer you will recite in the face of any adversity. Being able to apply love to a situation does not mean that you are a wimp, a wuss, or a pushover. It simply means that you do everything from a consciousness of love rather than fear or anger or confusion. If you would reflect for a moment on your housekeeping tasks, you know that the last task, the final task before the house is spic and span, is often the most difficult task to complete. You have done so much for so long, you simply want to rest. You also know that if you don't do it now, not only will the job not get done, you will only have to do it tomorrow, when you could feel worse than you feel right now. So gather all of your strength and tackle this last little detail, bringing in the light.

LET THERE BE LIGHT!

Light is knowledge. Where there is no knowledge, there is darkness. Light is the presence of day, where things can be seen and appreciated. Light is the power of God, the presence of life that is sustaining and nurturing. As you learn how to practice all of the things you have learned on the lower floors, you bring light to those who have not yet begun the journey or those who are only part of the way through. As you apply the principles to your life and it begins in take off in a new direction, you bring a light of hope to those who are watching you. When, however, you allow old habits, old thoughts, old fears to hang around and guide your actions, you, in effect, dance with the darkness! You don't want to do that. Dancing with the darkness can get you booted back down to the first or second floor. You don't want to be there! You want to be right where you are. If this is the case, then you must, with all due diligence, practice what you know and not allow yourself to be paralyzed by your old ways of doing things.

To say something and not back it up with action means you are, for one reason or another, paralyzed. Perhaps you have not told the absolute truth. Or maybe you are not clear and you have lost sight of your vision. That is what happened to Karen. She did not tell Stan the truth about what she was feeling for fear of upsetting him. She assumed responsibility for him and his life without telling the absolute truth—that she had outgrown the relationship. Karen had done her work and moved through love's house. She had rightfully made it through the third floor but was involved in a relationship with someone who was living in the basement, blaming other people for his situation, believing everyone else was the problem. Can a person who lives on an upper floor have a successful relationship with someone who lives on a lower floor, someone who has not done all of their work? Absolutely—sometimes!

REACH OUT AND TOUCH—BUT DON'T FALL!

The key in a relationship between two people who are living on different floors will be in your ability to stay centered. Will you be able to stay your course without getting caught up in your partner's stuff? If love is truly present, it will help you find a common space, some common ground on which you can stand. The tricky part for you may be in not trying to convince the other person that they must do what you are doing. The tricky part for them is not to feel threatened by what you are doing. Love will help you bring the situation into balance. The resistance will help you build your spiritual muscles. However, you must be on guard not to allow difference to descend into conflict. Karen, unfortunately, got caught up. Paralysis was the result.

It is not loving to ask people to do what they cannot do. You know what a person can do by watching what he or she does. Some people will ask for help. They will readily admit that they do not know what to do and would like some help in trying to figure it out. This is a second-floor person. This is a person who is at least showing some interest in getting it together. Whether they actually do so is another story. Basement lesson: willingness. There are those situations in which you need only be willing. If you are, life and the universe will give you the push that you need. Stan did not ask for help or support, a clear indication that he was not willing. Perhaps, like most basement dwellers, he was not even aware that he needed help. The most loving thing Karen could have done was stay in constant communication with Stan, letting him in on the what, why, and when of her true feelings to the best of her ability. She needed to acknowledge what she was feeling and express that to him. This would have kept her clear. This would have forestalled the paralysis. This would have invoked the power and presence of love. When you are living on the third floor of love's house, learning how to practice what you know, you must call on the power and the presence of love at every moment. If you do not, you will find yourself back on the steps between the second and third floors, working your way through some more of your stuff. That is exactly what happened to Karen, and it almost happened to Faye.

YOU ARE FREE TO BELIEVE
WHAT YOU CHOOSE TO BELIEVE!

Tim was a doctor. Faye was a nurse. That's how they met. She was a dedicated, very competent nurse, and he was a rising surgical star. Tim liked the way Faye worked. She was focused. She was thorough. They worked well together, he thought, and he would always request that she be assigned to work when he was in the surgical suite. One day, after almost a year of working together, he asked her out to dinner. It was wonderful, so they did it again and again. Tim always teased her about being so quiet. He liked it, however, because Tim was a great talker. What Tim didn't know was that Faye's silence was a learned behavior. She had grown up in a family where her father totally dominated her mother, even physically sometimes. Tim did not realize that what you see you become. He didn't know it, and Faye would not dare talk about it.

Faye had watched her mother go through years of mental, emotional, and sometimes physical abuse. Faye's father worked in a lumberyard, watched the baseball games, and drank beer. To Faye's father, everything had to be just right. He demanded that things be a certain way. Unfortunately, he forgot to tell her mother what that way was, and she was too afraid to ask. In many ways, Faye felt like that about Tim. That everything had to be just so, just right. To Faye's credit, she had more or less figured out what that was to Tim's satisfaction. Still, she felt that he had commanding power over her, power about which she could not speak and did not know what to do. So when he asked her to marry him, or when he told her she was gonna marry him, she obeyed.

By the time they came back from their honeymoon Faye had begun to ask herself if she had done the right thing. All her friends said she had done the right thing. Her mother said she had. His mother said she had. Such a quiet little thing, married to a surgical genius! How could she be wrong! They had a big, beautiful wedding because Tim and his family paid for everything. How could this be wrong? But there was this feeling in her gut, there were bells ringing ever so slightly in her mind. At first Faye resisted, but when she found herself shutting down, she allowed herself to examine what she was feeling. The feeling became clearer and clearer as months went by. Tim was more than dominating. He berated. He berated her in such a way that it took her a minute to understand that he was in fact berating her. *"Oh, you're such a good nurse, how come you didn't take the time to become a doctor? You could have been a doctor. Then we could have really worked together." "Your hair is pretty, but if it was shorter, or perhaps streaked, it would look much nicer."* Things like that. According to Tim, Faye was always okay, but just not quite good enough.

It never quite clicked in her brain that he was never quite complimenting her in order to help her become a better person. Although Tim frequently said "I want to support you in being a better person," Faye had never figured out what was wrong with the person she was. She didn't think anything was wrong, but if her husband said she should do this maybe she should. The thing is, she knew what her ears were hearing. Her brain was understanding, but her body was screaming Red Alert! Red Alert. The more she tried to ignore it, the louder the alarm rang. Faye's internal alarm became so loud, she began to get hives. Your body never lies. It will tell you exactly what you need to know every step of the way. On the third floor, you must listen. You must investigate. You must find the cause of the alarm and respond to the information. Faye was new to the third floor, and she hadn't quite figured any of this out yet.

YOU CAN'T HIDE THE TRUTH!

Three years into the marriage, Tim began insisting that Faye stop work and have children. It was time, according to Tim's schedule, to have children. Every time he said it, bells and whistles went off in her head. Faye was paralyzed. She didn't know why, but she knew she was not ready. Tim took away Faye's birth control pills because he said it was time. Because Faye knew it was not time for her, she got another prescription from another doctor and kept the pills in her locker at work. She wondered how long it would take Tim to realize she was still taking the birth control pills. The hives got worse and the bells and whistles continued to blow. It was four months before he confronted her. "What's wrong with you? Why can't you make any babies?" Bells, whistles, lights, and hives all seized her brain before she had a chance to think. Because she was not thinking, the words just sort of fell out of her mouth. The fall was pretty loud, too, "I don't wanna have your children. I don't even like you! You are too much like my father!"

Tim was stunned! No, he was shocked! No, he was hurt! Scratch that, his ego was too big for him to be hurt. He was incensed! The bells and whistles had stopped, and Faye could feel the hives going away. Once you get the courage to say what you need to say, the rest of the courage you need comes to you. Tim asked her what she meant. If you don't want to know a thing, don't ask a thing! Tim asked. Faye told. She told him that he was demeaning, condescending. She went on to say that he was an egomaniac. She further informed him that his helpful hints and tips directed at her self-improvement were getting on her nerves. As angry as Tim was, he listened, he actually listened. Then he told Faye she was having a hormonal imbalance, perhaps from the abrupt cessation of birth control pills. He told her he would get her a prescription for something and that she should lay off white sugar for a while. She looked at him as if he had grown two heads, called him an idiot, and stormed out of the room. Somewhere in the back of his brain, Tim thought to himself, *"She's pregnant, Oh, my God! She's pregnant! That's why she's having these mood swings!"* On the way into the meantime, some people go deaf!

They barely spoke for the next two days, which meant that Tim was not trying to improve Faye or her appearance in any way. But the air between them was so thick, there was so much stuff floating in the air, you could see it, almost touch it.

Tim was getting a little nervous. This was not like Faye, he complained to his mother. He had a very different take on the minor confrontation, which he also related to his mother. He had gotten damaged goods! She never did anything for herself unless he told her how to do it! She was so smart, but she never went for a bigger position, and she never achieved anything worth mentioning! Yes, she was a nurse, but they were glorified slop queens. Skilled maybe, but his wife should be a surgeon. His wife had the ability to be a well-paid surgeon. Instead she was content to be second best. Had he made a mistake? Yes! He was talking so loud, he did not hear Faye come into the room. That was the first mistake. The second was saying, "Hi, baby! Can I get you anything?" when *he knew* that she was not speaking to him.

Tim's mother was the kind of mother who did not like to see her only son upset. His mother was the kind of mother who did not like the idea that some little tootsie, whose wedding she had paid for, was upsetting her high-achieving only child. She figured that she and Faye needed to have a woman-to-woman talk. Actually she said, "I'm gonna fix this brat!" Now, of course, she did not tell her son she was going to talk to his wife; she just figured she would talk to her and get her straight. Besides that, she was getting older and wanted some grandchildren with whom she could spend some quality time before all of her teeth fell out!

Did Faye realize what a catch she had? Tim's mother wanted to know. There were hundreds of thousands of women who would be proud to be married to a brilliant surgeon. There were probably twice that many who would know how to treat him. Did she realize how lucky she was? Did she realize how good he was being to her? The bells and whistles started and then they stopped. Faye was not angry, nor was she upset. She was clear. Very, very clear. She was clear for the first time in a long time, because she actually heard what Tim's mother was saying. You see, you must listen to what people say, not to what you hear. You must listen to the words, not the inflection with which they speak. You must listen to the questions people ask when they are upset, because those questions will reveal to you who this person is, who they think you are, and who you think you are.

MASTERY MAKES THE HEART GROW STRONGER!

Faye listened. She heard, she saw. She understood that she had not yet mastered self-acceptance or self-love. As a result, she had subjected herself to being berated, degraded, and oppressed. Because she never got clear about what it was that she wanted in a relationship, she accepted the first thing offered to her, not really knowing what it was. Because she had watched her mother and father do this, she believed she had to do it. Faye had lived most of her life doing what other people wanted her to do. She was finally shifting out of that pattern, and people were upset with her. Now here's the real beauty of making it to the third floor—being there does not mean you will never again have a problem in your life, with yourself, or in a relationship. Since, however, you are learning how to do things, when stuff comes up in your life on the third floor, you know what to do and you are willing to do it. The how, which you have come to learn, is with love. Do it with love, and do it immediately! Faye packed, and she left.

Faye knew it was time to spend some time on herself. Conscious that she was living in love's house, she knew that she had missed a few steps and that she had to go back and clean up some stuff. The truth of the matter is, this had nothing to do with Tim. He was only voicing to Faye the things she had thought about herself. She knew that and accepted it. You see, on the third floor you have mastered acceptance, and you are willing to practice it. How do you do that? You don't get mad at people when they tell you what you already know. You don't go into denial or the belief that people should not say certain things to you. People can say whatever they want to say! The issue is how are you going to respond. Faye responded by taking steps toward self-correction. The Four P's. She wasn't quite sure if she wanted to end her marriage, but she knew she needed some time and space to think about it. She took three weeks. In that time, she did not go to work. She did not speak to Tim. She would leave him a voice message every day just to let him know she was doing fine and that they would talk soon.

It was four weeks after the woman-to-woman talk that Faye spoke to Tim. The first thing she did was ask his forgiveness for leaving so abruptly. Excellent third-floor behavior: Tell the truth, admit you made a mistake. Do not apologize for doing what you needed to do, but ask forgiveness for causing the other person any difficulty. Faye then told Tim exactly how she felt. She told him exactly what she wanted. She told him what she intended to do to get what she wanted. Then she told Tim what she expected of him in the process, and asked him if he was willing to support her. Faye told Tim that she realized she loved him, but that she also knew they had a lot of work to do on their relationship. Tim agreed and asked for her support. Together, they worked to make their third-floor experience a loving one.

When a master makes a shift, everything and everyone in the environment will shift. On the third floor you are not upset to be in a third-floor meantime experience. You are willing to be engaged in the experiences you are having and are not freaked out about them. You can instantly reflect on those situations in which you were totally freaked out about things not looking the way you wanted them to look. You remember your response. You are cognizant of the need to take time to look at you and your experiences with an open mind, lest you move forward doing what you do, the way you do it, without realizing the grief you are causing yourself. By the time you get to the third floor, you have totally surrendered your passive/aggressive tendencies. You are now receptively aware and purposefully active, in that order.

Trust is what will make your tenancy on the third floor pleasant and meaningful. Hopefully you have actually learned to trust yourself, God, other people, and the process of life. As a result, whether you are in a relationship or not, you will feel just fine. Whether you have money or not, you know you are going to make it. You know that the pendulum of life swings both ways, and that sooner or later, it will—no, it must—swing in your direction.

In the meantime, you are rolling along, doing what you can do, feeling okay about knowing that things are going to change for the better. This is called the *Row Your Boat* experience. Row, row, row your boat. Do what you can do. Gently down the stream. Don't get yourself upset. Experience your experience.

Don't fight the flow. Merrily, merrily, merrily, merrily. Stay up, stay in tune. Life is but a dream, and you realize that you are the dreamer. As the dreamer, you know you can change your scenario any time you wish. When you wish to change, you will, and with all the information you have gathered on your journey through love's house, change is inevitable.

PROCRASTINATION IS A THIEF!

Jean and Andy were definitely in love, no doubt about it. They were both young—she was thirty-one, he was thirty-five. What do you mean, that's not young? Of course it is if you consider the fact that you don't have any real sense until you are thirty. They had both been busy building their careers. He was an editor with a major publishing firm. She was a producer with a major television station. They had fun together. They had good communication between them. They had a brilliant future to which they were both looking forward. They kept putting the wedding off for reasons related to their careers. Besides that, there was no urgency, no hysteria. They knew they wanted to get married; they simply were not in a rush about it.

It was right in the middle of a newscast when Jean got the call. What kind of an emergency?!!! Andy had been rushed to the hospital. He had had a heart attack. Much to everyone's surprise, a few hours later, this young vibrant man was dead at the age of thirty-five. Jean was devastated. More than that, she was very, very angry. She was angry with herself for not seizing the opportunity when she had it; she was angry with Andy for dying; she was angry with life for robbing her; and she was very angry with God for putting her through this! She went through the funeral. She went through his apartment. She went through his things. She went back to work a week later. Jean was very efficient. She was almost as efficient as she was angry.

There are some things that are so painful that when you feel them come up in your body, you think you are going to die. You think that it is not possible for you to live through the experience and come out on the other end with a mind or a heart. You are afraid of this kind of pain. You are afraid of what it might do to you. You cannot think about the pain. You cannot speak about the pain. The only logical thing you can do when you start to feel the pain is stuff it. Jean stuffed her pain with food.

Within nine months of Andy's death, Jean had gained more than sixty-five pounds. None of her friends would dare say anything to her. They all noticed changes in her behavior. They also noticed that she was a little more moody than usual. They all attributed it to the fact that she was making this big adjustment to life without Andy. Jean noticed she had become very lethargic. She just attributed it to the fact that she was working so hard. It wasn't until a young man that she worked with asked her out on a date that the bells and whistles went off in her head. He was a new executive producer who had been transferred from another station, and he didn't know her story. No one was surprised that she turned him down by almost biting his head off, because everyone else at the station knew what had happened. They all knew, but nobody would say anything about it, not to her and not to the young producer. Jean was still a pretty woman despite the weight. She was still an excellent producer. No one would say anything about her weight or about her snippiness because they knew what had happened.

It got to the point where Jean would just go off at the drop of a dime, so everybody stayed out of her way. They sort of put their heads down when she passed, and sort of got away as fast as they could when she walked into the studio. She noticed their changes too. The poor producer was too new to notice anything, so he kept pursuing Jean. Eventually they began to talk, first about work, then about each other. One day he noticed the engagement ring on her finger and asked her about it, thinking it was the reason she would not go out with him. One way or the other, he liked Jean and wanted to be her friend.

The moment he asked the question, the pain exploded in Jean's body. She all but attacked the producer, saying some very inappropriate things. He simply waited until she was finished before asking, "Why are you so angry?" That really set her off on a tirade. She was screaming about how angry she was not. The entire studio stilled. The pain had hit the boiling point and spilled over onto the producer's head—she hit him. He backed up, and she hit him again. He grabbed her hands, took her in his arms, and refused to let her go. Everyone in the studio stopped breathing. Jean stopped fighting. She put her head on his shoulder and cried. She cried for a very long time because it was the first time she had cried since Andy had died.

Surrender to the feelings. Acknowledge them and express them. If you don't do it voluntarily, you will do it involuntarily, and sometimes inappropriately. On the third floor, you must live in total honesty. You must tell the absolute truth about everything, all of the time. If you choose not to, if you choose denial or judgment, the pain you will feel in your body will be so intense you will explode. Third-floor experiences are not about right or wrong. They are about strength and courage.

They are not about the support of image or ego. They are about being vulnerable. Unconditional love makes you vulnerable to experiences and people. Unless you are vulnerable, you cannot be open. If you are not open, you cannot know love in the many forms it can take. On the third floor, the gist of all your experiences will be to accept the fact that whatever you do in love is the absolute best you can do at the moment. You must be okay with that because it is the absolute truth.

Chapter 12
REARRANGE THE FURNITURE

stella spent seven years in a relationship with Matt. At the end of the seven years she was a single mother of two who, like so many others, had spent a few good years in a relationship with a pretty decent man. When Matt left, Stella dedicated her life to raising the children. She was a firm believer that if you raise a child right, you will not have to fix an adult. She was determined to give them her best. In the process of doing do, she never let another man into her life.

At the time they separated, Stella was still young. She told herself that she didn't want to set a bad example for her children by having various men running in and out of her life. Why she thought she couldn't find just one mate and settle down, I can't tell you. Why she thought she had to bring everybody home to spend the night is a mystery to me. Where she was when the second-floor lesson of expectations equals results was being taught, I cannot tell you. But neither you nor I have to know these things, Stella does. The truth of the matter is that Stella was angry. She went to church angry. She went to the single mother's support group angry. She was very active in her children's lives, although she was angry. She became totally immersed in the care and welfare of her children as a clever disguise that allowed her to deny her anger. In the meantime, she was also denying herself the pleasure, joy, and companionship of a relationship that she really wanted but was afraid she could not have.

Children don't exactly make great husbands or wives. They are okay companions, but there are some parts of a loving relationship that children cannot provide. Stella made her children her mate and her companions, and while she learned a lot about unconditional love and patience, she didn't learn enough to dispel the anger she had been carrying for so long. It was a long time, which passed very quickly. Before Stella realized that her children were teenagers, a young woman was calling for her son. Well, he was seventeen. He was getting ready for college. He was a good kid, who got good grades and never gave his mother a moment of trouble. Yet for some reason, Stella was very uncomfortable with her son's new love interest.

An uncomfortable mother can make your life quite difficult. She really doesn't mean to, but she does. Stella began to monitor her son's movements very closely. This included restrictions on the weekends, imposing curfews during the week, and monitoring, that's right, monitoring his telephone calls. Fifteen minutes a day, that was it. If you exceeded your fifteen minutes today, it would be deducted from tomorrow's fifteen minutes. You see what I mean! She was very uncomfortable. Such a good son he was! He put up with it only because he really loved and respected his mother. At least he did until she refused to let him go away on a fully chaperoned ski trip. Is that girl going? Yes. Well, then, you can't go!

Even a good son with good grades can reach his limit. This seventeen-year-old, who had one foot out of his mother's door and into the college door, had reached his. *"You're just mad because I have somebody and you don't! That's why you haven't been on a date in ten years! That's why you don't make yourself up, or go out! That's why you consumed your life with me, but I'm not going to be here, and you will be alone!"* On the third floor, the truth will come at you from the most unlikely sources! It will jump up in your face. Shake its finger at you and put all of your business in the street. If you have been in denial of the truth, it will cut its way straight through your stuff and sting you so hard, you will want to strike out, but you will be unable to. You may even try to respond with something like, *"Don't you dare raise your voice with me!"* That's weak, and it will not stop the truth from coming at you!

"You're just jealous of our relationship with Daddy. You want us to hate him like you hate him. You are mad because he has a new life and a new wife. Even when he tries to be your friend, you won't let him. If you don't stop being mad at him, you are going to lose me the same way you lost him!" I'm sorry, but she asked for it. Children are so clear, so perceptive, they can see right through you like an x-ray machine. They know what you do, and sometimes why you do it. Stella had raised her children to be independent thinkers. She liked that about them. She had raised them not to challenge authority, but to speak their truth when those in authority were violating principle and integrity. She was proud of that in her children. What she did not realize was

that everything she taught them to apply to the world also applied to her!

She had never spoken an ill word about their father, but she was engaged in a silent tug of war for their affection. Whenever the children went to visit him, they returned with all kinds of gifts and what Stella considered frivolous things that she could not provide for them (remote control cars, designer jeans, stereos, and so forth). She thought he was buying their love while she was working hard to build a home for them. Whenever it was something important, Dad would show up. He would say the word, and the children would scramble. Every time he did, Stella would get angry all over again that he had left her for a younger woman.

Deep down inside, Stella was somewhat happy that they had a loving relationship with him. He had always supported them financially, although sporadically at first. The moment, however, he got himself and his life together with *that woman,* Stella never had to call for the check. The truth of the matter is that Stella was trying to punish him for leaving her. She had decided that by leaving her with two children, he had ruined her life. For that, she determined, he needed to be punished. Each time he saw her, how hard she worked, how dedicated she was, how her life was absolutely centered on the children, she prayed that he would feel guilty. Apparently he didn't.

What you give, you get! When you live on the third floor of love's house, you will get it so quickly, you will have no choice but to accept full and total responsibility for yourself and your actions. You no longer have the privilege of being able to blame, hide stuff, or avoid. The spotlight is on you! It's hot! It's uncomfortable! You are trying to remember your lines—the lines you want to follow from this point on in your life. You know you are being watched, and you want to get it right. Forget right! You are in the meantime. Even in a third-floor meantime, nothing is right, and everything is all right, even though it looks all wrong! You've got a little more moving to do. Just a wee bit more cleaning. More important, you are ready to reassess whether you still want what you once thought you wanted. This is all third-floor behavior—allowing your stuff to come to the light so that you can make the necessary shifts, lovingly.

WHY DO I DO WHAT I DO?

We have been taught that it is our job in life to go out and find the perfect partner, when in fact our job is to find the perfection in ourselves. Because I did not know just how perfect I was, my fear was that people were going to bail out on me. I thought that if I opened my heart to them, they would take what they wanted and bail out. Through the many experiences I have had in all kinds of relationships, I have learned that people don't just bail out. They must have a reason to bail out. If they don't have a valid reason, they will manufacture one, just to get out—to get out of the way of love. There was a part of me, a part of my own psyche, that said, *"If you give people everything they want, they won't leave you like your mother did!"* When I tried it, I became a mindless people pleaser, avoiding the pain of having people bail out. I did whatever I thought it would take to keep them with me, near me. Eventually I got on their nerves and they bailed out anyway. I thought it was love. They thought it was suffocation. In the end, I got rejected or left. They got to escape the grasp of my needs cleverly disguised as love.

Some people jump into the relationship arena, pass go, collect the two hundred bucks, and are never seen or heard from again. Then there are those of us who have been engaged eighteen times and have never made it to the altar. There are also those of us who have done our spiritual work, who have created a purposeful, meaningful life, those who have waded through the stuff, cleaned it up, and still cannot find or maintain a loving, committed relationship. There are no guarantees!

There is no guarantee that at the end of the day, after all of the work you have done, you are either going to get a partner, have a relationship, or save the relationship you are in. The thing about the third floor is that those concerns are no longer critical for you. Having a relationship or being in love is no longer a critical or key aspect of living. This does not mean you do not want a relationship. It means you will not lose sleep over not having one. What's critical for you on the third floor is healing yourself in order to serve and support as many people as you can, in any way that you can. You have shifted out of the basement's physical attraction, needy, clingy, I gotta have you, ooh baby baby stuff into love is here all the time. Love is what I am. Love is what I give. Love is what I receive. You see everything as love. You see money as love. You see compliments as love. You see people as love. On the third floor what you are working toward is how to deal with every situation that comes up, until you really find that one partnership that makes you more than you already are.

Here is a major mistake we sometimes make. We think that

we can pray and meditate so long and so hard that God will send somebody to love us. You cannot move toward finding yourself, loving yourself, just for the sake of finding and loving someone else. You must do it for the sake of doing it. You must love, honor, and respect you for the sake of it—no strings attached. This would have made absolutely no sense to you anywhere but on the third floor. At the lower levels, you were still dealing with too much stuff. Now you are ready. Ready to make the shift from conditional love to unconditional love. You are now ready to be with yourself rather than by yourself. You have been through a meantime process in which you have become self-aware and self-reflective in order to make the necessary changes or shifts that will result in spiritual transformation. You are no longer in search of physical, emotional, or sexual satisfaction only. You want the true, full experience of love. If this is what you are going for, this is what you will get.

PRACTICE MAKES PERFECT!

It's one thing to study spirituality out of a book, or to be in a learning environment where you are being supported, where the teacher is there telling you what to do and how to do it. In a learning environment everybody in the room has the same goal, the same mind-set. This is the beauty of being in a learning environment. But why do we gather information? Why do we want to learn? We learn so that we can go out and put what we know into practice. We're not going to practice in the classroom —that is a false environment. In the classroom you develop the skill. In the world you hone the skill. In the outside world where people can't even spell the thing you just studied, you are going to do more than learn theory. In the world you are going to deal with people who have no idea what you are talking about. Does this mean that your information is faulty? Is it an accurate indication that the theories don't work? Absolutely not! It means that you must continue on the journey, put into practice all that you have learned. Eventually you will find yourself in a community or an experience where everybody wants to know what you know. Or where everybody knows what you know and is willing to help you facilitate further growth in it.

How can you take what you have learned about love and loving and apply it to every area of your life? You must be willing to meet resistance with love. This is how you will hone your skills. Find your center and stay grounded in it. Do not try to convert others to your way of thinking. When you find that you are the only person in a room who thinks the way you think, it doesn't mean that there is something wrong with what you do and how you do it. It means that every time you meet resistance, you have an opportunity to strengthen another love muscle. Don't doubt yourself. Don't question yourself. Know that the resistance is going to come up at different levels with different characters. Each time you face resistance it will evoke different feelings. Those feelings are the development of your stamina. One day very soon, the only feeling any experience will evoke is the opportunity to share, spread, give, or receive love.

SUDDENLY IT JUST HAPPENED!

Ralph, who is in his middle fifties, has been divorced for twenty-five years. During that time, he has had several long-term relationships that have all ended amicably, and he is still friends with every partner he has had. I mean they go out to dinner, send birthday cards back and forth, stop by the house at Christmas, and all of the rest. He has two children from relationships that he had when he wasn't married. He knows his children, has participated fully to the best of his ability in their lives. He has not always been the greatest financial support to them, but they never make a serious move without discussing it with their pop.

Ralph and his daughter have a famous relationship. They are really truly friends. But then Ralph has many friends. There is no place you can go in the country where somebody doesn't know Ralph. Not only do they know him, you would hardly hear anyone, not one single person, say one derogatory word about this man. All he does is love and serve people. It doesn't matter who you are; if there is anything Ralph can do to help you, he will do it, willingly and gladly, with no strings attached. Any time you call, any time you need him, anything you need that he has, he will give it to you. He does not do it to his detriment either. If he doesn't have it, he doesn't hesitate to say, *"I don't have it now, but I'll have it by this date. Can you wait?"* This man is total, complete, unconditional love with a name and two legs!

I hate to go on and on about him, but I really want to give you a picture of what third-floor loving looks like. If Ralph comes across something he thinks you would like or that would be interesting to you, he'll buy it and send it to you in the mail. We had a friend who had misplaced her teenage daughter once. She had an idea of where the girl was but no means to get to the place. I called Ralph. I asked him to try to get in touch with the young woman. He jumped in his car without a second thought. He didn't find her, but the effort was there. As a result of his ability to love, everything Ralph needs comes to him in the perfect way.

On the third floor of love's house, you become a teacher. Ralph is a teacher. He teaches others by the way he responds to his experiences. He uses love to demonstrate that all things can come together for the good of everyone involved. This is probably the reason he has had several female friends who were potential partners, but with whom he chose not to get involved. He could have, but he didn't. He chose not to take himself through the process of trying to make it work romantically when he was very clear that it was not his goal. How did he get so clear? He did a thorough job of cleaning the house on the way to the attic. He cleaned away urgency, need, and attachment to his way. He learned patience and total trust in the process of life. He learned to listen to his body and honor what he felt, without making excuses and without avoiding what he knew was necessary for him to do or say at any time.

He had a job once where his supervisor treated him like an indentured servant. She lived a step below the basement! She behaved wickedly. You notice I did not say she was wicked, just that she behaved that way. She was, however, very insecure and threatened by everyone and everything. Ralph did everything in his power to make her feel comfortable. Whatever she demanded of him, he did it without feeling bad. He would always say, "Whatever the lesson is here, I'm gonna get it!" No matter what she did, he turned the other cheek with no anger and no resentment. Sometimes I would listen to him in horror. Then when I met the woman, I knew she needed to be slapped. Now I know that is not very spiritual, but we all have our human moments. Ralph had no malice. He kept saying, "I'm gonna get it! I'm going to get the lesson!"

When you pour love into something, it is going to bring up everything that is unloving. When you put peace into the mix, it is going to magnify everything that is not peaceful. She couldn't take it! She could not take Ralph's sunny disposition and the love he poured into his work or onto her. When she had taken all she could take, she found a reason to terminate him. It was a flimsy reason, one that would never have survived even the most minute challenge, but Ralph decided not to fight. He said, "It's June. I'll take the summer off. I'm sure something will turn up by the fall."

Two weeks after Ralph was fired, the supervisor happened to mention to somebody that she had dismissed Ralph, and she gave the reason. The person immediately said, "That's not true! That is not what happened; this is what happened!" That person, the person who knew the truth, contacted Ralph, hired him, and almost doubled his salary. In the meantime, he was not required to begin work until the fall. The lesson is that there are people who will dump their stuff all over you. You cannot allow it to alter who you are or what you do. If you know who you are, a little discomfort should not frighten you or disturb you. Just keep loving yourself and everyone else. I think it's only fair to mention that in the meantime, while Ralph was engaged in a meantime test, he met a wonderful woman, and they are transforming life together.

IT'S ALL A PART OF THE DIVINE PLAN

The meantime is not about waiting to find a relationship. It's about building a better relationship with yourself. It is a process of self-reflection and self-awareness. It is a process within which you must work if you want to see results. The meantime is a means by which we can learn how to recognize all relationships as vehicles of spiritual healing and transformation. It is a love tool, divinely designed to tune our spirits to the highest octave of love. When you don't have a job, you have to love yourself. When your sister, your mother, your best friends stop speaking to you, you have to love yourself. Love is active, which means that if you engage in the process of self-love, you will move from where you are to where you want to be.

The meantime is a process that results in movement and change. It is change that brings spiritual enlightenment, that prepares you to share your life from a consciousness of balance and harmony. The meantime is what every soul requires in order to remember its divine identity. In order to acknowledge, accept, and embrace your true identity, you must be ready. You must be ready to see things from a different perspective, to do things in a different consciousness, to receive things with an open heart and mind. Readiness is the indication that you have learned something from your past experiences and that you are prepared to apply what you have learned. What you have learned and not learned, about yourself—your strengths, your weaknesses, your interactions with others—will determine the efficacy and severity of your meantime experiences.

You can find yourself in the meantime in any area of your

life. When you do, the solution you need may be different, but the process for surviving it is always the same:

1. Love yourself no matter what! Never let what is happening or the fear of what could happen rob you of your ability to love yourself. Realize that your meantime is bound to create confusion in your thinking. However, you must also realize that where you are is exactly where you need to be. You are being guided back to love, to self-love.

2. Feel what you feel and acknowledge that you are feeling it. Before you reach out to avoid the pain, reach in and feel it. Feel any hurt, pain, confusion, or weakness. Feel your vulnerability, and acknowledge that you feel vulnerable. Once you feel whatever it is that is going on inside you, let yourself know that it is perfectly okay to feel it. Do not judge yourself. Do not tell yourself you shouldn't. Feel it! Acknowledge it! Ride it out!

3. Express what you feel verbally or in writing. You will discover that it is absolutely imperative to express your feelings in the meantime. You must tell someone what you feel. If you try to hold it in, it will choke you! When this happens, more likely than not what you are trying to hold in will spill out in a very inappropriate way, at the most inappropriate time. You can save yourself a great deal of stress, and possibly some embarrassment, simply by choosing how you want to express what you feel. Write it out! Talk to a friend! Call Dial a Prayer! But by all means, never try to ignore what you feel or act as if the feelings do not exist.

4. Get clear about what you want. What do you want to do? How do you want to feel? How can you create the experience for yourself? What is it that you believe is keeping you from the experience? What are you willing to do to have the most peaceful version of the experience that is possible? Yes, I know these are more questions, but they are questions you must ask if you want to get out and stay out of the meantime.

5. Do not look for or expect anyone to make your meantime better or less painful. You need to spend some time with yourself and gather up the little pieces that you have given away. If you bring another person into the middle of the process as a means of distraction, you could very well misdiagnose the cause of your ills.

While the circumstances that take each of us to the meantime are unique and individualized, the process leading up to and of being in the meantime is quite universal.

You will not know what the problem is. Then you will know what the problem is, but you will not know what to do about it. Then you will know what to do about the problem, but your stuff, your issues, will prevent you from doing it. Then you will be forced to look at your stuff and sort through it in order to reach a solution. Then you will know what to do, but not how to do it. Then you will be called upon by the forces of life to do what you know you can do, must do all of the time.

In the meantime, there are certain very specific and pointed questions you must ask yourself:

What am I responding to?

Have I told the truth to myself? To everyone who is involved?

What is my vision?

What am I expecting of myself? For myself?

What is my intention?

Can I love myself no matter what happens?

Can I love others no matter what they do?

In the meantime, your experiences and lessons are designed to support you in developing and clearly articulating answers to these questions. The reason the process and the questions are so important in the meantime is that they will help you do one or more of the following things:

You will find your center, your *Self,* and learn to accept it.

You will stop making the same mistakes in your relationships.

You will learn to recognize your recurring issues through relationship experiences.

You will become equipped to dismantle your fantasies about love and loving.

You will find the true value and meaning of love.

The meantime is not about trying to fix your stuff. Yes, you will spend a great deal of time dismantling it, but fixing it is not the goal. The goal is learning to embrace the love. There is nothing to fix because God accepts everybody exactly as we are. On the third floor we will learn to do the same. Rather than thinking we must fix our stuff, we can use the meantime to rearrange it. This is done by determining who you choose to be in relationship to your experiences. If you have been a victim, giving your past your power and strength, you can rearrange it. If you have been an enemy, fighting, resisting, denying, struggling with your past experiences, you can rearrange them. If you have been a co-conspirator, using what has happened to you as a barrier that will not allow new experiences in, you can rearrange how you think about what you have done and where you have been. Become a student of your experiences, study what they have taught you. Become a teacher of your experiences by sharing with others what you have learned. Become a lover of your experiences by realizing that everything that you are, you are because you made it through the past.

The more able you are to incorporate what you have learned on the lower levels into what you do, the closer you will move toward being a true expression and example of love. This does not, however, mean you will not have the normal, nerve-wracking experiences that every other human being must face. It does not mean that you will float or sprout wings. It does not mean you will have whiter teeth or fresher breath! Even on the third floor, you will cry sometimes. But now you can cry with an agenda. You can cry because you now are moving closer to the goal, the goal of remembering who you are and why you came here in the first place. There will still be those experiences when you want to grab someone by the throat and shake the living daylights out of them. But you won't do that! You will know that you must forgive them and yourself. There will be those times when all you want to do is sit and reflect, feel, and ask questions. This will be a very good sign! The more time you spend sitting in the presence of your *Self*, the greater appreciation you will have for the time you will spend in the attic.

THE ATTIC

step back. Take a look around. Everything is in tip-top shape. It looks good. You look good. You've done good! You have made it all the way to the top—to the *Love Is Sweet* suite. There are two mantras—prayers, if you will—that you can take with you into the suite. They come from a very powerful book entitled *A Course in Miracles*. They are, "I am entitled to miracles" because "I am as God created me to be." You are a miracle, and for that matter, so is everyone else.

Chapter 13
PUT YOUR FEET UP AND RELAX!

the attic of life's house is the consciousness with which children live, totally trusting, totally free, totally accepting of self and others. Children don't know what's wrong until someone else tells them to believe it's wrong. Children don't know people are ugly until they hear someone else's version of what ugly is. The attic of life's house is about living with a childlike heart through which all things are good, even after you have been told otherwise. It is here, in the attic of love's house, that we see, feel, and learn to recognize the presence of God in our soul and in all other souls.

In the attic, you have made a commitment to shift your consciousness into a state of love, unconditional self-love. You have realized that if you are not willing to make this shift, you will always be wanting, waiting, hanging out in perpetual limbo, waiting to see whether who and what you want will ever show up. You understand that, as a human being, you have the tendency to people-please, dance around the truth, doubt yourself, and become involved with a host of things that masquerade as love. Because you know this about you, you commit your total being to the elimination of all of the things that have held you in a space of conditional love by examining your expectations about love. This means looking at what you want and what you expect that you will have to do to get it. There should be a natural shift in our consciousness as we mature in life, but sometimes it does not happen. We carry our childhood programming into our search for love. "Get out of the way!" You *expect* to be shoved around. "Don't talk back!" You *expect* not to be heard. "Can you wait until I finish?!!!" You *expect* to put the needs of others before your own. Examine your experiences. Remember the emotions you experienced. Reflect on what you did in the past. Express those feelings to yourself. Forgive yourself for not expressing them at that time. Create a new response. Develop new expectations of yourself.

Throughout your journey, you have had attic experiences. There have been those times when you have allowed yourself to be totally open, totally vulnerable to the experience of love. At those times, you were not concerned about what might happen or what could happen. You were relaxed. You were confident. Then your human stuff kicked in and you shifted into fear. Relationships bring up our deepest fears. The fear of failing, being abandoned, being yelled at, and not being lovable enough. These expectations, most of which we are totally unaware of, form the inner conflict we experience when we want love in fear.

This is the experience of wanting something while you are afraid you cannot have it or keep it. Asking for something when you are afraid that you do not deserve it or are not worthy of having it. Looking for something, afraid that if you get it, it will hurt you. Each of these are blocks that are eliminated as you shift your perceptions and expectations to unconditional love. In the attic of love's house you vow to never again allow fear to rob you of the experience of love.

THE BATTLE IS NOT YOURS!

When Pamela was young, she was very heavy, very knock-kneed, and she couldn't dance or jump rope. The children teased her mercilessly. She stayed heavy into her teens, which means she could not get a date. She had a few friends, people who were not cruel enough to cast her out of humanity. It was in these young girls that she confided her deepest feelings, including the fact that she was sweet on one guy. He was a handsome guy. Tall, athletic, the works. There's no crime in liking somebody! We are free to like anyone we choose, particularly when we are sixteen. The crime is committed when your helpful friends try to hook you up with the tall, athletic guy who thinks you are a freak of nature.

The crime was brutal! It was vicious! This guy not only laughed out loud when he heard, he followed Pamela around the school encouraging other people to laugh at her with him. Now, when you can't dance or jump rope, you certainly can't run! When you can't run, you walk away, acting as if you don't hear the cruel, brutal, vicious comments being spewed at your person from the object of your affections. Your friends try to chase them away, but athletes turn everything into a sport—including teasing people they don't like. You walk as fast as you can in an attempt to get away, but your knees are not cooperating. Miraculously, the athlete's attention is taken away by a more attractive female specimen.

Pamela stopped liking that guy almost immediately, but she did not allow the experience to make her stop liking all people. Every now and again, a fellow would catch her eye, but she never, never said anything to anyone about it. She held it all inside, believing that she was ugly, fat, unlovable, and all the rest. When you have a good heart, however, life does not turn its back on you. One day, much to Pamela's pleasure and surprise, a bold young man walked right up to her and asked her out. Could you fall on the floor and hoot! Pamela was thrilled! She was shocked! She took one look at the young man and realized she had a big problem. He was not of the same race as Pamela. Well now, this was a real meantime dilemma! If you have been waiting for seventeen years for a guy to ask you out, just how picky should you be when one finally asks you? Pamela couldn't figure it out, so she didn't try. In the meantime, she had a wonderful date.

That was just the beginning. For some strange reason, Pamela could not attract or hold the attention of men of her own race, when at the same time, other men, of all nationalities, found her both pleasant and attractive. Well into her thirties, Pamela hung out in the international dating arena. She had a ball! She learned so much about herself and other people. She also got to travel quite a bit. Every now and then, she would ask herself why men of her own ethnic background were not interested in her. She never got a plausible answer, so she kept dating whoever showed up. And you know what? She had the same issues and challenges as her girlfriends who were involved in same-race dating. She had the same issues to overcome within herself. Ultimately Pamela's meantime became a powerful lesson in acceptance and tolerance. She has remained single, but she is looking in all available places.

Children who are not taught to love themselves and who don't experience the acceptance, tolerance, mercy, and forgiveness of love can tease and reject one another. Children who receive that criticism have a powerful healing to experience. They must learn about forgiveness and the mercy of love. Few children are taught how to do this. Instead they take on the criticism and rejection as evidence that something is wrong with them. The whole issue, across the board, no matter who you are, is a lack of love. We teach our kids to love their parents. We teach them to love the other members of their family. We teach them to love things. What we do not do is teach our children to love people. We try to teach them what is and is not nice to do, but we don't get to the core, the core that teaches a love that is grounded in Spirit.

Because we live in a society that gives us a view of perfection, anything that doesn't match that view of perfection we must reject. As children, we learn that very early. Children are not taught that the true meaning of love is at the core. That the true essence of love is the intangible connection of the soul. We teach our children to read Bible verses and to memorize the books in the Bible. We teach them what to say, how to say it, and when to say everything that will give the world the impression that they are being properly raised. What we are not teaching our children are the principles. We are not teaching them the attitudes. We are not teaching them the activity of love. They hear us talking, and when we talk, we criticize, we judge, and we are intolerant, unaccepting, and unmerciful because we, the adults, don't remember the truth about love.

YOU'RE ON A MISSION!

"My only purpose for being on the planet is to awaken to my God Self, to celebrate life, and to do what brings me joy!" In the meantime, we must learn to live among people who don't believe this statement, to work through the stuff within us that keeps us from believing this statement, while we hopefully endeavor to discover the light in our souls that will help us embody this statement. When you look around the world today, it is really hard to believe that love can heal the ills with which we are plagued. How can love heal cancer, heart disease, or AIDS? How can love feed the hungry children? Or end violence in the street? It sounds so simplistic to say that love is the key to healing. I mean, how can love fix the national deficit? Actually, if we tell the truth, it sounds ridiculous! However, it is just as ridiculous to believe that what we are doing and have been doing will yield results any different from those we have already received.

We have all but eliminated the concept of love from the essence of life. Yes, we teach love in the family and in the church, but we dare not teach it in the schools or government agencies. We actually believe we can separate love from all places and any activities in which people are present. Perhaps the manner in which we selectively ignore the concept of love is a reflection of the intent to ignore God. No one is bold enough to outwardly admit we should ignore the Creative Force of life; however, we have made it very clear that God has to be relegated to certain arenas, on certain days, as if we really believe God will not, cannot, is not to be dealt with in all arenas, all of the time. It is pretty obvious that we believe love can be regulated. Why not God?

Then there is the very tiny issue that most living beings have very different concepts of what love is, or what it should be. How do we reach a consensus? How do we find a common denominator upon which we can agree with regard to what love is and what it can do? Far be it from me to prescribe a healing formula for the world! I will dare to say, however, that I believe if we each start doing our individual work, clearing our individual stuff, releasing our individual fears, I believe that love will hear the call and respond. Where better to start than in our relationships, those alliances we form in an effort to give and receive love? Where better to invoke and practice the principles of love—truth, trust, forgiveness, acceptance, nonjudgment, and peace? In the meantime, while we are trying to reach a consensus about love, we can each practice loving principles. We can each invoke the presence of love as the foundation of every choice and decision we make. We can each move from a conscious intent to reveal love in every word we speak and every action we take. In doing so, we would awaken the truth and love of God in our hearts. We would find more things to celebrate and be joyous about. We would be living from a much simpler perspective, but I for one do not think this approach to life is ridiculous. In fact, I know that this is the goal of meantime experiences: to teach us how to live, embracing the simple truth about life and God while engaging in joyous celebration of ourselves and each other. This is the goal we must keep in mind as we move through life, God's house, to the attic.

When you reach the Love Is Sweet Suite, you have a very important mission. It is to teach love. Yes, you do some of it on the third floor, but now you must dedicate your life to it. You must actively go out and find people who need to know about love. You must bathe yourself in love. You must brush your teeth with it. You must use it as cologne. You must pour love into things and onto people, through your thoughts, words, and deeds. Let me repeat that. Your thoughts! Your words! Your deeds! At this level of your development, you cannot even think an unloving thought! That is just how powerful you have become. You have so cleared your subconscious mind of stuff that no matter what you think love will manifest.

Think love. See love. Invoke love from the attic of life. You are in good company, you know. You have lots of support and assistance. This is where the Christ lives. This is where Buddha lives. This is where Krishna, Muktananda, and the archangels Michael, Ariel, Uriel, and Gabriel live. This is where the wise old grandmothers live, the medicine women, and the healers. This is where White Eagle lives. This is the realm of Spirit. This is the highest faculty of your mind. When you make it through all of your human stuff to this level of consciousness, you are keeping company with the masters. You, my dear, have become the light of the world—the loving light. I beseech you to do everything in your power to let your light shine.

Inner Visions Worldwide, Inc.

Where we believe . . .
"There is a universal power seeking an outlet through you!"

• WORKSHOPS • LECTURES ON TAPE • PRISON MINISTRY •
• CORRESPONDENCE COURSES • SUPPORT GROUPS •
• 24-HOUR PRAYER LINE • CLASSES and other activities •

We invite you to become a member of the
Spiritual Life Maintenance Network
Receive membership discounts on Inner Visions activities and products
Annual Dues $37.50

❏ YES! I WOULD LIKE TO BE A MEMBER!

(PLEASE PRINT ALL INFORMATION REQUESTED)

Name: _____

Address: _____

City: _____ State: _____ Zip: _____

Phone: _____ FAX: _____

Form of Payment: ❏ Check/M.O. ❏ Discover ❏ Visa/MC ❏ American Express

Account Number: _____ Expiration Date: _____

Cardholder's Name: _____

Cardholder's Signature: _____

✦

❏ I have a friend/family member I would like to enroll in the
INNER VISIONS PRISON MINISTRY.

(Members receive a monthly newsletter and supplementary reading materials).

Name: _____

Correctional facility: _____

Identification #: _____

Address: _____

City: _____ State: _____ Zip: _____

Enrolled by: _____ Relationship: _____

Please ask prison ministry enrollee to place Inner Visions on the approved mailing list.

Visit our web site at: http://Innervisionsworldwide.com

926 Philadelphia Avenue, Silver Spring, MD 20910 ✦ (301) 608-8750

BLESSING & GREETINGS

Inner Visions Worldwide Network
for Spiritual Life Maintenance

WHAT DO YOU DO IN THE MEANTIME?
There are hundreds of thousands of meantime scenarios
in which you could find yourself at any time.
If you are in the *Meantime* between jobs, between relationships,
between the test and the results, between the diagnosis and the treatment,
we want you to know what to do!

Working Through the Meantime: A Guidance Workbook
We can support you in learning:
What to Do ✦ How to Do It ✦ When to Do It ✦ When You Are in the Meantime!
Paperback ✦ 120 pages ✦ $12.00

We also invite you to become a member of the
INNER VISIONS WORLDWIDE NETWORK FOR SPIRITUAL LIFE MAINTENANCE

✦ Learn How to Apply Spiritual Principles to Your Life
✦ Learn How to Use Affirmative Prayer to Create a Shift
in Your Consciousness
✦ Learn How to Start and Maintain a Support Group
✦ Learn How to Connect with Like-Minded People
✦ Receive 10 Commentaries Annually
✦ 24-Hour Access to Our Prayer Line
✦ Membership Discounts to All Inner Visions Activities
and Workshops
Annual Dues $37.50

❑ PLEASE SEND ME **Working Through the Meantime** ($12.00 + 2.00 Shp. & Hand.)
❑ PLEASE ENROLL ME AS A MEMBER ($37.50 annual/ $65.00 for 2 years)

(PLEASE PRINT ALL INFORMATION REQUESTED)

Name: _____
Address: _____
City: _____ State: _____ Zip: _____
Phone: _____ FAX: _____
Form of Payment: ❑ Check/M.O. ❑ Discover ❑ Visa/MC ❑ American Express
Account Number: _____ Expiration Date: _____
Cardholder's Name: _____
Cardholder's Signature: _____

All information provided to Inner Visions Worldwide Network is held in absolute confidence.
Feel free to call before your place your order.

Visit our web site at: http://Innervisionsworldwide.com

Post Office Box 3231, Silver Spring, MD 20918-0231 ✦ (301) 608-8750

In the Meantime:
The Music That Tells The Story

*featuring Faith Evans • Yolanda Adams
Donnie McClurkin and Nancey Jackson with London
Community Gospel Choir • Kelly Price • Maxi Priest
Montell Jordan and Monifah • Howard Hewitt
Angelo & Veronica • Tulani Kinnard • Terry Bradford*

with motivational messages from

Iyanla Vanzant

CD/cassette IN STORES NOW
or call TOLL FREE (888)466-3800

With more than 3 million copies of her books in print, America can't get enough of

Iyanla Vanzant

ACTS OF FAITH
Fireside, 0-671-86416-5, $11.00
Simon & Schuster, Hardcover Gift Edition, 0-684-83236-4, $22.00
Simon & Schuster Libros en Español, 0-684-83143-0, $11.00

FAITH IN THE VALLEY
Fireside, 0-684-80113-2, $12.00
Simon & Schuster, Hardcover Gift Edition, 0-684-85048-6, $22.00

THE VALUE IN THE VALLEY
Fireside, 0-684-82475-2, $13.00
Simon & Schuster, 0-684-80287-2, $22.00

ONE DAY MY SOUL JUST OPENED UP
Fireside, 0-684-84134-7, $14.00

DON'T GIVE IT AWAY!
Fireside, 0-684-86983-7, $11.00

YESTERDAY, I CRIED
Simon & Schuster, 0-684-86424-X, $22.00